Invitation to Struggle

Invitation to Struggle
Congress, the President, and Foreign Policy
THIRD EDITION

Cecil V. Crabb, Jr.
Louisiana State University

Pat M. Holt
Former Staff Director,
Senate Foreign Relations Committee

A Division of Congressional Quarterly Inc.
1414 22nd Street N.W., Washington, D.C. 20037

Library of Congress Cataloging-in-Publication Data

Crabb, Cecil Van Meter, 1924-
    Invitation to struggle: Congress, the president, and foreign policy / Cecil V. Crabb, Jr., Pat M. Holt. — 3rd ed.
        p.   cm.
    Bibliography: p.
    Includes index.
    ISBN 0-87187-478-4
    1. Presidents—United   States.   2. United   States.   Congress.   3. United States—Foreign relations—1945- I. Holt, Pat M. II. Title.
JK573 1989
353.03'72—dc19   88-15031
                                                                      CIP

CONTENTS

PREFACE

The Constitution . . . is an invitation to struggle
for the privilege of directing American foreign policy.

—Edward S. Corwin
The President: Office and Powers

As the United States begins its third century under the Constitution, this quotation by one of the nation's most eminent constitutional authorities remains applicable to the foreign policy process. Indeed, the "struggle" identified by Corwin for control of the foreign policy machinery may be even more intense today than in earlier stages of American history.

The contest between the White House and Congress for a dominant position in the conduct of foreign affairs is one of the constants in the nation's history. At the end of the eighteenth century, President George Washington complained about what he viewed as Senate obstructionism in dealing with the proposed Jay Treaty with England. By contrast, some legislators were convinced that "His Majesty" (as Washington was sometimes described by his critics) was attempting to exclude legislators from meaningful participation in an important diplomatic undertaking. More than a century later, the struggle was exemplified by the conflict between President Woodrow Wilson, who advocated American membership in the League of Nations, and his opponents in the Senate. Wilson's diplomatic defeat over the Treaty of Versailles following World War I had damaging consequences for the United States and the rest of the world.

The credibility of the administration of President Lyndon B. Johnson was ultimately destroyed, in no small measure because of mounting opposition in Congress to U.S. participation in the Vietnam War. Inevitably, perhaps, the period after this war was an era of unprecedented legislative activism in foreign policy. Many legislators believed, correctly or not, that among the "lessons of Vietnam" was the necessity for

Congress to assert its prerogatives more decisively in foreign affairs. During the 1970s, presidents Nixon, Ford, and Carter repeatedly complained about congressional efforts to limit their diplomatic freedom of action.

The Reagan White House encountered a continuation of this trend. Three examples from the Reagan administration support this conclusion: the development of new weapons systems, such as the MX missile, the B-1 bomber, and the Strategic Defense Initiative ("Star Wars"); negotiations over arms control; and American policy toward the Middle East and Central America. The diplomacy of the Reagan administration was marked by disunity and disarray because of repeated instances of intra-executive conflict. This conflict reached its culmination in the Iran-contra affair, which received prominent media coverage for several months during President Reagan's second term. In turn, that development encouraged—if, in fact, it did not virtually guarantee—renewed efforts by Congress to impose limits upon the diplomatic activities of the president and the chief foreign policy aides.

Evidence from the diplomatic record of the United States since World War II leaves little doubt that the nation's foreign policy process continues to reflect an invitation to struggle between the president and Congress. To date, efforts to attenuate or eliminate the problem have had little or no impact upon it. This struggle will *remain* a feature of the American foreign policy process for an indefinite period of time. At times this struggle is likely to have momentous consequences for the ability of the United States to achieve its foreign policy goals.

Following the pattern established in earlier editions, this third edition of *Invitation to Struggle* was written primarily with two groups of readers in mind. For those interested chiefly in substantive problems in recent American diplomacy, the study provides insight into a number of such instances, especially those confronting the United States since the Vietnam War. For readers whose interest is centered on the foreign policy process of the United States, the study supplies a succinct and contemporary analysis of that subject. The extensive reading list at the end of the book should prove useful to readers desiring to undertake more thorough research and reading on selected aspects of the nation's foreign policy.

Again consonant with the successful format of earlier editions, this new edition contains eight chapters. Three provide general and theoretical discussions, while five consist of case studies illustrating various aspects of presidential and congressional powers in the foreign policy field. The third edition contains several new case studies as well as others that have been extensively revised to reflect recent developments.

Chapter 1 provides the reader with a broad discussion of the roles of the president, the State Department, and other influential members of the executive bureaucracy in the formulation and administration of foreign policy. The basic focus of this chapter is the dominant position maintained by the chief executive in the decision-making process.

In Chapter 2 we analyze the constitutional and historical powers and responsibilities of Congress in foreign affairs. The chapter focuses on the impact of the Vietnam conflict in motivating Congress to assert its powers more forcefully in the sphere of external policy. The congressional assertiveness observed in foreign relations since the Vietnam War can be best understood within a broad historical and constitutional context.

The first case study (Chapter 3) deals with the effort by the United States and the Soviet Union to devise one or more international agreements dealing with anti-ballistic missile (ABM) systems. This issue highlights the prerogatives of the president and the Senate—and, indirectly at least, of Congress as a whole—in the treaty-making process. This chapter also deals with a new issue in executive-legislative relations—the roles of the president and the Senate in interpreting treaties.

Chapter 4 examines the specific issue of American military assistance to Saudi Arabia, within the larger context of the Arab-Israeli conflict. This case study is especially useful in calling attention to the impact of lobbying, and of public opinion generally, on the diplomatic decision-making process.

A recurrent and still controversial topic is the subject of Chapter 5: the commitment of the nation's armed forces abroad. As the evidence presented in the chapter indicates, the American people and their leaders remain uncertain about when, why, and where armed force should be employed to achieve national policy goals. As much as any single issue since World War II, this two-fold question—whether armed force ought to be applied overseas and who ought to make the decision—epitomizes the invitation to struggle between the White House and Capitol Hill in the foreign policy process.

Another difficult and recurrent problem for the American democracy, the proper role of agencies comprising the intelligence community within the U.S. government, is examined in Chapter 6. To date, no consensus has been achieved concerning the legitimacy of activities by the CIA and other members of the community, especially in covert action abroad. As the experience of the Reagan administration clearly indicates, neither executive nor legislative officials have been able to formulate and impose effective controls upon intelligence agencies, thereby ensuring that their operations in fact serve the national interest. Many of the reasons for this failure are identified in the case study.

Another new case study, focusing upon the roles of the president and Congress in foreign economic policy, is provided in Chapter 7.

While the specific focus in the chapter is American trade policy, the discussion makes clear that this subject can be meaningfully understood and discussed only in the larger context of internal economic policies and developments. This case study clearly illustrates the growing inter-relationship between domestic and foreign policy within the American democracy.

As in earlier editions, the final chapter offers an assessment about the nature and implications of the invitation to struggle in regard to the foreign policy of the United States today and in the years ahead. It should come as no surprise to the reader that the rivalry between the executive and legislative branches for primacy in the field of external policy will almost certainly continue to be a prominent feature of American diplomacy.

Chapters 1, 2, 4, and 8 of the third edition were written by Cecil V. Crabb, Jr. Chapters 3, 5, 6, and 7 were written by Pat M. Holt. As always, the authors are greatly indebted to many individuals who have contributed directly and indirectly to this new edition. Their assistance has been invaluable and is gratefully acknowledged.

The comments and suggestions received by the authors from students, faculty members, government officials, and interested citizens have been extremely useful and have been reflected in changes incorporated in this edition. In particular, we thank James S. Magee, Philip Rogers, and Thomas Yantek for their valuable critiques of the manuscript. The editors and staff of CQ Press have provided indispensable advice and guidance at every stage. Specifically, the authors wish to thank the director of CQ Press, Joanne Daniels; the managing editor, Nancy Lammers; and our production editor, Kerry Kern.

While acknowledging the essential contributions of others, the authors accept sole responsibility for any errors of fact or judgment that may be found in these pages.

Cecil V. Crabb, Jr.
Pat M. Holt

The Process of Foreign Policy Making

   A unique feature of the governmental system of the United States is that its powers are divided among separate executive, legislative, and judicial branches. From the perspective of constitutional theory, these are often described as equal and coordinate branches of the government. In practice, however, their powers and influences are not equal, especially in the foreign policy sphere. The purpose of Part I of this study is to provide a context within which congressional efforts to play a more influential role can be understood.

   Throughout American history, the judiciary has largely been content to play a passive role in the foreign policy process. When the Supreme Court has concerned itself with foreign policy questions (which it does rarely), it has nearly always taken one of two positions: Either it has declared foreign policy issues to be political questions that are not susceptible of resolution by the judicial system,[1] or it has forcefully upheld the exercise of executive power.[2] Over the years, a series of Supreme Court decisions has thus reinforced the claims of successive presidents that in foreign affairs the chief executive is the dominant organ of government. Insofar as fears about the emergence of an "imperial presidency" have resulted from vigorous and unrestrained presidential leadership in foreign affairs, that phenomenon has received strong impetus from the constitutional interpretations of the Supreme Court.[3]

   Both the diplomatic experience of the United States and certain provisions of the Constitution therefore dictate that we begin our inquiry into the making of foreign policy by focusing upon the role of the executive branch. Although recent years have witnessed a new congressional militancy in foreign relations, the fact remains that the president is still in charge of American foreign policy. For the most part, Congress's powers are limited to telling the White House what it cannot do beyond the country's borders. The power to decide what the United States will undertake in its relations with other countries and in carrying out specific programs, such as arms control or the promotion of democracy abroad or mediation in the Arab-Israeli dispute, continues to reside with the chief executive. As we shall see in Chapter 1, an incumbent president has at his disposal a variety of instruments that create an unequaled position for influencing the diplomatic policies of the United States. More than at any other time in American history, perhaps, the nation's influence abroad now depends upon presidential decisions—including, of course, decisions about whether to work collaboratively with Congress in the foreign policy process. Hence, Chapter 1 deals with the president's role in the making of foreign policy.

In the American constitutional system, Congress is also assigned a number of responsibilities that impinge directly and indirectly upon foreign affairs. Despite the opinion expressed by many legislators in recent years that their views have been ignored by the White House, the U.S. Congress has more power to influence foreign affairs than any other national legislature in the world. In addition to its constitutional prerogatives, Congress has acquired over the course of two hundred years extraconstitutional powers and informal techniques for affecting the course of foreign relations. One tendency since World War II—the erosion of the distinction between domestic and foreign affairs—has significantly enhanced the influence of Congress. Chapter 2 provides a discussion of the formal and informal prerogatives of Congress in the foreign policy field, and it identifies and analyzes the forces that have produced the new congressional militancy in external affairs.

Notes

1. In 1855, a federal judge ruled that the interpretation of a treaty was a "political question" and thus was not among the powers that were "confided by the people to the judiciary . . . but to the executive and legislative departments of our government." *Taylor v. Morton*, 23 F. Cas. 784 (C.C.D. Mass. 1855) (No. 13,799). See also an earlier case, *Foster v. Neilson*, 2 Pet. 253 (1829).
2. Two landmark decisions affirming the president's prerogatives in foreign relations were the *Prize Cases*, 67 U.S. (2 Black) 635 (1863), and *United States v. Curtiss-Wright Export Corp.*, 299 U.S. 304 (1936). Several decisions during the late 1970s and early 1980s sustained that position. In *Edwards v. Carter*, 436 U.S. 907 (1978), the Supreme Court upheld the right of the president to dispose, through the treaty process (thus requiring the consent

of the Senate), of property belonging to the United States, as provided for in the Panama Canal treaties that had recently been negotiated by the Carter administration. In another case, growing out of the Iranian hostage crisis of 1979-1980, the court upheld the president's authority over several billion dollars of Iranian assets, which had been frozen after the hostages were seized. In *Dames and Moore v. Regan,* 453 U.S. 654 (1981), the court stated that in the foreign policy field Congress had accorded the chief executive more freedom to settle claims with foreign countries than was the case in domestic affairs. In *Agee v. Haig,* 453 U.S. 280 (1981), the Supreme Court upheld the right of the executive branch to deny a passport to a former employee of the Central Intelligence Agency whose writings were viewed as endangering the lives of current CIA agents and as detrimental to national security.

The Supreme Court has not yet ruled on the constitutionality of the War Powers Resolution of 1973, which sought to limit the president's power to use the armed forces abroad without the consent of Congress. During the Persian Gulf crisis of 1987, several legislators sought to get a federal court to rule that the Reagan administration had not complied with the resolution, but they were not successful. For more detailed discussions of and commentary on these cases, see Warren Christopher, "Ceasefire between the Branches: A Compact in Foreign Affairs," *Foreign Affairs* 60 (Summer 1982): 990-995.

3. The concept of the imperial presidency, which has come into wide currency since the Vietnam War and Watergate crises, is actually a variation on a very old theme in American history: pervasive apprehension about the abuse of executive power. This fear strongly colored the attitudes of those who wrote both the federal and the early state constitutions, in which the powers of the chief executives were severely limited. In the context of the Vietnam and Watergate experiences, the idea of the imperial presidency suggests a president who routinely infringes upon the constitutional authority of the legislative and judicial branches; who believes the presidency to be above the law, particularly in the conduct of foreign relations; who manipulates and deceives Congress and the American people in order to accomplish domestic and foreign policy objectives; and who surrounds the operations of the executive branch with a wall of secrecy. As a leading student of the presidency has asserted, this conception of the presidential office implies a "radical transformation" in the American system of government, which is founded upon the doctrine of separation of powers. Arthur M. Schlesinger, Jr., *The Imperial Presidency* (Boston: Houghton Mifflin, 1973), viii. This study provides a detailed analysis of the emergence of the imperial presidency during two hundred years of U.S. history.

Yet it must also be emphasized that—especially since the administration of President Franklin D. Roosevelt—the American people have fundamentally accepted the idea of a strong or forceful president who takes the lead in meeting internal and external challenges energetically and successfully. Perhaps even more today than in the 1930s, citizens look to the White House, rather than to Congress or the courts, for the dynamic leadership required to solve urgent national problems.

Insofar as it is regarded as constitutionally and ethically objectionable, therefore, the imperial presidency has two specific connotations: behavior by the chief executive and his subordinates that is patently illegal or of questionable constitutional validity; and the failure of the chief executive to achieve his major policy goals. It is, for example, interesting to speculate about whether President Lyndon B. Johnson would have been viewed as epitomizing the imperial presidency if the United States had *won* the Vietnam War, since many of Johnson's acts during that conflict were comparable to those of President Roosevelt during World War II and of President Abraham Lincoln during the Civil War.

CHAPTER 1

The Executive Branch and Foreign Affairs: Locus of Decision Making

As the United States entered its third century under the Constitution, the president of the United States was in some respects the most powerful official in the contemporary world. This was an ironic situation, because the nation's founders had been extremely wary of executive power. Little doubt exists that, in their minds, the dominant organ of the new system of government was to be Congress. Yet after two hundred years of experience, it seems undeniable that the locus of the foreign policy decision-making process in the United States is the White House. In foreign affairs, the president has become what one commentator has called the "ultimate decider" and the "decision maker of last resort." [1]

In practice, all presidents depend upon a corps of official and unofficial advisers to assist them in managing foreign relations. Historically, the State Department has been the agency which, under the president's ultimate direction, is in charge of the foreign policy of the United States. Since World War II, however, the State Department has faced increasing competition from many other executive agencies—such as the Defense Department, the Central Intelligence Agency (CIA), and the president's own staff—that have become active in the foreign policy field.

As the subsequent discussion will show—and as was dramatically illustrated by the Iran-contra affair during President Ronald Reagan's second term—the achievement and maintenance of unity within the executive branch in dealing with foreign policy issues have become a perennial challenge for national leaders. Various mechanisms and devices created since World War II—which will also be discussed—have thus far failed to solve the problem and have, in some respects, perhaps compounded it.

An even older problem confronting officials involved in foreign policy decision making is coordinating the actions of the executive and legislative branches. The two problems are related, for executive-legislative cooperation in foreign affairs is, to a significant degree, dependent upon the maintenance of unity among the leading members of the executive bureaucracy in dealing with foreign policy issues.

Despite widespread concern about the "imperial presidency" since the Vietnam War, it seems evident that the president continues to serve as what some commentators have called the nation's "diplomat in chief." The chief executive's dominant position stems from a combination of formal constitutional and informal or extraconstitutional powers that will be identified and examined later in this chapter.

Concepts in Foreign Policy

Foreign policy refers to the external goals for which a nation is prepared to commit its resources. This definition distinguishes between a nation's foreign policy and a variety of hopes, visions, and dreams (such as universal democracy and perpetual peace) that may be espoused by individuals and groups within the society. Unless the objective—in the case of the United States, for example, deterring Soviet aggression, protecting the security of members of the North Atlantic Treaty Organization (NATO), assisting in the economic development of India, or preserving access to the Persian Gulf oil fields—involves some application of the economic, military, intellectual, or other resources of the nation, it cannot be seriously viewed as forming part of its foreign policy.

A closely related term is the *foreign policy process*. This denotes a complex and often time-consuming series of steps by which officials in the executive and legislative branches formulate external goals or objectives and decide upon the most appropriate means for reaching them. More specifically, the foreign policy process may be thought of as entailing, in the usual case, six distinct steps or stages.

1. Officials, and often the public as well, perceive an external challenge or problem that is viewed as affecting the interests of the United States. This challenge might be evidence of Soviet expansionism, a political crisis in the Middle East, human rights abuses by a foreign government, or a rising level of national armaments.

2. The president and his advisers attempt to identify the challenge clearly and to determine precisely how and to what degree the interests of the United States are affected by it. For example, what would be the effects of more cordial relations between the Soviet Union and Iran, or

of growing political violence in South Africa, or of mounting economic problems in Mexico? (Since the Vietnam War especially, there has been a greater reluctance to believe that the diplomatic or security interests of the United States are directly involved in such matters.)

3. Executive officials formulate and consider alternative courses of action or *policy options* available to the United States for responding to the external challenge. They evaluate these options in the light of the likely consequences and implications of each. In the end, the president has the responsibility of choosing the course of action the government will pursue.

4. Steps are taken to implement or carry out the policy chosen by the president. Doing so may involve diplomatic moves by the State Department and U.S. ambassadors abroad; military programs and activities by the Department of Defense; intelligence studies and a variety of other operations by the CIA and other members of what is called the "intelligence community"; propaganda and informational programs by the United States Information Agency (USIA); economic measures by the Treasury Department; a new food aid program, in which the Department of Agriculture plays a key role; legislation or appropriations by Congress; and other possible steps to achieve the declared objective abroad. It is virtually certain that the achievement of any foreign policy goal today will require the collaboration of several executive agencies and some form of congressional participation, if only in the provision of funds.

5. The success of the policy in achieving its goals is reviewed. What major problems have been encountered in the attempt to realize the policy's objectives? What steps could be taken to improve the policy or its implementation? Is there another option that, on balance, would be preferable? Efforts to answer such questions are made by the State Department (including U.S. officials overseas), the White House staff, and other executive agencies; by committees of Congress, which often investigate problems in the foreign policy field; by citizens' organizations and "think tanks" (such as the Council on Foreign Relations and the Rand Corporation); by foreign governments and political movements; and by individual citizens, political commentators, and informed students of the nation's diplomacy.

6. Policy makers determine the future of the policy. The decision may be to continue the existing policy largely unchanged; to modify it, in the belief that major changes are required; or to abandon it, on the grounds that it cannot achieve U.S. goals abroad. Thus, to take a hypothetical case, in the American approach to arms-control issues with the Soviet Union, the president and his advisers may decide that the nation's position on disarmament is in the main satisfactory and ought to be continued; or that substantial changes need to be made in current

U.S. policy toward arms-control questions; or that the prevailing policy does not achieve American objectives abroad and ought, therefore, to be replaced by a totally new set of proposals designed to achieve the reduction of Soviet and American military arsenals.

It must be recognized that, like certain concepts in physics, such as "frictionless bearings" or a "perfect vacuum," the above model of foreign policy decision making is an ideal type, almost never found in its pure form in the real world of decision making. In reality, the foreign policies of the United States (and of other countries) sometimes are continued for no better reason than habit, bureaucratic momentum, or public resistance to change. Nearly always, subjective and emotional factors influence policy decisions, as when President Lyndon B. Johnson said about a particular challenge abroad that it was "just like the Alamo!" Unquestionably also, the White House, the State Department, Congress, and other participants in the foreign policy process may and do develop strong vested interests in an existing policy. At every stage, misperception, erroneous information, and faulty interpretation of events abroad may influence the outcome of the decision-making process.

Former Secretary of State Dean Acheson said, after he left office, that the exact process by which foreign policy decisions are actually made within the United States government is "unknown and unknowable." Former presidential adviser Clark Clifford called the process by which foreign policy decisions were arrived at by President Johnson "unfathomable." After North Korea invaded South Korea in late June 1950, President Harry S Truman did not engage in a prolonged process of formal decision making before concluding that the United States must resist the attack; rather the formal decision-making process was used to ratify the presidential decision after it had already been made. Critics charged that this was also frequently the case with decision making in the Vietnam War during the Johnson administration. At some point all presidents have demanded that their advisory machinery produce viewpoints and policy recommendations consonant with their own prior inclinations. Allowing for these qualifications, it is nevertheless the case that decision making in the foreign policy field generally approximates the sequence of steps that has been described.

Another concept in the field of foreign policy, one which has come to the fore especially since World War II, is *national security policy.* This embraces activities, both abroad and in domestic affairs, that are designed to protect the independence and integrity of the United States. At its most basic level, national security policy is concerned with the defense of the nation against actual and potential enemies. Construed more broadly, it involves preventing threats to national sovereignty, collecting and evaluating information about the behavior of potential enemies, creating and maintaining military alliances, and supplying friendly countries with arms and other forms of aid.

A famous Prussian general of the Napoleonic period, Karl von Clausewitz, has said, "War is the continuation of politics by other means." [2] One of the implications of this dictum is the idea—exemplified today by the "cold war" between the United States and the Soviet Union—that political and military relations among nations are two sides of the same coin. Political or diplomatic decisions sometimes lead to armed conflicts among nations; in turn, the results of war—and one nation's perception of another's military strength—crucially affect what diplomats are able to achieve at the conference table.

Awareness of these relationships led to the creation in 1947 of the National Security Council (NSC), the highest presidential advisory agency for national security policy. While NSC's membership has varied, its members currently are the president (who serves as chairman), the vice president, the secretary of state, and the secretary of defense. Other civilian and military officials may be, and frequently are, invited to participate in its deliberations. The NSC staff is directed by a presidential assistant. Beginning with the Eisenhower administration in 1953, the position was elevated into the presidential assistant for national security affairs. The best known and most influential occupant of this position was Henry Kissinger under the Nixon and Ford administrations. Kissinger converted the NSC staff into a kind of rival State Department; although he was not a member of the National Security Council, Kissinger operated as a de facto cabinet officer. Conversely, in the Nixon-Kissinger era, the influence of the State Department declined significantly. While other national security advisers have been less influential than Kissinger, the position has become an extremely influential one in the foreign policy field. (It should be noted also that, in contrast to cabinet officers, the president's national security adviser is *not* confirmed in the position by the Senate.)

The NSC was created to integrate diplomatic, military, financial, and other factors into a unified national security policy for the United States. It is important to note that the NSC is solely an *advisory organ to the president.* Chief executives utilize the NSC in very different ways. Some, like President Dwight D. Eisenhower, have been strongly "staff oriented" in arriving at decisions and so have relied heavily upon the NSC. Others, like President Johnson, relied more frequently on informal advisers and friends.

The membership of the NSC was deliberately composed by Congress to preserve and underscore a fundamental principle of the nation's constitutional system: civilian control over the military establishment. All members of the NSC are civilians, and, although military officers (such as members of the Joint Chiefs of Staff) may be invited by the president to attend NSC sessions, the military point of view is normally conveyed to the president through the secretary of defense. However, the president may also, and not infrequently does, consult the nation's top military commanders directly in the determination of national security policy and strategy.

Another important term in the field of foreign policy is *diplomacy*. This concept is somewhat ambiguous and often causes widespread public confusion. At the risk of oversimplification, we may say that it is frequently used in two different ways. Diplomacy can refer to the entire range of a nation's external relationships—routine diplomatic communications between governments, summit conferences among heads of state, the recognition of one government by another, cultural and scientific exchange programs, and so on. Alternatively, diplomacy often has a more limited connotation: the resolution of disputes and conflicts among nations by peaceful methods. In this latter sense, diplomacy is conceived of as a substitute for war and violence; it is a method of preventing the settlement of international quarrels with armed force.[3]

Americans have traditionally been suspicious of diplomacy and of the officials engaged in it. In the public mind, diplomacy is associated with Old World political values and machinations held to be at variance with the democratic ethos of the New World. One argument invoked to justify an isolationist stance in foreign affairs has been that Americans lacked skill and training in diplomacy; hence, in any encounter with the wily diplomats of the Old World, the United States would almost certainly lose. This point of view was reinforced by the results of several diplomatic conferences during World War II, such as the meetings at Yalta and Potsdam in 1945, which many Americans interpreted as diplomatic victories for the Soviet Union. This historical frame of mind no doubt contributes to the poor image that the State Department tends to have with the American public and with Congress.[4]

The President's Constitutional Authority

The preeminent position of the chief executive in the U.S. foreign policy process stems from two broad sources of power: those conferred by or implied in the Constitution; and those that are outgrowths of tradition, precedent, or historical necessity. Let us examine each of these categories in detail.

From the beginning of the republic, constitutional authorities have debated whether the Founding Fathers intended to make the conduct of foreign policy largely an executive responsibility, whether they meant for Congress to be the dominant organ, or whether they desired some kind of balance of power between the two branches.[5] Yet it is beyond contention that the intention of the Founders has been less important in determining what happened than numerous other influences, such as the impact of forceful personalities upon the presidential office, the crises confronting the nation at home and abroad, and the decisions of the Supreme Court. Irrespective of what the Founders desired, the tendency has been toward executive preeminence in nearly every aspect of the foreign policy process.

The constitutional position of the president in foreign affairs rests upon several important provisions. Article II, Section 1, vests the executive power of the government in the president. It also requires that the president take an oath to "preserve, protect and defend the Constitution of the United States," implying a responsibility for the preservation of national security. Sections 2 and 3 of this article specify the president's powers, of which the most relevant to foreign policy are that the chief executive serves as commander in chief of the army and navy, can make treaties with foreign governments, can appoint ambassadors and other representatives of the United States abroad, and can "receive ambassadors and other public ministers" of other governments.

Commander in Chief

The Constitution (Article II, Section 2) also designates the president as "Commander in chief of the Army and Navy"—which today also includes the air force. Like other constitutional provisions, this grant of authority engendered much controversy. Does it mean that the president should function symbolically or ceremonially as head of the armed forces (like the British monarch in modern history), while leaving the determination of military strategy and the deployment of the armed forces to others, possibly to Congress? (The case studies in Chapter 5 focus upon the demands of Congress regarding the use of the armed forces for foreign policy ends.) Or does it mean that the chief executive actually determines military strategy and tactics?[6]

American diplomatic experience has left no doubt about the answer. Successive presidents since Lincoln have interpreted their authority in this realm broadly and dynamically. Their position as commander in chief of the armed forces has become one of their most influential powers in the foreign policy field. Over the course of its history, the United States has been involved in approximately 125 "undeclared wars" and other instances of violent conflict abroad conducted under presidential authority. For example, in 1846 President James K. Polk ordered the army to occupy disputed territory along the Rio Grande, unquestionably (and almost certainly by intent) provoking Mexico into war. Early in the twentieth century, despite strong congressional opposition, President Theodore Roosevelt sent the American navy on a cruise around the world. (His implicit objective was to impress Japan with U.S. naval might.) On his own authority, President Franklin D.

Roosevelt ordered the navy to shoot on sight any German submarines that entered the hemispheric "security zone." President Truman personally made the decision to use two atomic bombs against Japan in 1945; in 1950 he again ordered U.S. armed forces in the Pacific to repel North Korea's thrust into South Korea, thereby involving the United States in one of the most prolonged and expensive undeclared wars in its history.

Early in his administration, President Eisenhower threatened Communist China and North Korea with the possible use of nuclear weapons if they resumed hostilities in the Korean conflict. Eisenhower was also the first of several chief executives to make major military commitments to the government of South Vietnam, ultimately leading to massive U.S. involvement in the conflict between North and South Vietnam.

In the most dangerous cold war encounter since World War II, President John F. Kennedy in 1962 presented the Soviet Union with an ultimatum demanding the removal of its nuclear missiles from Cuba. Kennedy placed the U.S. air force on worldwide alert and interposed the navy between Cuba and the Soviet ships that were apparently bringing new missiles to the island. Little doubt exists that Kennedy was prepared to use whatever degree of force was required to eliminate this Soviet threat.[7]

During the closing months of his administration, following the Soviet invasion of Afghanistan, President Jimmy Carter issued the so-called Carter Doctrine, pledging the United States to defend the security of the oil-rich Persian Gulf area. A few weeks later, he ordered the Pentagon to undertake a mission designed to rescue U.S. citizens being held as hostages in Iran. Congress and the American people were not informed of this mission until after it had been launched and had failed to achieve its objective.[8]

President Reagan reiterated and strengthened the Carter Doctrine, in effect placing the Persian Gulf area under the military protection of the United States. Subsequently he dispatched naval forces to shield Kuwaiti oil tankers from attack by Iran, in an effort to keep the region's oil flowing to the United States and its allies.

A president's decision *not* to use armed force, or to terminate military hostilities and enter into negotiations for a truce or for a peace treaty, can have significant effects upon the nation's relationships with other countries. This was illustrated by President Carter's refusal to embroil the United States in several conflicts in black-ruled African countries. After first deciding to intervene militarily in Lebanon's troubled political situation, President Reagan later withdrew the nation's forces from that country.

With the concurrence of the Senate, the president also appoints and promotes the highest military officers; and on his own authority, he can relieve military commanders of their posts, as President Truman did in his widely publicized dismissal of Gen. Douglas MacArthur during the Korean War. While ultimate authority to determine the size and nature of the U.S. military establishment resides with Congress, the president plays a crucial role in that decision. The presidential budget message to Congress—along with many other communications to the legislative branch and the testimony provided to congressional committees by executive-branch officials—usually have a decisive impact upon legislative attitudes and behavior.

To the minds of many Americans, by the mid-1960s White House reliance upon the armed forces to achieve diplomatic objectives, often with little or no consultation with Congress, symbolized the imperial presidency. Limiting this presidential prerogative has been a major goal of those legislators who advocate a more influential role for Congress in foreign affairs. A noteworthy step in that direction was the passage of the War Powers Resolution in 1973. It will be examined in detail in Chapter 5.

Treaty-making Power

Article II, Section 2 of the Constitution gives the president the power, "by and with the Advice and Consent of the Senate, to make treaties, provided two-thirds of the Senators present concur." The ability of the chief executive to enter into formal agreements with other countries in the form of treaties—and less formal accords and understandings by means of executive agreements—is another influential tool of presidential leadership.

Controversy has always surrounded the meaning and requirements of this constitutional provision. For example, is the process of negotiating treaties an exclusively executive function, or does the "advice and consent of the Senate" mean that the Senate plays a role in the negotiation process, as well as the ratification of treaties? Again, diplomatic experience provides the answer. Presidents have nearly always taken the view that the executive branch "makes" or negotiates treaties and then submits them to the Senate for its consideration. In the post-World War II period, senators (and occasionally even representatives) have been invited by the White House to participate in international negotiations. This practice reached its zenith in the peace treaties for the minor Axis powers following World War II. President Jimmy Carter employed the device in the negotiations for the new Panama Canal treaties during the 1970s. Moreover, the case study of the ABM treaty (Chapter 3) provides other examples of the phenomenon.

After a treaty has been negotiated and signed by the parties to it, the agreement is submitted to the Senate for its consideration. At this stage, the Senate has several choices. After deliberation and debate, the

Senate can *approve* the treaty by the required two-thirds majority. (Throughout American history, the vast majority of treaties has received senatorial approval.) Conversely, the Senate can *reject* the treaty, by failing to give it a favorable two-thirds vote. In reality, the Senate very rarely takes this course of action. Then the Senate may *change* the treaty, by attaching amendments, reservations, and understandings to it.*

After the Senate has approved a treaty, it must be *proclaimed* by the president before it becomes law. It is a popular misconception to say that the Senate "ratifies" treaties. The Senate plays a key role in the ratification process, but in the end the treaty becomes law only after it has been proclaimed by the president.

Throughout the entire process of treaty making, the chief executive retains the initiative. The president decides to undertake the negotiations, appoints the negotiators and monitors their work, approves the treaty's provisions and submits it to the Senate, and proclaims the treaty as law. At any stage the president may withdraw the treaty from active Senate deliberation, or the president may refuse to proclaim a treaty that has already been approved by the Senate, if the White House believes its provisions are detrimental to the national interest. This was the action taken by President Woodrow Wilson toward the Treaty of Versailles, because of the objectionable amendments and resolutions added to it by the Senate.

Can a president also terminate an existing treaty? This question was posed by the action of the Carter administration in December 1978 when it established full diplomatic relations with the People's Republic of China and concurrently notified the Republic of China (Taiwan) that the security treaty with that government would be allowed to lapse. Predictably, Carter's action precipitated considerable public and congressional opposition. Since the security pact with Taiwan had been approved by the Senate, some legislators argued that it could be terminated only with the concurrence of the Senate or of Congress as a whole. Initially, this viewpoint was supported by a U.S. district court, but on December 13, 1979, by a vote of 7-2, the Supreme Court reversed the

---

* An *amendment* to a treaty changes its language and provisions, thereby probably requiring its renegotiation with the other parties to it. *Reservations* and *understandings* specify the American interpretation of its provisions. For example, in several international agreements, the United States has specified that the accord does not supersede the Monroe Doctrine, under which Washington has historically protected the defense of the Western Hemisphere. In Senate deliberations on the SALT II arms limitation agreement with the Soviet Union in 1979, several senators insisted upon an understanding that the Soviet Union would adhere to pledges (given orally) not to expand certain components of its military strength. As we shall see in Chapter 3, in consenting to the new Panama Canal treaties, the Senate appended certain conditions to its approval of them. In reality, with the passage of time the differences among these various categories of changes have become increasingly indistinct.

decision, holding that the president had the constitutional authority to terminate the defense pact with Taiwan. In writing about the decision four members of the Court held that the controversy was a political question that was not subject to judicial determination and that had to be resolved between the president and Congress.[9]

Another issue that has arisen is: Who has the power to interpret (or reinterpret) the meaning of treaties between the United States and foreign nations? Predictably perhaps, executive officials have contended that this power also belongs to the president, while many legislators have taken the position that it belongs to the Senate (or, as some view it, to the Senate and the president, jointly). This issue will be examined further in the case study on the ABM treaty.

Executive Agreements

In lieu of formal treaty accords with other countries, an incumbent president may enter into *executive agreements* with them.* Although executive agreements are not mentioned in the Constitution, they have a venerable tradition going back to the earliest days of the republic. Some of them have had a momentous effect on the course of American foreign relations. Some notable examples are President Franklin D. Roosevelt's destroyers-for-bases deal with Great Britain in 1940; the agreements with the Soviet Union and other allies during World War II (notably those reached at the Yalta and Potsdam conferences); a series of understandings, beginning in the Truman administration, by which the United States assumed a de facto commitment for the security of Israel; the understandings between President Carter and Chinese Deputy Premier Deng Xiaoping leading to cultural and scientific exchanges between the two countries; and the understanding between the United States and several Persian Gulf countries to maintain the military security of the region in exchange for continued access to Persian Gulf oil.

According to one estimate (and estimates vary widely), between 1946 and 1976 the United States entered into 7,201 executive agreements with foreign countries (excluding over sixty secret agreements that the State Department reported to Congress between 1972 and 1977)—far more than the number of treaties signed during the same period.[10] Perhaps no presidential prerogative in foreign affairs has gen-

---

* Under the Constitution a distinction can be made between a treaty and an agreement (or compact) with other countries, although the differences are not always legally and practically clear. An *executive agreement* is an understanding between heads of state or made under their authority; it may be either written or oral; and many agreements ultimately require congressional approval (as in providing funds for their implementation) before they can become effective. Many executive agreements (for example, those related to the sale of surplus agricultural commodities abroad) are negotiated pursuant to authority delegated by Congress. These are sometimes described as *statutory agreements.*

erated such concern on Capitol Hill in recent years as the practice of entering into such agreements without legislative knowledge, scrutiny, or concurrence. As Senator J. William Fulbright, D-Ark., a former chairman of the Senate Foreign Relations Committee, has lamented:

> The Senate is asked to convene solemnly to approve by a two-thirds vote a treaty to preserve cultural artifacts in a friendly neighboring country. At the same time, the chief executive is moving military men and materiel around the globe like so many pawns in a chess game.[11]

In 1972, Congress passed the Case Act, which requires that all executive agreements be reported to Congress. If Congress objects to an agreement, it may then take such action as seems indicated. Despite such legislation, it would be difficult to demonstrate that Congress has yet been able to impose effective limits upon the president's power to enter into agreements with other governments.[12]

Appointment Power

Article II, Section 2 of the Constitution also provides that the president "shall nominate, and by and with the Advice and Consent of the Senate, shall appoint Ambassadors [and] other public Ministers and Consuls." An ambassador serves as the *alter ego* of the head of state abroad; hence, it is expected that the president will select those individuals for this post who share his conception of the nation's role in foreign affairs. The same constitutional requirement also applies, of course, to the secretaries of state and defense, as to other cabinet heads, and to lower-level department officials, normally down to and including assistant secretaries. To date, however, the appointment of the president's national security adviser has not required confirmation by the Senate.

As they have with the treaty power, resourceful chief executives throughout U.S. history have discovered methods for circumventing limitations upon their appointment power. One such device is for the president to make an interim appointment; the individual so appointed may hold office and perform important duties while the Senate is not in session. After the Senate reconvenes, the president has three choices: he may submit the name of the interim appointee for confirmation; he may allow the interim appointee's period of service to end and may nominate another individual (perhaps one more acceptable to the Senate) for the position; or he may decide not to fill the position at all.

The chief executive may also, and frequently does, use cabinet officers to undertake diplomatic assignments. In 1979, President Carter relied upon Secretary of the Treasury Michael Blumenthal to arrive at certain understandings with the People's Republic of China before the United States opened an embassy in that country.[13] In the same time period, Secretary of Defense Harold Brown assured the governments of Saudi Arabia and other Persian Gulf states that, in light of the revolutionary upheaval in Iran, their security would be protected by the United States.[14] Similarly, President Reagan called upon Defense Secretary Caspar Weinberger to carry out diplomatic assignments.

The appointment of personal representatives is another device presidents have used to bypass senatorial confirmation of diplomatic officials. During World War II, President Franklin D. Roosevelt relied heavily upon his personal aide, Harry Hopkins, to conduct negotiations both with Great Britain and with the Soviet Union. The distinguished public servant W. Averell Harriman served as the personal representative of several presidents during and after World War II. During the Iranian hostage crisis in 1979-1980, White House aide Hamilton Jordan conducted secret negotiations for President Carter with intermediaries who had contacts with the revolutionary regime in Tehran. In the Reagan administration, presidential envoy Philip C. Habib spent several months in efforts to gain a peace agreement in strife-torn Lebanon; still later, the president called upon Habib again in an effort to reach an understanding that would restore political stability and peace to Central America.[15] From time to time presidents have also used the vice president—and sometimes the first lady—as diplomatic envoys.

Recognition of Foreign Governments

Article II, Section 3 of the Constitution gives the president the power to "receive Ambassadors and other public ministers" from foreign countries. The power of the president to recognize other governments is derived from this provision.

In normal diplomatic relations between two nations each gives formal recognition to the legitimacy of each other's government by the exchange of ambassadors (or ministers) between them and the establishment of embassies (or legations). Therefore, the decision as to whether to receive diplomatic representatives from other countries—and, hence, to accord formal recognition to their governments—belongs solely to the president. In practice, the Senate can frustrate the exercise of this power, as when it refused to confirm President Truman's designated ambassador to the Vatican, but such cases are exceptional. On the other hand, President Franklin D. Roosevelt decided to accord formal diplomatic recognition to the Soviet Union in 1933, after its Communist regime had been in existence for more than fifteen years. At the end of 1978, President Carter recognized the People's Republic of China, thereby ending the long period of estrangement that had existed between the two countries.

For many years two theories have existed about the criteria that should be employed in deciding whether the president should recognize another government. What might be called the classic international law conception holds that such recognition should depend primarily upon whether the government in question is stable, has established its authority throughout the country, and is fulfilling its international obligations. If so, it should be recognized, irrespective of the nature of its government or its ideological system. Applying this traditional standard, most governments, unlike the United States, recognized the People's Republic of China soon after the end of the Chinese civil war in 1949.

The other view—the Wilsonian or distinctively American approach—holds that recognition should depend upon the nature and character of the government in question. Specifically, it relies upon such criteria as whether the government enjoys popular support, whether it respects the rights of its citizens, and whether its conduct accords with international law. In 1913, President Woodrow Wilson invoked such principles when he refused to recognize the new government of Mexico, headed by Victoriano Huerta (a regime Wilson called "a government of butchers"). Basically the same reasons dictated America's refusal for many years to recognize the Communist regimes in the Soviet Union and China.

If the president can recognize foreign governments, he can by the same token withdraw or withhold recognition. In extreme cases, presidents have sometimes dramatically severed diplomatic relations with another country, as President Woodrow Wilson did with Imperial Germany before the United States entered World War I. Another presidential option is to withhold recognition for an indefinite period, perhaps until a country achieves internal political stability or modifies its behavior. Alternatively, the president can send a warning to another country by calling the American ambassador home "for consultation." President Carter, for example, recalled the U.S. ambassador to Moscow, Thomas J. Watson, to express anger at the Soviet Union's invasion of Afghanistan. Conversely, the president can require foreign diplomats in the United States to leave the country if their behavior becomes unacceptable to the White House.

Informal Techniques of Leadership

In addition to these constitutional powers, the chief executive possesses certain informal and extraconstitutional techniques for the management of foreign affairs. According to some students of the presidency, these may be even more important than his constitutional powers in accounting for the dominant foreign policy position of the chief executive. Five of these are especially important.

First, the president has unequaled access to the information sources required for effective decision making. Information is available to the White House from many sources, including departments and agencies within the executive branch, embassies and other overseas posts, the intelligence community, and foreign governments. The scope and nature of the information at the president's disposal about events and tendencies abroad are among his most influential resources for affecting the course of American diplomacy. Moreover, presidents are often able to withhold this information even from Congress under the doctrine of executive privilege.* However, as we shall see more fully in Chapter 2, the legislative branch has made increasing efforts to acquire its own sources of information in order not to remain dependent upon information supplied by executive officials.

Second, a noteworthy trend in the evolution of the presidency has been the growing importance of the chief executive's role as a *legislative leader*. Article II, Section 3 of the Constitution requires the president periodically to provide Congress with "information of the State of the Union." His annual State of the Union address, however, is merely one among literally hundreds of messages and recommendations sent from the White House to Capitol Hill. Even more important may be the president's Budget Message, normally a document of several hundred pages, containing detailed recommendations for expenditures in all spheres of domestic and foreign governmental activity. As a rule, Congress uses these recommendations as a guide to its own deliberations. Although in the end it may depart from them in some respects, congressional action is massively influenced at all stages by the wishes of the president.

After Congress has approved a budget, the president still possesses discretion in the administration of the funds available to the executive branch. For example, after encountering considerable opposition to his request for expanded economic and military aid to El Salvador in 1983, President Reagan and his advisers stated that by "reprogramming" budgetary allocations and shifting funds from one program to another they would manage to acquire the funds the White House needed to achieve the administration's goals in Central America.[16] Such tactics, it must be emphasized, may be successful in the short run, but where funds are involved in the long run the president is dependent upon congressional willingness to provide them. Some recent presidents have also impounded (or refused to spend) funds appropriated by Congress for diplomatic purposes not approved by the White House. The fre-

---

* Under this doctrine, the president and his principal aides cannot be compelled to testify before Congress, or to make papers and other records public, if to do so would impair the confidentiality of advice given to the president or would be damaging to national security. Members of Congress sometimes oppose particular applications of this doctrine or accuse presidents and their subordinates of abusing it. Nevertheless, Congress has generally acknowledged the necessity of the doctrine for the successful, orderly, and secure operation of the federal government.

quent use of this power by President Richard Nixon led Congress to pass the Congressional Budget and Impoundment Control Act of 1974, which limited the chief executive's discretion in this realm.

The ability of a chief executive to "manage" Congress—or to maintain at least minimally collaborative relations with it—has become a major criterion by which the success of a president is measured. Even by his own admission, President Carter neglected his legislative responsibilities. Both his domestic and his foreign policy programs suffered from that neglect. On the other hand, President Reagan's reputation as the "Great Communicator" during his first term owed much to his ability to persuade an often reluctant Congress to support his policies.[17]

Third, perhaps the most effective technique available to the president for managing foreign relations is the ability to influence public opinion. Even before the era of modern communications media, chief executives understood the potency of this tactic. President Theodore Roosevelt once observed:

> People used to say to me that I was an astonishingly good politician and divined what the people are going to think. . . . I did not "divine" how the people were going to think; I simply made up my mind what they ought to think, and then did my best to get them to think it.[18]

As a molder of public opinion at home and abroad, the president is in a uniquely favorable position vis-à-vis Congress and other potential rivals (most likely, only a president could be called a "Great Communicator"). Routinely, the activities and statements of the chief executive are given extensive coverage by the news media. The president's actions and statements dominate the news outlets; responses by rival political figures to major presidential addresses, for example, usually attract only a fraction of the audience that heard the president. When the White House believes it desirable, the president can almost always obtain time on national radio and television to inform the public about a crisis or some significant development in foreign affairs and describe the steps he proposes to take to deal with it. According to one informed student of public opinion, once a president has made a foreign affairs decision that becomes known to the public, he automatically receives the support of at least 50 percent of the people, irrespective of the nature of the decision.[19] Despite recent fears of the imperial presidency, the American people continue to believe that the president is and should be in charge of foreign policy. Conversely, as the demise of the Carter administration suggested, they have little forbearance for a chief executive who appears to be indecisive and to have lost control of events abroad.

At one time or another, every president in the past fifty years has been accused of managing the news to achieve his foreign policy objectives.[20] President Franklin D. Roosevelt used his radio "fireside chats" with extraordinary effectiveness to rally public opinion behind his policies. During the Cuban missile crisis in 1962, President Kennedy made a dramatic national TV speech, informing the nation about the construction of Soviet missile sites in Cuba and presenting his strategy for responding to the threat. During the early 1980s, President Reagan repeatedly relied upon his communication talents to rally public support behind his program for substantial military expansion.

Fourth, one of the oldest bases of the president's power is his role as a political leader. Normally, a president is automatically acknowledged to be the leader of his political party. Congressional, state, and local candidates usually value his endorsement in their political campaigns, and there may be considerable pressure on them to support the president's policies in order to win that endorsement. The president can also make many "patronage" appointments to federal office (though the number of these appointments has declined over the past half-century), and he is naturally inclined to favor political friends and allies. Moreover, White House influence can be useful to legislators and others in dealing with the federal bureaucracy. Perhaps most crucially, leaders and members of the president's party are constantly aware that the results of the next presidential election will depend substantially upon the president's record in dealing with major internal and external issues.

Finally, the president is sometimes able to commit the nation to a position or course of action in foreign affairs regardless of what others may wish. This power was vividly illustrated by President Theodore Roosevelt's actions in building the Panama Canal. Roosevelt was determined to "make the dirt fly" in Panama—that is, to get the canal built despite the opposition of legislators and others. He authorized construction to begin even before the Senate had approved the Hay-Bunau-Varilla Treaty (1904), which gave the United States the right to construct a canal across the Panamanian isthmus. He later noted:

> If I had followed traditional, conservative methods I would have submitted a dignified State paper ... to Congress and the debates on it would have been going on yet; but I took the Canal Zone and let Congress debate; and while the debate goes on the Canal does also.[21]

During the crisis over the Soviet threat to Greece in 1947, President Truman committed the United States to a policy of "containment" of communism, and in a speech on the Senate floor, Sen. Arthur H. Vandenberg, R-Mich., declared:

> The overriding fact is that the President has made a long-delayed statement regarding Communism on-the-march which must be supported [by Congress] if there is any hope of ever impressing Moscow with the necessity of paying any sort of peaceful attention to us.[22]

In short, once the chief executive has put a policy in motion, it is extremely difficult for Congress or public opinion to repudiate it. Presi-

dent Reagan has understood and used this technique on several occasions. Many members of Congress, for example, were uneasy about
Reagan's Central American diplomacy; they were apprehensive about
possible involvement in "another Vietnam" in the Western Hemisphere,
and they believed that the precise goals of the Reagan administration's
policy in the region had not been clearly specified. Nevertheless, after
Reagan had publicly asserted that there was a Communist threat to the
security of Central America, and after he had pointedly informed Democrats in Congress that they would bear a significant part of the responsibility for Communist gains in the region, even his critics at that time
were reluctant to deny the White House the resources it was seeking to
counter Communist activity. The Democratic party, having been accused of "losing China" to communism after World War II, was especially sensitive to the charge that it was again showing indifference to
the consequences of Communist gains abroad.

Even beyond both constitutional grants of authority and informal
modes of executive leadership is this reality: The president of the
United States is the head of state and the leader of perhaps the most
powerful nation known to history—the dramatically visible symbol of
that nation. In contrast to the way in which it structures the other two
branches of the government, the Constitution vests the executive power
of the United States *in a single person:* the president. For millions of
people at home and abroad, the White House serves as the focal point of
decision making in the U.S. government. When citizens ask, "Who is in
charge here?" they almost immediately, perhaps instinctively, answer,
"The president." It is to the Oval Office that they look for dynamic
leadership in formulating responses to external problems. Implicitly,
even Congress concedes that it is incapable of providing the kind of
unified and decisive leadership required to navigate the troubled waters
of international relations safely in the late twentieth century.

The Foreign Policy Bureaucracy

Within the executive branch, many entities other than the White
House are involved in the making of foreign policy. Chief among these
is, of course, the State Department, but account must also be taken of
the intelligence community, the military establishment, and a host of
other agencies.

The State Department

The executive agency most broadly and directly concerned with
foreign affairs is the Department of State, headed by the secretary of
state, who is generally regarded as the highest ranking cabinet officer.
Under the authority of the president, the department conducts relations

with more than 150 other independent nations around the world, with international organizations such as the United Nations, and with regional bodies such as the Organization of American States (OAS). It operates more than 150 embassies and diplomatic missions overseas, as well as some 140 consular posts. Yet the State Department's operating budget has always been one of the smallest of any executive agency. In the 1989 fiscal year, for example, it was $1.95 billion—considerably less than 1 percent of the funds allocated to the military.

Traditionally, the State Department's primary concern has been political relations with other countries. Its five regional bureaus, plus another bureau for international organizational affairs, serve as the channels for communicating policy decisions to U.S. embassies abroad and for receiving communications from them. Since World War II, there has also been a significant expansion in the department's functional bureaus, those that deal with problems and issues cutting across national boundaries. For example, the department now has a bureau that is concerned with the impact of public opinion on foreign policy, and another for oceans and international environmental and scientific affairs. Two recent additions have been bureaus for human rights and humanitarian affairs and for international refugee affairs.[23]

Another postwar development has been the department's recognition of a growing congressional role in foreign policy. An assistant secretary for congressional relations is now assigned specific responsibility for maintaining constructive relations with Congress, and this function has become an increasingly important and time-consuming dimension of State Department activities. The Office of Congressional Relations collects and analyzes information on legislative attitudes toward foreign policy issues; it provides services requested by members of Congress, such as foreign travel arrangements; and, when required, it plays a prominent role in White House lobbying on Capitol Hill for the president's foreign policy program. State Department services to Congress sometimes take curious forms. Former secretary of state Acheson pointed out that legislators often feel compelled for domestic political reasons to oppose certain external programs, such as foreign aid. In one case the department helped a legislator resolve that dilemma "by the promise of a powerful speech against the foreign aid bill when it came up for final vote in the House. We [the State Department] duly wrote it and all parties profited!"[24]

In 1961, Congress established the Agency for International Development (AID) to administer bilateral economic aid programs. Initially it was housed within the State Department; later, it was made part of the International Development Cooperation Agency. While it is thus administratively separate from the State Department, in carrying out its mission AID still takes its policy guidance from the department.

Routinely, newly elected presidents announce that they regard the secretary of state as their chief foreign policy adviser and expect this official to provide overall direction to the government's activities in foreign affairs. Yet in practice, a decline in the State Department's preeminence in the foreign policy field since World War II has been evident to all observers. The department's reputation with the White House, with other executive agencies, with Congress, and often with other governments has been chronically poor. In the minds of some presidents, the State Department has epitomized bureaucratic inertia, devotion to tradition, and lack of imagination.[25] Ever since the administration of President Franklin D. Roosevelt, presidents have been prone to bypass the State Department, using one device or another to make crucial decisions without consulting it.[26] As we shall see, coordinating mechanisms, like the National Security Council, have emerged as powerful rivals to the State Department for dominance in the foreign policy field. Indeed, at times a condition of anarchy appears to exist among the executive agencies involved in foreign relations. Countless studies have been made in recent years of the State Department, and hardly a year passes that the department does not experience major or minor organizational changes, designed in part to restore its primacy in the foreign policy process.

The erosion of the State Department's position can be explained by many factors and developments, some internal to the department and others outside it. Critics of the department have complained that it has failed to adapt its procedures and ideas to a rapidly changing world, leaving the White House no choice but to look elsewhere for creative policy recommendations. The involvement of an increasing number of other executive agencies in foreign relations has diluted the State Department's authority and responsibility. Finally, unlike other departments and agencies of the national government, the State Department suffers from the disability of having no domestic constituency to argue or lobby for its programs and activities abroad. Its policies toward Cyprus or South Africa or Israel often engender strong *negative* reactions by pressure groups within the United States. What such groups are against overseas is often considerably clearer than what they advocate positively.[27]

On Capitol Hill, the State Department is likely to be regarded by legislators as a troublemaker, for it advocates costly foreign economic and military aid programs, which are frequently unpopular with the voters. In addition, the department is often viewed as the "Department of Bad News." Virtually every year since World War II, it has had to report to Congress and the American people on some actual or potential crisis in the Middle East, some Soviet threat to U.S. security, or discouraging information about threats to democracy within the Third World.

Many Americans believe that if the State Department were organized and run more effectively, the country would be more successful in achieving its external goals. The frustration felt by members of Congress and their constituents on foreign policy issues is expressed in attacks on the State Department—and this fact in turn adversely affects the department's morale and performance.

The Intelligence Community

The agencies and bureaus that collect and analyze information on foreign affairs for the executive branch are collectively known as the *intelligence community*. As specified in Executive Order 12333, issued by President Reagan on December 4, 1981, the intelligence community consists of the Central Intelligence Agency; the National Security Agency; the Bureau of Intelligence and Research in the Department of State; the Defense Intelligence Agency and the intelligence offices of the army, navy, air force, and marine corps in the Department of Defense; the Federal Bureau of Investigation; intelligence offices in the Department of Energy and the Department of the Treasury; and "staff elements of the Director of Central Intelligence." [28]

Intelligence is a minor part of the activities of some of these agencies in terms of their budget and personnel, even though it may be important in the total flow of information. The function that makes the FBI part of the intelligence community is counterintelligence—that is, the identification of covert foreign agents in the United States and the defeat of foreign efforts at espionage and subversion. The main contribution of the Treasury Department is economic, financial, and monetary information.

As every reader of the daily headlines is aware, in recent years public controversy has surrounded the activities of the CIA and other members of the intelligence community. Charges have been made that intelligence agencies have sought to assassinate political leaders abroad; that they have supported attempts to overthrow foreign governments (for example, in Central America); and that they have infringed upon the rights of U.S. citizens. On the other hand, the intelligence agencies have also encountered criticisms (particularly after the Iranian revolution in 1979) that they have failed to provide policy makers with objective and up-to-date estimates that would have enabled them to anticipate major developments abroad and to respond effectively to them.

Two general observations about intelligence activities in the United States are worth making here. First, today, as in the past, the intelligence function is recognized by officials in both the executive and the legislative branches, and by a majority of citizens, as essential to the national security and to the achievement of diplomatic objectives. The

CIA was established in 1947 in large part because of vivid recollections by the American people and their leaders of the military disaster at Pearl Harbor, which was (rightly or wrongly) viewed as the result of an intelligence failure. Most informed Americans are aware of the adverse consequences of a crippled or inadequate intelligence service. In 1983, a terrorist attack against U.S. marines in Lebanon, resulting in the death of 241 men, dramatically called attention to the dangers implicit in a lack of advance information.

Second, the need for effective intelligence operations conflicts with such traditional democratic concepts as open diplomacy, freedom of the press, and public disclosure of information, which are no less important in the foreign policy process. The tension in a democracy between these two kinds of requirements is real, continuing, and perhaps inescapable. If, as is suggested in Chapter 6, congressional efforts to monitor and regulate intelligence operations have been less than satisfactory, the reason may be that the dilemma has no simple or easy solution.

Propaganda and Informational Programs

Another executive agency that plays a key role in foreign affairs is the United States Information Agency (USIA). Like AID, USIA is administratively separate but takes its policy guidance from the State Department. Its mission is to conduct propaganda and informational programs abroad on behalf of the United States. Perhaps its best-known activity is the Voice of America, the nation's worldwide radio network. In addition, the USIA engages in a variety of other activities and programs, such as the production and distribution of films; the preparation of press releases; the sponsorship of cultural, scientific, and other kinds of exhibits and lectures; and the operation of cultural centers and libraries overseas.

Ever since its creation in the early postwar period, controversy has surrounded the mission of the USIA, growing out of the conflict between two conceptions of the agency's mission. One view holds that it was intended to be primarily a propaganda instrument of the government, and as such, its dominant function ought to be to portray the internal and external policies of the United States in the most favorable light possible. The other conception is that USIA's principal mission is to engage in a "campaign of truth," as the program was designated by the Truman administration, and it should therefore be factual and objective in its depiction of the United States, with no attempt to gloss over shortcomings and failures. The underlying assumption of this latter approach is that objectivity is "the best propaganda" for a democratic nation. The conflict between these two schools of thought has impeded the effectiveness of U.S. propaganda and informational campaigns in the past and will likely continue to do so in the future.[29]

The Military Establishment

Among national policy makers and informed citizens, World War II produced a realization that was not always present in earlier eras of U.S. diplomacy: The military establishment plays a vital role in the foreign policy process. Previously, both civilian and military officials tended to separate political and military questions sharply, as illustrated by President Franklin D. Roosevelt's view that the resolution of political questions arising during the war ought to await the outcome of military hostilities.[30] After the end of the war, when a new political-military conflict known as the "cold war" had erupted among the erstwhile allies, Ameican officials recognized the indissoluble link between these two aspects of national policy.

Following a prolonged study, the Department of Defense was created in 1947, and other reforms of the military establishment were undertaken. While the traditional pattern of separate military services was preserved, they were placed under the jurisdiction of a single department, headed by a civilian secretary of defense. The Joint Chiefs of Staff, consisting of the commanders of each of the military branches and a chairman, was created to formulate unified military strategy.

In the late 1980s, some 2.2 million men and women were serving in the armed forces of the United States. For fiscal year 1989, the Reagan administration asked Congress to appropriate $332 billion to operate the Department of Defense. According to projections, military spending in the years following was likely to rise above this level because of the steadily growing cost of new weapons and equipment, such as aircraft carriers and support vessels, strategic missiles and bombers, and transport aircraft.

If the decline in U.S. military strength had become a matter of national concern during the Carter presidency, under President Reagan a different problem existed. This was whether the president and his advisers were too prone to conceive of external challenges confronting the United States in military terms and to prefer military solutions for complex diplomatic issues. To put the problem differently, in the light of the traumatic experience of the Vietnam War, how was the Reagan administration going *to use* the nation's growing armed strength for diplomatic ends?[31]

Even during the Korean and Vietnam wars, however, U.S. public opinion and governmental policy remained strongly supportive of one basic constitutional principle. A civilian, the president, is the commander in chief of the armed forces; the members of the National Security Council are civilian officials; and the foreign policy process is controlled by civilian officials. No convincing evidence exists that the fundamental constitutional precept of civilian control over the armed forces is in jeopardy.

Other Executive Agencies

A striking and highly significant development since World War II has been the increased interest and involvement in foreign relations by many departments and agencies within the executive branch other than those that have been discussed so far. The departments of Agriculture, Commerce, Defense, Treasury, Transportation, Interior, and Labor all have responsibility for problems with a foreign policy dimension. For example, the Agriculture Department has played a pivotal role for many years in the Food for Peace program, which ships food products to needy countries; it promotes agricultural exports to countries such as Japan; and it has sent hundreds of experts abroad to assist less-developed societies in raising their agricultural output. As has always been the case, the Commerce Department seeks to expand American business, investment, and trade opportunities abroad. The Treasury Department is concerned with fiscal and monetary issues, such as the soundness of the dollar overseas. The Transportation Department has some responsibilities in the determination of international airline routes. Even the Interior Department conducts programs that impinge upon foreign affairs, such as water reclamation projects involving the United States and Mexico.

A growing number of smaller and less publicized federal agencies have functions giving them a role in foreign relations. The National Aeronautics and Space Administration (NASA) sponsors programs that affect the global balance of military power and America's ability to monitor the military activities of other countries. The Arms Control and Disarmament Agency is responsible for preparing reports and recommendations to the president on arms-limitation proposals. The Department of Energy is concerned about such issues as the nation's access to foreign supplies of oil and the safe disposal of nuclear waste products by all nations.

This proliferation of executive agencies involved in foreign affairs has had a parallel in Congress, as we shall see more fully in Chapter 2. Today, there is hardly a legislative committee or subcommittee whose work does not relate in some way to foreign affairs, and the result is a serious potential for conflict between the White House and Congress on foreign policy questions. This poses an increasingly difficult problem for the creation and maintenance of unified governmental efforts abroad.

Coordination of Foreign Policy

Senator Vandenberg once told officials of the Truman administration that members of the Republican party wanted to cooperate with the White House on behalf of a "bipartisan foreign policy," but they could do so only with "one secretary of state at a time." The problem to which the senator alluded has become more acute since that time. The

Carter administration's response to the collapse of the Iranian monarchy in 1979, for example, became, in the words of one report,

> the subject of fierce internal debate [within the executive branch], with many officials asserting that interagency disputes and bureaucratic compromises have hampered the efforts of Mr. Carter and his top advisers to fashion and carry out an overall strategy.[32]

According to former secretary of state Alexander Haig, conflicts among President Reagan's chief foreign policy advisers were such that the United States had become a "ghost ship" drifting aimlessly upon the sea of international relations.[33]

During President Reagan's second term, an even more vivid example of intra-executive conflict and disunity in the foreign policy field was provided by the so-called Iran-contra affair. In this episode, the president's national security adviser, together with members of the National Security Council staff, high-ranking officials of the CIA, and others, arranged to sell arms to the government of Iran, in direct opposition to the president's publicly stated policy. They then used the proceeds from these sales to subsidize the activities of the "contras," an anticommunist force seeking to overthrow the Sandinista regime in Nicaragua. These activities seemed to give U.S. foreign policy a schizophrenic quality. Furthermore, they may have violated certain statutory requirements governing the supply of U.S. arms to the contras. To some, they suggested the existence of a group of executive-branch officials who were "out of control" and who either did not understand, or refused to be bound by, either presidential directives or the law.[34]

At one stage, according to Secretary of State George P. Shultz, a state of "guerrilla warfare" existed among the president's foreign policy aides. Shultz (together with Secretary of Defense Weinberger) had protested the actions of the officials involved in the Iran-contra affair, but these remonstrances had no discernible effect. As for President Reagan, the evidence is unclear as to whether he had given tacit approval for the provision of clandestine aid to the contras, or whether the officials had done so without his knowledge or authorization. Either case had troubling implications. In the former, the president might have been party to an illegal act, which could be grounds for impeachment; in the latter, the president would appear to have been "disengaged" from the process of decision making and unaware of what was going on around him. Whatever the president's precise role and responsibility, virtually all observers agreed that the episode had seriously weakened the nation's diplomatic credibility and its role as a global leader. Most also acknowledged that mechanisms like the NSC had not solved the problem of executive disunity in the foreign policy field.

There have been a few examples of an impressive degree of unity in the White House's approach to major foreign policy issues. An outstand-

ing one was the Kennedy administration's handling of the Cuban missile crisis in 1962. Its response to the discovery of nuclear-armed Soviet
missiles in Cuba was a model of diplomatic decision making; and yet in
the early stages of the crisis, there was considerable disagreement
among President Kennedy's advisers over what actions to take. Ultimately, the members of Kennedy's foreign policy team did reach substantial unanimity on the course of action to be followed, and this was
unquestionably one of the factors contributing to the achievement of
U.S. goals in the crisis. In retrospect, however, what was remarkable
about the episode was the rarity of the unity among decision-making
officials. Such a high degree of intra-executive unity on foreign policy
questions has seldom been seen again.

Presidents and Their Advisers: Four Models

On the basis of historical experience, it is possible to identify four
reasonably distinct patterns or models of relationships between chief
executives and their foreign policy advisers. Each pattern has both
assets and liabilities for the effort by the United States to achieve its
foreign policy objectives.

1. *The president as his own secretary of state.* This model is
associated particularly with the presidency of Franklin D. Roosevelt.
FDR was, in some respects, the most charismatic and politically adroit
chief executive in U.S. history. Although he possessed only limited
background and experience in the foreign policy field, as time passed he
increasingly took the conduct of external affairs into his own hands. For
example, Roosevelt had almost unlimited confidence in his ability to
arrive at lasting agreements with "Uncle Joe" Stalin, and, more generally, to create the kind of new world order he hoped would follow World
War II. FDR's secretary of state, Cordell Hull, therefore largely confined his efforts to a few assigned areas of foreign policy, such as
generating support on Capitol Hill for Roosevelt's diplomatic moves and
cultivating cordial relations with Latin America. The president himself
made crucial foreign policy decisions, often without even consulting the
State Department; negotiated with foreign leaders; attended summit
conferences; and otherwise conducted foreign relations. Hull and other
members of FDR's inner circle were often left in ignorance of the
president's foreign policy moves and intentions. Any coordination of the
administration's foreign policy activities (and frequently there was very
little) was provided by Roosevelt himself.

FDR's determination to be his own secretary of state undoubtedly
added to the burdens of his office, contributing to his declining health
and vitality. Moreover, many diplomatic historians believe that a number of Roosevelt's diplomatic decisions reflected a lack of understanding

of key international issues and were detrimental to U.S. interests. His penchant for secrecy meant that there was no immediate accountability to Congress and the electorate for foreign policy moves. At the same time, it must be remembered that FDR led the nation during wartime, when a high degree of secrecy customarily surrounds military and diplomatic moves. It must also be noted that, in the U.S. constitutional system, a president is free to function as the secretary of state at any time, and nearly all presidents in fact do so on some occasions.

2. *The hierarchical model.* This pattern is illustrated by the approach to diplomatic decision making taken by President Truman. Truman had even less experience in foreign affairs than Roosevelt, but unlike his predecessor, he did not hesitate to acknowledge his limitations in this respect. Truman followed the ritual of declaring that his secretary of state would be responsible for the conduct of foreign relations, under his own direction. However, in contrast to most presidents, Truman actually adhered to this principle. Time and again he defended his secretary of state from critics inside and outside the government and supported him against rival claimants within the executive branch. This State Department-centered model of decision making clearly has advantages, as shown by the fact that the Truman administration accomplished some of the most noteworthy diplomatic feats of the post-World War II era.

In this model, the president assumes ultimate responsibility for directing foreign affairs, but he delegates the day-to-day conduct of foreign relations to the secretary of state, who in turn relies upon the State Department bureaucracy for expertise and guidance. The secretary of state is also given the authority to coordinate foreign policy activities throughout the executive branch. (The National Security Council was created during Truman's administration, but its role in foreign policy decision making was minimal during his term of office; he was known to be unenthusiastic about the NSC mechanism.) It may be seriously questioned whether, with the widening circle of executive agencies involved in foreign policy decision making, it is any longer possible to return to this model.

3. *The consensual model.* The Johnson administration of the 1960s is a good illustration of this pattern. Its outstanding trait was the overt unanimity among the president's foreign policy advisers in formulating policy toward the Vietnam War and most other developments abroad. Under the tragic circumstances of his accession to the presidency, LBJ believed that he was obliged to continue the diplomatic policies of his predecessor, and President Kennedy had left no doubt that he viewed Communist control of Southeast Asia as highly detrimental to U.S. diplomatic and security interests. President Johnson was determined to prevent that development.

Despite his background of service in Congress, LBJ possessed little first-hand knowledge or experience in the sphere of foreign relations. Moreover, as a product of the populist political tradition, he was suspicious of the State Department and of foreign affairs generally—a realm populists believed to be a distraction from the principal business of domestic affairs. President Johnson defined his chief goal as the creation of the Great Society in the United States. LBJ also valued loyalty among his aides; he expected unwavering support from them, and he did not take kindly to evidence of dissent from his administration's policies. The result was what some commentators have called "groupthink," a more or less forced and virtually monolithic agreement among his advisers. For several years, Johnson used techniques of direct and indirect coercion to maintain this show of unity, but the result was to prevent full and frank discussion by executive officials of controversial foreign policy issues—above all, the Vietnam War. Dissenters, such as Under Secretary of State George Ball, found themselves ostracized and increasingly relegated to the sidelines. Failing to get a hearing for their views within LBJ's official family, dissenters resorted to leaks to the press in order to present their ideas and policy recommendations. Adherence to this model of decision making contributed to the perpetuation of a policy abroad that, in the end, resulted in a dramatic and serious diplomatic defeat for the United States.

4. *The rival State Department model.* The diplomatic record of the Nixon administration illustrates the fourth approach to foreign policy decision making. As a chief executive who was keenly interested in foreign policy, and had acquired impressive experience in this sphere, President Nixon had decided by the 1970s that fundamental changes were called for in the nation's approach to external problems. (Many of Nixon's substantive proposals were contained in what came to be called the "Nixon Doctrine.") He was extremely suspicious of the State Department and doubted its ability to provide the diplomatic leadership required in the era following the Vietnam War. Accordingly, Nixon selected as his national security adviser Henry Kissinger, who possessed outstanding academic credentials, had a clear conception of the direction in which he believed U.S. foreign policy ought to move, and had the ambition and skill needed to make his viewpoints prevail in the inevitable bureaucratic infighting. Like Nixon, Kissinger doubted both the ability and the willingness of the State Department to provide creative diplomatic leadership. Meanwhile, President Nixon appointed a largely unknown individual, William P. Rogers, to head the State Department, in the deliberate expectation that Rogers would be a weak and ineffectual secretary of state. In the Nixon White House, therefore, Kissinger quickly emerged as the principal spokesman, articulator, negotiator, and highly visible public symbol of the administration's foreign policy.

This White House-centered model of decision making signified the fact that the president was extremely interested in foreign affairs, was actively involved in the decision-making process, and was determined to impose central direction and coordination upon the nation's diplomatic activities. Kissinger created and operated the "rival State Department" with President Nixon's full encouragement and support. Yet, as many legislators and commentators complained at the time and afterward, Kissinger had never been confirmed as secretary of state by the Senate, and he often conducted himself as though he had no real accountability to Congress or the American people for his performance. To this day, the State Department has not regained the status it enjoyed in an earlier era, and perhaps it never will.

Conclusion

In conclusion, three observations may be made about the decision-making models considered here. First, presidents are free to use their advisers in any way they choose. Congress may create new administrative structures, like the NSC, but it cannot determine how—or even whether—a particular president will utilize such mechanisms in the decision-making process.

Second, a president may use different models at different times. For example, President Truman did rely somewhat more upon the NSC toward the end of his tenure in office than he had earlier.

Third, coordinating mechanisms and devices are perhaps in the end less important than individuals in determining whether the executive branch achieves and maintains a high degree of unity in dealing with foreign policy problems. No one of these models per se guarantees unity among the major participants in the foreign policy process, nor is one inherently superior to the others. The model that is employed, and the contribution that it makes to the foreign policy process, will to a considerable degree be determined by a particular president's administrative style and preferences. In the final analysis, durable unity within the government on foreign policy questions will likely be a function of a shared conviction that the policy adopted best promotes the interests of the United States in foreign affairs.

Notes

1. Roger Hilsman, *The Politics of Policy Making in Defense and Foreign Affairs* (New York: Harper and Row, 1971), 18. General works on the presidential office are Joseph Besette and Geoffrey Tullis, eds., *The Presidency in the Constitutional Order* (Baton Rouge, La.: Louisiana State

University Press, 1981); Edward S. Corwin, *The President: Office and Powers, 1787-1957* (New York: New York University Press, 1957); Clinton Rossiter, *The American Presidency* (New York: Harcourt, Brace and World, 1956); and Robert E. DiClerico, *The American President*, 2d ed. (Englewood Cliffs, N.J.: Prentice-Hall, 1983).

2. Clausewitz was the author of the celebrated treatise *On War*, in which he examined the relationships between armed conflict and the political process. For an illuminating condensation of his thought, see Roger A. Leonard, ed., *Clausewitz on War* (New York: Capricorn, 1968).

3. For a more detailed discussion of the meaning and connotations of diplomacy, see Elmer Plischke, "The New Diplomacy: A Changing Process," *Virginia Quarterly Review* 49 (Summer 1973): 321-345.

4. For fuller elaboration of this point, see the discussion on the "different worlds" that the State Department and Congress occupy, in Smith Simpson, *Anatomy of the State Department* (Boston: Houghton Mifflin, 1967), 152-183.

5. For a succinct discussion of this long-standing controversy, see the report prepared by the Library of Congress for the House Foreign Affairs Committee, *Background Information on the Use of the United States Armed Forces in Foreign Countries*, 91st Cong., 2d sess., 1970. A more detailed treatment of the significance of individual constitutional provisions is provided in *The Constitution of the United States of America: Analysis and Interpretation* (Washington, D.C.: Library of Congress, 1973).

6. A useful compendium of conflicting interpretations of the president's authority over the armed forces is provided in Senate Foreign Relations Committee, *Hearings on the War Powers Legislation*, 92d Cong., 1st sess., 1971. See also Pat M. Holt, *The War Powers Resolution: The Role of Congress in U.S. Armed Intervention* (Washington, D.C.: American Enterprise Institute, 1978).

7. An informative discussion of the presidential use of the armed forces to achieve diplomatic goals since World War II is Herbert K. Tillema, *Appeal to Force: American Military Intervention in the Era of Containment* (New York: Thomas Y. Crowell, 1973).

8. The context, meaning, and implications of the Carter Doctrine are discussed in Cecil V. Crabb, Jr., *The Doctrines of American Foreign Policy: Their Meaning, Role, and Future* (Baton Rouge, La.: Louisiana State University Press, 1982), 325-371. The ill-fated mission to rescue the hostages in Iran is discussed in detail in Jimmy Carter, *Keeping Faith: Memoirs of a President* (New York: Bantam Books, 1982), 459-513.

9. See the column by James Reston in the *New York Times*, December 20, 1979, and the editorial, "Unmaking a Treaty," January 20, 1980. For summaries of the Supreme Court's decision in the case, see the *Washington Post*, December 14, 1979, and the *Congressional Quarterly Weekly Report*, December 15, 1979, 2850.

10. Loch Johnson and James M. McCormick, "Foreign Policy by Executive Fiat," *Foreign Policy* 28 (Fall 1977): 118-124. This article provides a comprehensive and illuminating discussion of presidential reliance upon executive agreements since World War II and of Congress's response to that practice.

11. Ibid., 117.

12. Ibid., 118.

13. *New York Times*, March 2, 1979.

14. Ibid., February 13, 1979.

15. See W. Averell Harriman and Elie Abel, *Special Envoy to Churchill and Stalin: 1941-1946* (New York: Random House, 1975); Hamilton Jordan, *Crisis: The Last Year of the Carter Presidency* (New York: G.P. Putnam's Sons, 1982); and, for reports on Habib's diplomatic activities in the Middle East, *New York Times,* July 23 and November 2, 1982.

16. President Reagan's budgetary maneuvers in responding to upheaval and violence in Central America are discussed by Tom Wicker in the *New York Times,* March 1, 1983.

17. For more detailed discussion of lobbying by governmental agencies, see *The Washington Lobby,* 4th ed. (Washington, D.C.: CQ Press, 1982).

18. Quoted in Sidney Warren, *The President as World Leader* (New York: McGraw-Hill, 1964), 23.

19. Daniel Yankelovich, "Farewell to 'President Knows Best,'" *Foreign Affairs* 57 (1978): 670. Yankelovich contended that "automatic" public approval of presidential leadership in foreign affairs was declining, but President Reagan subsequently utilized his skills as a communicator in convincing the American public that he would reverse the decline of the nation's power abroad. For an analysis of these skills, see John Herbers, "The President and the Press Corps," *New York Times Magazine,* May 9, 1982.

20. David E. Haight and Larry E. Johnston, *The President: Roles and Powers* (Skokie, Ill.: Rand McNally, 1965), 275-281; Leon V. Sigal, *Reporters and Officials: The Organization and Politics of Newsmaking* (Lexington, Mass.: D.C. Heath, 1973); Doris A. Graber, *Media Power in Politics* (Washington, D.C.: CQ Press, 1984); Robert B. Sims, *The Pentagon Reporters* (Washington, D.C.: National Defense University Press, 1985).

21. Quoted in Thomas A. Bailey, *A Diplomatic History of the American People,* 8th ed. (New York: Appleton-Century-Crofts, 1969), 497.

22. Arthur H. Vandenberg, Jr., ed., *The Private Papers of Senator Vandenberg* (Boston: Houghton Mifflin, 1952), 344.

23. For an informed and provocative analysis of the State Department since World War II, see Barry Rubin, *Secrets of State: The State Department and the Struggle over U.S. Foreign Policy* (New York: Oxford University Press, 1985).

24. Dean Acheson, *Present at the Creation: My Years in the State Department* (New York: W. W. Norton, 1969), 93.

25. Perhaps no modern president was more inclined in this direction than Kennedy; see Theodore C. Sorensen, *Kennedy* (New York: Harper and Row, 1965), 287-290.

26. A recent example was the Carter administration's diplomacy during the Iranian crisis of 1979. According to one report, the president sent a high-ranking U.S. military officer attached to NATO to confer directly with Iranian military leaders; this official "was told by the White House to bypass the United States Embassy" in Tehran. Nor was the embassy informed about discussions between members of the White House staff and Iranian diplomatic officials in the United States. See the dispatch by Richard Burt in the *New York Times,* January 12, 1979.

27. For a more detailed analysis of the State Department's postwar decline, see Robert Pringle, "Creeping Irrelevance at Foggy Bottom," *Foreign Policy* 29 (Winter 1977-1978): 128-140.

28. *Weekly Compilation of Presidential Documents,* vol. 17, no. 49, 1336-1348. One commentator has pointed out that the concept of the intelligence community is actually rather amorphous, since nearly every executive agency engages in some form of information gathering. For a comprehensive

and objective discussion of the intelligence function, see Jeffrey T. Richelson, *The U.S. Intelligence Community* (Cambridge, Mass.: Ballinger, 1985). The evolution of the U.S. intelligence system during and after World War II is discussed in Allen Dulles, *The Craft of Intelligence* (New York: New American Library, 1965). Other useful information may be found in Lyman B. Kirkpatrick, Jr., *The U.S. Intelligence Community: Foreign Policy and Domestic Activities* (New York: Hill and Wang, 1973); and David Wise and Thomas B. Ross, *The Invisible Government: The CIA and U.S. Intelligence* (New York: Random House, 1974).

29. Background on U.S. propaganda and informational programs since World War II is provided in John W. Henderson, *The United States Information Agency* (New York: Praeger, 1969); and Terry L. Deibel, and Walter R. Roberts, *Culture and Information: Two Foreign Policy Functions* (Beverly Hills, Calif.: Sage, 1976). Recent information on the USIA's activities and programs may be found in Senate Committee on Foreign Relations, *Certain USIA Overseas Activities,* 98th Cong., 1st sess., 1983, S. Rept. 1983; and in House Committee on Foreign Affairs, *Oversight of the U.S. Information Agency,* 98th Cong., 2d sess., 1984. Useful commentaries are Frank A. Ninkovich, *The Diplomacy of Ideas: U.S. Foreign Policy and Cultural Relations* (New York: Cambridge University Press, 1981); Morrell Heald and Lawrence Kaplan, *Culture and Diplomacy* (Westport, Conn.: Greenwood Press, 1979); Garth Jowett and Victoria O'Donnell, *Propaganda and Persuasion* (Newbury Park, Calif.: Sage, 1986); and Leo Bogart, *Premises for Propaganda* (New York: Free Press, 1976).

30. See Gaddis Smith, *American Diplomacy during the Second World War* (New York: John Wiley and Sons, 1966), 12-16. For an expression of this viewpoint by a high-ranking military leader, see Omar N. Bradley, *A Soldier's Story* (New York: Holt, Rinehart and Winston, 1951), 536.

31. A number of studies have appeared in recent years questioning the defense policies of both the Carter and the Reagan administrations and criticizing the organization of the U.S. military establishment, contending that it has in fact done little to promote a unified national defense policy. Among these studies are James Fallows, *National Defense* (New York: Random House, 1982); James Coates and Michael Kilian, *Heavy Losses: The Dangerous Decline of American Defense* (New York: Penguin, 1986); Barry Blechman and William J. Lynn, eds., *Toward a More Effective Defense* (Cambridge, Mass.: Ballinger, 1985); The Boston Study Group, *Winding Down: The Price of Defense* (San Francisco: W. H. Freeman, 1982); Donald M. Snow, *National Security: Enduring Problems of U.S. Defense Policy* (New York: St. Martins, 1987); George E. Hudson and Joseph Kruzel, eds., *American Defense Annual, 1985-1986* (Lexington, Mass.: Lexington Books, 1985), and see later publications in this series; Robert W. Polle, Jr., ed., *Defending a Free Society* (Lexington, Mass.: D. C. Heath, 1984); Asa A. Clark, ed., *The Defense Reform Debate: Issues and Analyses* (Baltimore: The Johns Hopkins University Press, 1984); and Arthur T. Hadley, *The Straw Giant: Triumph and Failure—America's Armed Forces* (New York: Random House, 1986).

32. Dispatch by Richard Burt, in the *New York Times,* January 12, 1979.

33. Alexander Haig, *Caveat: Realism, Reagan, and Foreign Policy* (New York: Macmillan, 1984). Haig's tenure as President Reagan's first secretary of state was marked by continuous squabbling among cabinet heads and White House aides; after eighteen months in office, he resigned and was replaced by George Shultz.

34. During the spring and summer of 1987, committees of the House of Representatives and the Senate jointly conducted a detailed investigation of the Iran-contra affair; see Senate Select Committee on Secret Military Assistance to Iran and the Nicaraguan Opposition, *Report of the Committees Investigating the Iran-Contra Affair,* 100th Cong., 1st sess., 1987, S. Rept. 100-216. Other useful accounts of the affair are the summary of events prepared by the staff of the National Security Archive, *The Chronology* (New York: Warner, 1987), and *The Tower Commission Report* (New York: Bantam Books-Times Books, 1987). The Tower Commission was a group of three men, chaired by former senator John Tower, appointed by President Reagan to look into the affair not long after it came to light.

CHAPTER 2

Congress and Foreign Affairs: Traditional and Contemporary Roles

In mid-October 1987, the Senate passed a $3.6 billion authorization bill to finance the operations of the State Department for the next fiscal year. During the course of debate on this measure, ninety-eight amendments were offered, of which eighty-six were adopted. As one report expressed it, these amendments enabled legislators to express "outrage, support, concern and frustration" about almost every conceivable aspect of American foreign relations. One amendment called upon the president to seek reimbursement from those nations (chiefly the NATO allies and Japan) whose ships were being protected by the U.S. navy in the Persian Gulf. Another exempted anticommunist newspapers and other publications from the U.S. trade boycott against Nicaragua. Others demanded that the president close the offices operated by the Palestine Liberation Organization (PLO) in Washington and New York City, and condemned Chinese persecution of Tibetan nationalists and political dissidents. (One amendment that was rejected asserted that U.S. acceptance of the Panama Canal treaties in 1978 had been a major mistake.)

Meanwhile, congressional dissatisfaction with the condition of the nation's external foreign policy was expressed in another way: Congress made a deeper cut in the State Department's operating budget than had been made in some thirty years—a reduction that the department said would require large-scale layoffs of personnel. (It was observed, however, that the $84 million reduction in funds represented less than half the cost of a single B-1 bomber.)[1]

These actions illustrated the determination of the legislative branch to play a greater role in the foreign policy process. Since the

Vietnam conflict especially—because of the belief that actions by the
"imperial presidency" were in large measure responsible for American
involvement in that traumatic episode—legislators have been determined to take back what many of them view as the historic prerogatives
of Congress in foreign, no less than in domestic, policy. At a minimum,
they want Congress to be accepted as a "partner" with the president in
the conduct of foreign relations; some legislators even aspire to make
Congress the dominant organ of the government in the foreign policy
field. In any case, it seems indisputable that congressional activism has
now become a permanent feature of American foreign relations.[2]

Congressional Assertiveness:
The Challenge and the Problems

All informed students of recent U.S. foreign relations are aware
that the milestones in the nation's diplomacy in the years after World
War II—establishment of the UN (1945), the Greek-Turkish Aid Program (1947), the Marshall Plan for European recovery (1948), the
NATO treaty (1949), and the Point IV program of aid to the developing
countries (1949)—emerged as the result of collaboration between executive and legislative policy makers. Over the next twenty years, however,
congressional influence in foreign relations declined, reaching its nadir
at the time of the Vietnam War. Yet by the mid-1970s, presidents
Richard Nixon and Gerald Ford—joined sometimes even by some legislators—were complaining about the "restraints" that Congress had
imposed upon the executive branch's ability to respond to foreign crises.
During the 1980s, President Reagan similarly deplored legislative efforts to limit his freedom of action in Central America and the Middle
East.

According to an informed commentator, Congress has "always been
uncertain about its role in the field of foreign affairs."[3] Can Congress
become a dynamic and effective force in foreign relations? Can it, as
some proponents of a more influential legislative role advocate, operate
as a partner with the president in foreign affairs? A revitalization of
legislative influence in external affairs faces numerous major and minor
obstacles.

There is, first of all, a problem that has impeded effective legislative participation in the foreign policy process for more than two centuries—since even before the founding of the republic—and may be a
more formidable obstacle today than at any other stage in American
history. In 1777, the Continental Congress established a five-member
Committee for Foreign Affairs to conduct external relations. Yet, as the
study found, "partisanship and personalities, frequent changes in personnel and the use of special committees, impaired the efficient func-

tioning of the committee and made a coherent policy impossible."
Legislative management of foreign relations was characterized by "fluc-
tuation, . . . delay and indecision." As much as any other single factor, it
was the mismanagement of foreign affairs *by Congress* that led to the
calling of the Constitutional Convention in 1787.[4]

Contemporary evidence indicates that the same conditions—a diffusion of power and responsibility in Congress and an inability to
coordinate its activities in foreign affairs—are no less present today
than they were then.[5] Indeed, they may have become worse since the
end of World War II, as political party ties have weakened, the power of
committee chairmen has declined, the number of legislative subcommittees has proliferated, and individual legislators increasingly attempt to
"leave their mark" on selected areas of foreign policy. Sen. Barry
Goldwater, R-Ariz., upon retiring from the Senate after many years of
service, said, "If this is the world's greatest deliberative body, I'd hate to
see the worst!" [6]

A few figures and examples will reinforce and illustrate the point.
During an investigation by the Senate Foreign Relations Committee of
the Johnson administration's conduct of the Vietnam War, one member
remarked, "There are nineteen men on [the committee], and they
represent 21½ viewpoints." [7] During the 1970s, the Carter administration's foreign policy efforts were beset by the divisions on Capitol Hill.
Distrustful of the Soviet Union, conservative groups in Congress opposed attempts to arrive at agreements with Moscow, such as the SALT
II treaty. By contrast, liberal legislators were calling for large reductions
in the national defense budget. A third group demanded across-the-
board reductions in all federal spending.[8]

During the first session of the 99th Congress (1985), the Senate had
sixteen standing (or permanent) committees, and nearly all of them
claimed jurisdiction over some aspect of foreign policy. For example, the
Committee on Agriculture, Nutrition, and Forestry had a subcommittee
on foreign agricultural policy. The Armed Services Committee had six
subcommittees concerned with foreign affairs, such as one on sea power
and force projection abroad. The Commerce, Science, and Transportation Committee had one subcommittee on business, trade, and tourism,
and another that dealt with the merchant marine fleet. The Finance
Committee had a subcommittee on international trade, while the Judiciary Committee had one on immigration and refugee policy. The Senate, lamented one experienced legislator, "has 100 separate power centers." [9]

The situation is similar in the House of Representatives. In the
drafting of a trade bill in 1986, six different standing committees played
a significant part. In addition to the Foreign Affairs Committee, they
were the Ways and Means, the Banking, Finance, and Urban Affairs,

the Energy and Commerce, the Education and Labor, and the Agriculture committees.[10] When Congress was called upon in the 1970s to respond to the energy crisis precipitated by the suspension of oil shipments from the Persian Gulf area, the House leadership discovered that more than *eighty subcommittees* had jurisdiction over some aspect of the energy problem, leading to the observation that the term "subcommittee government" could be used to describe the operations of the legislative branch.[11]

Perhaps no chief executive since World War II struggled with a divided Congress more frequently, and over a wider range of foreign policy issues, than President Ronald Reagan. From the day he entered the Oval Office, legislators called upon the White House to renew the search for arms-control agreements with the Soviet Union. The pact that was finally signed in 1987 between the United States and the Soviet Union, reducing intermediate-range missiles on the European continent, was in no small measure the result of such continuing legislative pressure. On a different front, Congress approved a record-level national defense budget of some $300 billion. This included funding for continued research and development for President Reagan's controversial Strategic Defense Initiative (SDI), or "Star Wars," as it has been popularly called. If the project proved to be feasible (which many scientists doubted), it would ultimately cost untold billions of dollars over future decades. Moreover, many critics were convinced that it violated the Soviet-U.S. Anti-Ballistic Missile Treaty (a question dealt with more fully in Chapter 3).[12]

U.S. policy toward Latin America was another issue illustrating the presence of deep divisions and uncertainty on Capitol Hill concerning the direction of the nation's diplomacy. Determined to avoid "another Vietnam," Congress imposed restrictions upon the quantity and kinds of aid the Reagan administration could provide to anticommunist groups in Central America, notably to the contras opposing the Sandinista government of Nicaragua. President Reagan and his supporters viewed the contras as "freedom fighters," whose goal was the creation of a genuinely democratic government in Nicaragua.

A matter of related congressional interest—highlighted by the Iran-contra affair, which held the spotlight of public attention during much of 1987—was the imposition of new legislative restrictions upon the activities of U.S. intelligence agencies, especially upon those "covert" operations that in time usually became well publicized. One restraining factor, which President Reagan exploited on numerous occasions, was that the president's opponents on Capitol Hill recognized the risk of "losing" Central America to communism. (In the early postwar era, the Democrats had been accused of "losing" China to communism.) Accordingly, Reagan's critics in Congress were loath to terminate aid to the contras or to prohibit all forms of covert intervention in Central America.[13]

The experience of the Reagan administration raises a serious question about congressional ability to play an effective role in foreign affairs. To cite merely one example at this point (others will be given later), in 1984, for the third straight year, Congress was so internally divided that it was unable to pass the customary annual foreign aid bill. Deadlock on Capitol Hill made it considerably easier for the Reagan White House to gain piecemeal approval by the House and Senate for its foreign aid requests.[14]

Congress's Constitutional Powers

Like the executive branch, Congress has both formal constitutional and extraconstitutional prerogatives. For the Founding Fathers, Congress was unquestionably viewed as the dynamic organ of government, as the voice of the people, and as the depository of democratic ideals. For a number of reasons—not least, their colonial experience—they were profoundly suspicious of executive power. The American people and their delegates to the Constitutional Convention mostly believed that the abuse of power by executive officials (by King George III, the British prime minister, and the royal colonial governors) was largely responsible for the American Revolution. It is noteworthy that the powers and responsibilities of Congress are described in the first article of the Constitution; they are also specified in much greater detail than those of the president or the judiciary.

Did the Founding Fathers expect Congress to play the leading role in foreign, as well as in domestic affairs? Or, as the Supreme Court held in 1936, did they understand that these were two realms?[15] Constitutional authorities have debated this question for some two hundred years, and even today the answer remains unclear.* As Thomas Jefferson, the nation's first secretary of state, said, "The transaction of business with foreign nations is executive altogether." [16] The experience of President George Washington in trying to arrive at a unified position within the national government on the Jay Treaty with England in 1794 underscored his point. The treaty was approved only after "stormy sessions" in both houses of Congress.[17]

---

* Many commentators on American diplomacy draw a distinction in roles between the executive and the legislative branches in making and conducting foreign policy. Yet this traditional distinction is becoming increasingly difficult to draw and maintain in practice. The *conduct* of foreign policy—involving such questions as how foreign aid is actually administered or whether the president should use armed force to achieve a particular foreign policy objective—is not a matter that Congress today is willing to leave solely to the executive branch. In other words, how the White House *conducts* foreign policy will affect legislative attitudes and behavior in the *making* of foreign policy.

In any case, the Founding Fathers gave the legislative branch important constitutional duties in the foreign policy field. Of the eighteen powers given to Congress in Article I, Section 8, seven affect foreign policy directly; others are enumerated in Article II. Four of Congress's foreign policy powers are especially important. Two of them belong to the Senate alone, creating for it a unique role in the foreign policy process: giving advice and consent to treaties and confirming the executive's appointments. The other two are exercised jointly by the House and Senate: the power to raise and appropriate funds and the power to declare war.

Advice and Consent Prerogative

As we have already seen, the Constitution provides that the president may make treaties "by and with the Advice and Consent of the Senate ... provided two-thirds of the senators present concur." Why did the Framers require that agreements with other countries must receive a two-thirds majority vote in the Senate, when a simple majority was deemed sufficient for all other legislative acts (except impeachments and the overriding of vetoes)? The answer appears to be that this provision reflected the isolationist sentiments of the Founding Fathers—a "congenital distrust of Europe"—and illustrated the people's determination that the nation's involvement in international politics would remain extremely limited.[18]

Another question is why congressional participation in treaty making was limited to the Senate alone. From their experience under the Articles of Confederation, the Founders had become painfully aware of the consequences of foreign policy mismanagement by the entire Congress. The smaller, indirectly elected (until 1913), and more mature Senate—capable of resisting the whims of public opinion—was expected to serve as a kind of council of state to advise the president on foreign relations.

As noted in Chapter 1, the ratification of international agreements by the United States government is a multistage process, in which the Senate plays a critical role. It acts upon treaties submitted to it by the president, but it does not, as is often believed, "ratify" them.[19] It gives (or withholds) its "advice and consent," but treaties become part of "the supreme law of the land" (as they are designated in Article VI of the Constitution) only when they have been approved by a two-thirds vote in the Senate *and* proclaimed by the president.

Throughout the course of U.S. history, the vast majority of treaties has been approved by the Senate. Between 1789 and 1982, only nineteen treaties were rejected by the Senate, out of some 1,400 submitted to it.[20] (In some cases, the Senate neither approves nor disapproves a treaty; it simply refuses to act upon it. This is equivalent to rejection.) Occasionally, the threat of an adverse vote can induce a president to withdraw White House support for a treaty under Senate consideration, as occurred when President Jimmy Carter in effect withdrew the SALT II arms-control agreement with the Soviet Union in 1980. Although SALT II is, technically speaking, still "before" the Senate, senators know that a treaty cannot go into effect without the support of the president.

In the postwar period, it has become common practice for the president to invite senators to participate in the negotiations leading to major international agreements. This practice has come to be viewed as a way of imparting bipartisanship to foreign affairs and of enhancing the prospects for favorable senatorial action on any resulting treaty. Indeed, today the Senate probably expects to be routinely included in important treaty negotiations. Legislators have even undertaken diplomatic negotiations on their own, sometimes in the face of expressed presidential opposition to their actions, as we shall see in Chapter 8.

Another dimension of the treaty-making process became a matter of controversy between executive and legislative officials in the late 1980s. This was the issue of the *interpretation* of existing treaties. As will be explained in Chapter 3, certain provisions of the Anti-Ballistic Missile Treaty of 1972—especially those related to the development of a space-based defense system ("Star Wars") by the United States—had become matters of great contention between the Reagan White House and its critics. President Reagan's position was twofold: he contended that the construction of a Star Wars system was permissible under the 1972 treaty and that the interpretation of the terms of this or any other treaty is an exclusively executive prerogative. Opponents of Star Wars on Capitol Hill argued that the system would violate the ABM agreement. Even so staunch a supporter of a strong defense establishment as Senator Sam Nunn, D-Ga., said that the Senate was entitled to interpret the meaning of any treaty to which it has given its consent. At a minimum, the Senate and White House jointly should agree upon a treaty's meaning. President Reagan, however, showed no sign of being deterred by such legislative sentiments from moving ahead with the development of the Star Wars system.

The Senate's role in the treaty-making process has given the upper chamber a distinctive and prestigious position in foreign affairs. It was Senate opposition that led to U.S. rejection of membership in the League of Nations after World War I; and during the interwar period, powerful voices in the Senate expressed the isolationist sentiment that actuated the nation's foreign policy. During and after World War II, influential senators such as Arthur H. Vandenberg, R-Mich., and Tom Connally, D-Texas, cooperated with the Roosevelt and Truman administrations to lay the foundation for the active internationalist role that the United States assumed after 1945.[21] In the 1960s, the Senate (more specifically, the Senate Foreign Relations Committee) again took the lead in congressional opposition to the nation's role in the Vietnam War.

Throughout most of the nation's history, the House of Representatives was content to play a subordinate role in the foreign policy process. Membership on the House Foreign Affairs Committee was largely viewed as a symbolic assignment that few legislators coveted. As late as 1970, the chairman of the Foreign Affairs Committee expressed the opinion that the committee should normally support the executive branch's foreign policy positions.[22]

A noteworthy trend in recent years, however, has been an effort by the House to reverse this traditional role. Even though the House has no formal constitutional responsibility in treaty making, it has sought to use other powers, such as its predominant position in the appropriations process, to exert its influence in foreign relations. This viewpoint was illustrated in the remarks of Rep. John D. Dingell, D-Mich., early in 1979 in connection with the Panama Canal treaties:

> We in the House are tired of you people in the State Department going to your tea-sipping friends in the Senate. Now you good folks come up here and say you need legislation [to implement the treaties] after you ignored the House. If you expect me to vote for this travesty, you're sorely in error.[23]

Later, President Reagan's critics in the House demanded that he adhere to the provisions of the (unratified) SALT II treaty. They threatened to enact this demand into law, perhaps as an amendment to the Defense Department's budget, if the president refused to comply.[24]

Senators resent these efforts by the House to intrude upon their historic domain, and they continue to guard their constitutional prerogatives in the treaty-making process jealously. Sen. Frank Church, D-Idaho, a former chairman of the Senate Foreign Relations Committee, said of the representatives' actions, "Their nibbles end up being big bites, and we [are] being bitten to death." [25]

Confirmation Prerogative

The other (and much less influential) senatorial prerogative is the power to confirm executive appointments. In the minds of the Founders, this power and the power to approve treaties were interrelated. The Senate was expected to play a key role in the appointment of the officials who would engage in treaty negotiations. The Senate would thereby acquire a voice in framing the instructions given to these officials.[26] Within a relatively short time, however, this linkage broke down. Throughout U.S. history, the Senate has generally given routine approval to the president's diplomatic appointees. In 1981, for example, a not untypical year, out of 106,616 nominations for appointments by the president that were received by the Senate, 105,284 were confirmed,

33 were withdrawn, and 1,299 were left unconfirmed by the end of the legislative session. No nominee was rejected outright.[27] As a rule, the Senate operates upon the principle that an incumbent president is entitled to have a "team" in which he has confidence and whose members will support his program.

Occasionally, of course, the rule is broken. Early in his first term, President Reagan nominated Ernest W. Lefever to be assistant secretary of state for human rights and humanitarian affairs. A number of legislators and public groups questioned Lefever's dedication to the cause of international human rights. In the face of virtually certain senatorial rejection of his candidate, President Reagan withdrew Lefever's nomination.[28] Several years later, President Reagan nominated Robert M. Gates to serve as director of the Central Intelligence Agency. Because of his involvement in the Iran-contra affair, Gates was widely opposed within Congress, and President Reagan also withdrew his name from further consideration.[29]

Power of the Purse

What has historically been called the "power of the purse"—the weapon used by the British Parliament to establish its primacy over the monarchy—consists of two interrelated prerogatives: the power to *raise revenue* (by means of taxes, tariffs, and loans), granted to Congress in Article I, Section 8; and the power to determine how the funds shall be *spent*, in accordance with the stipulation in Article I, Section 9 that "no money shall be drawn from the Treasury, but in Consequence of Appropriations made by law."

Since all federal expenditures must be approved by Congress, it may increase funds for particular programs above White House recommendations; it may refuse to grant the funds needed for carrying out certain programs and policies; it may provide the required funds with the proviso that certain conditions be met; it may terminate programs already in existence; and it may exercise legislative oversight of programs, investigating such questions as whether they are achieving their objectives or whether their continuation is in the national interest.

A few brief examples will illustrate the scope and importance of the power of the purse in shaping external policy. In 1986, Congress reduced the Reagan administration's proposed defense budget by $17.6 billion— the largest cut in the White House's recommended defense budget in many years. Congress at first refused to accept President Reagan's request for funds to produce the Pershing II and MX missile systems; although funds for these systems were later restored, the amounts were smaller than had been requested. In the same year, the House nearly passed a resolution calling upon the executive branch to negotiate a freeze on nuclear testing with the Soviet Union (it was defeated by one vote). Congress also placed a ceiling of 315,000 on the number of U.S. troops that could be stationed in Western Europe; and in a related move, it made a moderate reduction in the financial contribution by the United States to the NATO defense program—thereby indicating the existence of widespread dissatisfaction on Capitol Hill with the level of contributions to NATO by other members of the alliance.

In succeeding years, Congress refused to approve—or placed very severe restrictions upon—military aid to the Nicaraguan contras, despite President Reagan's repeated insistence that support for them was essential to achieve the nation's diplomatic and security goals in the Western Hemisphere. In mid-1986, the House finally approved the president's request. The vote margin was only twelve votes, and the administration won this narrow victory only after an intensive "lobbying blitz" directed at wavering members of the House.[30] The following year, because of the revelations accompanying the Iran-contra affair (see Chapter 1), the Reagan administration's program of aid to the contras once again came under fire on Capitol Hill. When the evidence left little doubt that executive officials had evaded or violated the law in their efforts to support the contras, many legislators appeared determined either to cut off U.S. funds to the contras entirely or to impose extremely stringent limitations governing their use.

In 1986, Secretary of State Shultz complained vociferously about the budgetary cuts made by Congress in the administration's foreign policy programs. Shultz declared his intention to "drop everything else" in order to lobby for restoration of the funds. He asserted that the budget reductions by Congress impaired the nation's ability to promote democracy and economic progress in such countries as the Philippines, South Korea, and Thailand and jeopardized the ability of the United States to protect its embassies and citizens abroad from attacks by terrorists. In Shultz's assessment, Congress's action amounted to a "tragedy for U.S. foreign policy and national security." [31]

During President Reagan's second term, legislators used the annual debate over the Defense Department budget as another occasion for assertiveness in the foreign policy field. In 1987, for example, some of them expressed their opposition to the Star Wars proposal; others demanded that the White House move ahead energetically in the effort to arrive at an arms control agreement with the Soviet Union that would reduce the number of intermediate-range missiles in Europe. A number of Democrats in the Senate threatened to filibuster the defense spending bill unless their demands were accepted by the president. In turn, Republicans filibustered to keep Democratic demands out of the bill. Other critics of President Reagan's diplomacy threatened to reduce drastically the proposed $303 billion defense budget unless executive officials were more responsive to congressional complaints.[32]

During the same period, Congress voted to suspend U.S. aid to Pakistan, in an expression of legislative displeasure with that nation's apparent determination to acquire a nuclear arsenal. Some legislators were searching for a way to express their dissatisfaction with the Reagan administration's policies in the Persian Gulf area—especially its failure to involve Congress in the making of key decisions, some of which risked the possibility that the United States would become actively engaged in military hostilities.[33]

Both potentially and actually, the power of the purse is a highly effective instrument available to Congress for influencing the conduct of foreign relations. Even in recent years, however, it is doubtful that Congress has taken full advantage of this weapon in the struggle with the White House over the control of external policy.

Authorization and Appropriations Process. Federal programs that require expenditures for their implementation must be approved by Congress in two stages. As an example, take the annual foreign aid budget. The first major step in the process is for the program to be considered by the Senate Foreign Relations Committee and the House Foreign Affairs Committee. Theoretically, in this *authorization phase* these committees are concerned with such questions as: Does foreign assistance promote the diplomatic interests of the United States? Are particular foreign aid projects (in Bolivia, say, or Morocco, or India) justified? Is there a strong likelihood that the objectives of the program can be achieved? Following committee consideration and recommendation, authorization bills must be approved by the full House and the full Senate. If the bills differ, the two houses must agree upon a common measure before the authorization becomes law and this stage is completed.

Next, the foreign aid program must go through the *appropriations stage,* in which the funds are actually provided for its implementation. This is the province of the House and Senate appropriations committees. Custom has established that the House committee plays the dominant role in the appropriations process, and in the postwar period it has had a decisive voice in certain aspects of American foreign policy.

Theoretically, neither the House nor the Senate Appropriations Committee is concerned with the merits of a program that has already been authorized by Congress. The appropriations committees are supposed to concentrate upon such matters as whether sufficient revenues are available to finance the authorized programs. In practice, however, the jurisdictional and political lines between the appropriations committees and the authorizing committees have become indistinct, to the point of disappearing entirely. Between 1955 and 1965, for example, the foreign aid program encountered its most formidable opposition on

Capitol Hill from the Foreign Operations Subcommittee of the House Appropriations Committee, headed by Rep. Otto Passman, D-La., an outspoken and determined opponent of foreign aid. Each year the subcommittee subjected the foreign aid authorization to "Passmanization," a process of making massive cuts in the program. Passman accused executive policy makers of attempting to "grab the check," that is, forcing U.S. taxpayers to pay for all the social and economic needs of the world.[34]

By custom, the Senate Appropriations Committee functions as a "court of review" for the actions taken by its counterpart in the House. As a rule, some—occasionally most—of the cuts made by the House in foreign aid (and other programs) are restored by the Senate committee. The final amount in the appropriation bill must then be set by another agreement between the two chambers.[35]

Problems of Budgetary Procedures.   Students of the national legislative process, as well as many members of the House and Senate, have long recognized and deplored the fact that Congress's handling of the budget is fragmented and lacking in any sense of priority among the literally hundreds of budgetary categories. In an effort to remedy these longstanding defects, in 1974 Congress enacted the Budget and Impoundment Control Act.[36] This act created budget committees in the House and the Senate, whose responsibility it would be to prepare a tentative, and later a final, budget for each chamber. The latter would reflect decisions about spending priorities and would balance total expenditures against anticipated governmental revenues.

Without entering into a detailed analysis of the effects of this act, it may be noted that this attempt at budgetary control has thus far failed to achieve its objectives. Some observers, in fact, believe that the changes have made foreign policy measures, such as the foreign aid program, even more vulnerable on Capitol Hill than they were before. The process of budgetary accommodation now required, in the view of one commentator, "has the greatest impact on the weakest programs," making foreign aid "a prime target" (especially in a national election year). Lacking a strong domestic constituency, foreign aid is always a tempting target for budget cutters.

By many criteria, the power of the purse has been and remains the most potent weapon available to Congress for determining public policy. Yet even in the post-Vietnam era of congressional activism, it remains an underutilized instrument of legislative influence in foreign affairs. As we observed in Chapter 1, resourceful presidents can usually get access to funds for foreign policy undertakings, at least in the short run, by using emergency funds at their disposal, by reprogramming budgeted funds, and by other devices. Ultimately, the threat or actuality of reduced appropriations can of course restrain the president or compel changes in his conduct of foreign relations. Yet, as was evident when Congress dealt with the Reagan administration's policies toward Central America, legislators have often been inhibited from entirely cutting off funds for particular projects (such as the administration's aid to anticommunist groups in the region) by a powerful deterrent: fear that they would be held responsible by the president and the voters for any adverse consequences to the diplomatic interests of the United States. Nevertheless, in the long run, all chief executives are aware that nearly every worthwhile program in foreign affairs requires funds for its implementation; and if Congress does not provide those funds, the program has no future.

War Powers Prerogative

Constitutional Powers. Four consecutive provisions of Article I, Section 8 of the Constitution comprise the war powers of Congress. These confer the powers to "declare war," to "raise and support armies," to "provide and maintain a navy," and to "make rules for the government and regulation" of the armed forces. These provisions have served as the basis for forceful assertions of the congressional will in external policy. The Truman administration was widely criticized on Capitol Hill for ignoring legislative viewpoints and prerogatives when it involved the United States in the Korean War during the early 1950s. In time, the Johnson and Nixon administrations faced even more outspoken congressional disapproval of their escalation of the Vietnam War and of the invasion of Cambodia without the explicit approval of Congress. More recently, the passage of the War Powers Resolution in 1973 and efforts to limit the kinds of national commitments undertaken by the executive branch have indicated Congress's determination to influence the course of foreign relations by exerting its powers over the military establishment. During 1987, many members of the House and Senate insisted that Congress must be more fully involved in the Reagan administration's efforts to preserve access to the oil fields of the Persian Gulf area—efforts that unquestionably entailed the risk of war.

Declarations of War. Although the Constitution grants to Congress the power to declare war, several developments in modern international relations have combined to render this legislative prerogative largely a formality. In contrast to international practice for several centuries before the Constitution was drafted, in modern history nations have seldom declared war before engaging in hostilities. When Congress does issue a declaration of war (which it does rarely), the declaration simply recognizes that a condition of warfare *already exists;*

it is not an occasion for Congress to debate whether hostilities *ought* to exist.

Indeed, more than a century ago the Supreme Court held in a landmark case that the existence of a state of war depended upon prevailing conditions; the president was not required to await a declaration of war from Congress before responding to external threats.[37] Chief executives, especially in modern times, have frequently referred to "functional equivalents" of a declaration of war. Examples are the passage of the 1964 Gulf of Tonkin Resolution, which approved the president's use of armed force in responding to threats to U.S. security interests in Vietnam, and (during the Vietnam War) congressional enactment of the draft and the defense budget.[38]

Of the more than 125 violent encounters in which the United States has been engaged, only five have involved declarations of war by Congress. Most of these incidents of armed conflict have involved major or minor episodes in which the president or a local U.S. official employed the armed forces for foreign policy ends. Neither of the two prolonged and costly military engagements since the end of World War II—the Korean War (called a "police action" by the Truman administration) and the Vietnam War—was formally declared to be a "war" by Congress, primarily because the incumbent president did not request Congress to do so.

The creation of a worldwide network of military alliances since World War II has also eroded the power of Congress to declare war. Article 5 of the NATO agreement, for example, provides that the parties shall regard an attack upon one signatory as an attack upon all of them—a provision which, according to many commentators, is tantamount to the threat of "automatic war" by the United States. Despite laments on Capitol Hill about the tendency of modern presidents to bypass Congress in decisions to employ the armed forces abroad, some legislators have said that a declaration of war in each case involving military hostilities abroad would be inadvisable, since it might turn a limited war into a global nuclear conflict.[39]

Separation of Powers.   During the drafting of the Constitution, Congress was at first given the power to "make" war. This language was later changed to grant Congress the power to "declare" war. Suspicious as they were of executive power, the Founders recognized that the successful prosecution of a war would require *both* executive and legislative participation; one branch alone could not "make" war. (No one was more mindful of this than George Washington, who had endured many frustrating experiences trying to get coordinated policy and effective support from the Continental Congress during the Revolutionary War.) Accordingly, in the Constitution the chief executive is also given important military powers. In particular, the president is designated commander in chief of the armed forces. As with other constitutional issues, the precise balance or allocation of war powers between the two ends of Pennsylvania Avenue has been determined more by experience, precedents, and circumstances than by the intentions of the Founders or by contending legal theories. In this case, the overall tendency has been for legislative prerogatives to be eclipsed by executive initiative and leadership.

Included in the legislative war powers is the requirement that Congress "raise and support armies" and "provide and maintain a navy." Reflecting the American people's aversion to a standing army, the Constitution prohibits Congress from making appropriations for the army for longer than two years. (No such limitation exists with regard to naval appropriations.) This stipulation assured that the questions of the size and character of the armed forces would be subject to frequent legislative review.

Throughout modern history, Congress has seldom used its power over the military establishment to its fullest potential for the purpose of influencing the course of American diplomacy. From the end of World War II until the termination of the Vietnam War, the tendency was for Congress to provide the kind of armed forces requested by the White House. From the end of the Vietnam conflict until the late 1970s, defense spending was deemphasized in favor of expanded domestic programs. Toward the end of President Carter's term, however, a significant expansion in the national defense budget began, as a result of the revolution in Iran and the Soviet invasion of Afghanistan.

When President Reagan took office, he was determined to restore the nation's military strength, and so he called for a new intercontinental missile system (the MX), an expanded navy, a new "stealth" bomber, and later, the Star Wars antimissile defense system. The resulting annual defense budget of $300 billion and more provided numerous opportunities for congressional influence in determining the size and nature of the military establishment. Yet, as in the past, many legislators (including some who opposed the expansion of the military) were often reluctant to oppose the White House overtly on an issue directly affecting the national security of the United States. For example, several legislators who were skeptical about the proposed MX missile system ultimately voted to provide research and development funds for it. Similarly, once the president had committed American forces to the defense of the Persian Gulf region, many legislators were reluctant to deny the funds needed by these forces.[40]

The War Powers Resolution.   Mounting legislative dissatisfaction with the president's use of the armed forces for foreign policy ends was forcefully demonstrated in 1973, when Congress passed the War Powers Resolution over President Nixon's veto.[41] This resolution will be more fully discussed in Chapter 5, but a few general observations should be made here.

The resolution declared that its purpose was to ensure that the "collective judgment of both the Congress and the President will apply to the introduction of United States Armed Forces into hostilities," or into situations in which hostilities are believed to be imminent. Accordingly, it required that congressional consent be obtained for the prolonged use of U.S. troops in foreign conflicts; otherwise the president would be required to withdraw American forces.

In the relatively brief time that has elapsed since passage of the War Powers Resolution,* it is difficult to assess its impact upon American foreign policy. Advocates of a more influential congressional voice in foreign policy decision making have in general applauded the resolution, but other commentators (including a growing number of legislators) have been considerably less enthusiastic. Some have questioned whether, in the context of a foreign crisis, the resolution would really inhibit the president's reliance upon armed force to promote national security and diplomatic objectives; by the late 1980s, experience had tended to confirm these doubts. Other students of the U.S. constitutional system have argued that the resolution in fact *strengthened* the position of the president as commander in chief of the armed forces, by according him wide latitude to deploy them with little effective hindrance by Congress.

In recent years, chief executives have taken somewhat different positions regarding their authority over the armed forces. Presidents Ford and Carter acknowledged the legality of congressional restrictions on this authority, such as those contained in the War Powers Resolution, but nevertheless objected to them.[42] Other presidents, such as Johnson, Nixon, and Reagan, have insisted that this authority was derived *from the Constitution* and therefore could not be limited by statutes or congressional resolutions. President Reagan, in particular, has complied with the resolution only nominally or has not complied

---

* One provision of the resolution was nullified by the Supreme Court's 1983 decision, in an unrelated case, regarding the legislative veto. *Legislative veto* is the name given to the procedure whereby Congress *permits* executive officials to engage in certain specified activities (such as the president's commitment of the armed forces abroad), unless and until Congress revokes his authority to do so. Normally, Congress's "veto" of executive actions is cast on a case-by-case basis, as was contemplated by the provisions of the War Powers Resolution. The Court held that the legislative veto was an unconstitutional exercise of legislative power, since the Constitution specifically provided for the procedures that must be followed (that is, passage by both houses of Congress and the signature of the president) for the enactment of legislation. The decision affected numerous pieces of legislation. (See *Immigration and Naturalization Service v. Chadha,* 51 U.S.L.W. 4907, 1983.)

with it at all. In September 1982, for example, he ordered that a detachment of 1,200 marines be sent to Lebanon to engage in "peace keeping." He did not request congressional consent for this action. As the weeks passed, President Reagan and his advisers contended that withdrawal of the forces would raise serious questions about the nation's credibility and staying power under adverse conditions and would thus endanger national security and global peace. He also pointedly informed his critics that, if he were compelled to withdraw the troops, the responsibility for Communist gains in this and other areas would rest with them. Influenced by such arguments, Congress did sanction the marines' presence in Lebanon for eighteen months, pursuant to the War Powers Resolution—although the president withdrew them before that time, following a terrorist attack in which 241 marines were killed.[43]

In the Persian Gulf crisis of 1987, the Reagan White House sent a naval contingent to protect Kuwaiti oil tankers from attack. Initially the president insisted that there was no danger that U.S. forces would become involved in hostilities and that the War Powers Resolution therefore did not apply. After hostilities actually erupted in the Persian Gulf, the president's critics then had to face the accusation that their opposition to White House policy placed U.S. forces in danger and risked an embarrassing diplomatic defeat for the nation. Under these circumstances, the president's critics found themselves in a dilemma: either to support or acquiesce in the president's action, even though they doubted its wisdom, or to oppose it and risk being blamed for a possible diplomatic failure or worse. Nor were Reagan's critics able to produce alternative policies capable of commanding wide public support and of promoting the national interest.

The problem that the War Powers Resolution addressed was in many respects analogous to that confronting the United States during the 1930s, when Congress sought to keep the nation out of World War II by passing the Neutrality Act. In the end, that effort failed. Legal attempts to keep America out of the hostilities were inadequate to protect the nation's diplomatic and security interests. Supported by public opinion, President Roosevelt often circumvented such restraints—and in the process blamed Congress for the nation's lack of military preparedness. Perhaps the only effective constraint on the president's use of armed force for national security and diplomatic ends is the creation of external conditions that make such use unnecessary. But, as postwar experience has shown, that is a time-consuming and frustrating challenge, to which there is likely to be no easy solution.

Other Economic Powers

The Constitution confers upon Congress certain general economic powers, several of which are important in the conduct of foreign relations. These include the power to levy and collect taxes, to impose tariffs upon imports, to borrow money, to regulate interstate and foreign commerce, and to coin money and regulate its value. The significance of these powers has greatly increased as a result of the steady growth in the federal budget and the part played by the budget in the national economy. For example, legislative measures to control domestic inflation are a major influence in determining the value of the dollar overseas; they also influence such intangible but crucial developments as the degree of confidence that foreign governments have in U.S. leadership. The priority that Congress establishes between domestic and foreign spending is a major factor affecting the global strategic balance, the nation's ability to fight limited wars, and its capacity for responding to the economic needs of the Third World.

Throughout the 1970s, legislative attitudes reflected an opinion that appeared to have wide public support: domestic needs should be given priority over foreign policy needs by national policy makers. According to some critics of American interventionism, the United States should set its own house in order before it attempts to solve the world's problems.[44] This viewpoint (part of what was sometimes called the "post-Vietnam War syndrome"), however, was largely abandoned by the end of the decade, as a result of the Soviet invasion of Afghanistan, Moscow's intervention in Poland, revolutionary ferment in Latin America, continuing conflict in the Middle East, and other developments. After pledging in his 1980 campaign to "make America great again," President Reagan called for a substantial expansion in the national defense budget. The Reagan administration's approach to external policy was that the United States could afford whatever measures were necessary to maintain its strength and credibility as the leader of the noncommunist world.

Few of the economic prerogatives of Congress have more significant implications for foreign policy than its power to regulate commerce. The trade wars among the states under the Articles of Confederation had led to economic turmoil and instability—a primary reason why the Constitutional Convention was assembled. Congress, therefore, was given the exclusive power to regulate trade both among the states and between the United States and foreign countries.

Beginning with the Reciprocal Trade Program inaugurated by the Roosevelt administration, the United States has sought to maximize its foreign trade on the basis of reciprocal tariff concession agreements with other countries. Congress grants the president considerable discretion to negotiate these and other trade agreements. It also periodically engages in major revisions of the trade laws, often at the instigation of domestic industries that claim they are threatened by rising imports (automobiles from Japan, textiles from Hong Kong, fruits and vegetables from Mexico). Labor unions, farmers, business groups, and others seeking to improve their competitive positions add to the pressures on Congress to act in matters of trade. On several occasions in recent years, for example, the House and Senate have used various means to convey to Japan their concerns about the rising volume of Japanese exports to the United States and Tokyo's resistance to expanded U.S. sales in the Japanese market.[45] Such congressional warnings are sometimes welcomed by the president and his advisers when they are trying to win new trade concessions from other countries.

Incident to its power to regulate commerce, from time to time Congress investigates the behavior of U.S. business firms overseas. In recent years, it has inquired into allegations that American corporations bribed officials in other countries to obtain preferential consideration. Political intervention in the affairs of Chile by the International Telephone and Telegraph Company has also elicited detailed legislative investigation.[46]

Today, virtually all foreign policy activities have an economic dimension. Even with regard to ideological and ethical issues, such as human rights in the Soviet Union and racial equality in South Africa, Congress has used trade concessions, boycotts, and other economic instruments in its efforts to influence the course of events.[47]

The Oversight Function

Since the mid-nineteenth century, many students of the legislative process have pointed out that, in the words of one of them, "control of the government—the oversight function—is probably the most important task the legislature performs." As a result, "the bureaucracy lives under the heavy frown of congressional supervision all the time." [48] Although it is not specifically mentioned in the Constitution, the congressional power of investigation is a basic legislative function, one that Congress has relied upon repeatedly to influence foreign affairs. During the 1930s, for example, the investigation carried out by the Nye Committee into the nation's participation in World War I had a major impact on public opinion, strongly reinforcing the existing isolationist mentality.[49] During World War II, the Truman Committee (the Special Senate Committee Investigating the National Defense Program, headed by then Sen. Harry S Truman, D-Mo.) investigated problems related to the war effort; this committee's work was widely cited as a model of constructive investigation by Congress.[50]

In the early postwar period, committees of the House and Senate examined political, social, and economic conditions in Europe, and their reports played key roles in formulating the Greek-Turkish Aid Program (1947), the Marshall Plan (1948), and NATO (1949). Later, Congress looked into the question of why the United States "lost" China to communism. These inquiries yielded few positive results and impaired morale in the State Department and other executive agencies for many years.[51] One of the most influential legislative inquiries in recent times was conducted during the late 1960s by the Senate Foreign Relations Committee on America's participation in the Vietnam War. This exhaustive and well-publicized review served as a focus for the emerging internal opposition to the war and was a major factor in the Nixon administration's decision to bring the conflict to an end.

During the late 1980s, revelations associated with the Iran-contra affair led to exhaustive investigations of the Reagan administration's activities in the Middle East and Central America. These inquiries directed the attention of the news media and the public to the administration's policy in Central America; brought censure of the intelligence agencies for certain of their activities (such as mining Nicaraguan harbors); and strongly communicated legislative uneasiness about certain forms of interventionism by the United States in the affairs of Latin American nations. Nevertheless, they did not succeed in fundamentally changing the administration's diplomacy in the area.[52]

Informal Methods of Legislative Influence

In addition to its constitutional prerogatives, Congress has evolved certain informal, and sometimes extremely effective, methods of influencing the course of foreign relations. One of these is the ability of the House or Senate (or both) to pass resolutions expressing the opinions of legislators on diplomatic issues.* Such resolutions are not legally binding upon the executive branch, although expressions of congressional sentiment are noted and taken seriously by executive agencies. A noteworthy example of this procedure was the resolution endorsing a freeze on nuclear testing that was adopted by the House of Representatives in 1983. It is testimony to the ambiguous nature of such resolutions that both the pro- and the anti-freeze forces viewed its passage as a victory: Advocates claimed that the resolution compelled the Reagan administration to intensify the quest for arms control; opponents pointed out that the resolution had no legally binding effect.[53]

One way in which members of Congress inform themselves about foreign affairs is by making trips abroad for the purpose of first-hand observations. These trips are often referred to as "junkets," with the

---

* Resolutions expressing the opinions of one or both houses of Congress may take various forms. A *concurrent resolution* conveys the opinion of both houses on a particular question. However, it is not law and thus does not require the president's signature. Similarly, a *sense of the House* or a *sense of the Senate* resolution may express the viewpoint of one chamber on a question. While executive policymakers are interested in congressional sentiment, they are not bound by such resolutions.

implication that there is a large element of recreation in them. Shortly before the Memorial Day holidays in 1983, for example, it was reported that a number of legislators "were enjoying springtime in Paris—and Rome and Berlin and Athens and Budapest and Brussels and Prague and Geneva." Altogether during this period, fifty-nine representatives and seven senators were traveling to sixteen different countries (plus Puerto Rico), studying such diverse topics as the prospects for peace in the Middle East, Soviet advances in aircraft and technology (as seen at the Paris Air Show), and the possibility for negotiations among rival political factions in Central America.[54] One former State Department official has said that trips of this kind, despite their reputation, are extremely valuable; not only do they broaden legislators' horizons, but they also help Congress to be less dependent upon executive officials for their information about major developments abroad.

Sometimes, foreign governments encourage legislators to visit their countries in order to be better able to exert influence upon them.[55] One particularly newsworthy case occurred in 1987, when, at the invitation of the Soviet government, three members of the House visited a highly controversial, and hitherto secret, radar installation at Krasnoyarsk. The Soviet purpose was evidently to convince legislators that, contrary to the contention of President Reagan and his advisers, the installation did not violate the ABM Treaty; in so doing, the Soviets hoped to reduce support on Capitol Hill for the Star Wars scheme.[56]

Although the era of great oratory may have ended on Capitol Hill (and elsewhere), speeches by individual legislators are newsworthy and can sometimes have a potent effect on U.S. foreign policy. One conspicuous example was a widely publicized speech by Sen. J. William Fulbright, D-Ark., criticizing the diplomacy of the Johnson administration in the Dominican Republic.[57] A different sort of example was provided by Sen. Jesse Helms, R-N.C., an outspoken and ultraconservative senator, who evidently believed that President Reagan had to be "saved" from his own advisers. Helms not only made numerous speeches—sometimes amounting to filibusters—in the Senate, but he also raised questionable allegations about the activities of executive officials and used the rules of the Senate to block presidential nominations to diplomatic posts.[58]

Congress and Postwar Diplomacy

Since the late 1960s Congress has exhibited a new dynamism and militancy in exerting its prerogatives in external affairs. For the first two decades after World War II Congress was largely content to leave the management of foreign relations to the executive branch—thereby providing impetus for the emergence of the imperial presidency; when it

did play a significant role in foreign relations, Congress normally supported the diplomatic policies and programs advocated by the White
House. Recalling the decisive impact upon American diplomacy Congress had in earlier periods of the nation's history and concerned about
the steady accretion of executive power, many members of the House
and Senate have advocated a return to a more influential role in the
realm of external policy.

Congress's dynamic involvement in the foreign policy process must
be viewed from the perspective of the diplomatic experience of the
twentieth century. The post-Vietnam War era of legislative assertiveness in foreign relations, for example, may be regarded as another stage
in the "democratization" of American diplomacy that began under
President Wilson. Although he was not always consistent with his own
principle, Wilson believed in "open covenants, openly arrived at," in
involving public opinion decisively in the foreign policy process, and in
other measures designed to make the conduct of diplomacy consonant
with America's democratic values. As the branch of government most
representative of the people (as many legislators believe), Congress can
justify its diplomatic assertiveness by reference to such Wilsonian principles. The perspective of history also reminds us that there have been
many earlier periods of congressional activism in foreign relations—
such as the era of the Spanish-American War and the decade of the
1930s. In the latter period, not even President Franklin D. Roosevelt—
one of the nation's most skilled political leaders—was able to impose his
will upon a Congress strongly attached to isolationism.

The Expanding Role of Government

One factor contributing to growing congressional involvement has
been the expanding role of government in all spheres of life, both at
home and abroad. In 1946, the total annual expenditures of the U.S.
government were $62 billion; for fiscal year 1988, President Reagan's
proposed expenditures exceeded $1 trillion. The Pentagon's share of
this budget request was $312 billion—five times as great as the entire
1946 budget.

The emergence of the United States as a superpower after World
War II and its adoption of an internationalist foreign policy were other
developments of the same kind. Before the war, isolationism had been
the rule of U.S. foreign policy since the nation's founding. Normally,
congressional interest and participation in diplomatic issues were minimal. Indeed, it might be said that during the isolationist period, the
United States really had no foreign policy, as the term was defined in
Chapter 1. The United States was not then willing to commit its
national resources to achieve a set of external goals.

After World War II, however, even leading proponents of that approach acknowledged that the isolationist era had ended.[59] Its demise was symbolized by President Harry S Truman's address to Congress on March 12, 1947, inaugurating the policy of containment against expansive communism. In proposing a program of aid to Greece and Turkey to help them resist Soviet pressure, Truman put the choice squarely before Congress: Either it would support whatever measures were required to preserve peace and security abroad or it would risk widespread global instability and the possible outbreak of World War III.[60] Painful as the choice was for many legislators, Congress faced the realities of the postwar era and supported the measures dictated by America's emergence as a global power. Since that time, many other issues—the economic needs of the Third World, international trade questions, and threats to the global environment, to mention but a few—have provided further opportunities for Congress to leave its imprint on U.S. foreign policy.

Domestic Implications of Foreign Policy

The growing interrelationship between domestic and foreign affairs also provided impetus for congressional assertiveness in external policy. This phenomenon can be illustrated by the Food for Peace program, under which American agricultural products are sold or donated to countries in need. One study called this program "a popular form of foreign aid on Capitol Hill because it benefits the donor economy more than the recipient." With considerable encouragement from Congress, the Department of Agriculture seeks to dispose of agricultural surpluses abroad, thereby helping American farmers.[61] Another example of this interrelationship is the dependence of the United States upon access to foreign oil at reasonable prices. A State Department official noted that nowadays "no member of Congress can ignore foreign policy decisions and expect to be re-elected." Legislators can no longer say, "That's up to the president and Congress can't do anything about it." [62]

Impact of the Vietnam War

Perhaps more than any other single development, the nation's traumatic and divisive involvement in the Vietnam War convinced many legislators that presidential dominance in the foreign policy field must end. Rightly or wrongly, many people in the United States blamed the rise of an imperial presidency upon the Vietnam experience. Critics of the war contended that the Johnson and Nixon administrations manipulated and deceived Congress concerning the nature and extent of U.S. participation and misled the nation about the prospects for victory.[63] As President Johnson repeatedly stated, Americans were not accustomed to losing wars. Inevitably, perhaps, the Vietnam experience led to a new era in executive-legislative relations, in which Congress insisted on more effective restraints upon presidential power. For many years thereafter, congressional and public apprehensions about "another Vietnam" strongly colored legislative viewpoints and actions on foreign policy issues.

Implicit in the impulse toward congressional activism in foreign affairs has been the idea that the exertion of a more independent and forceful role *by Congress* enhances the prospects for international peace, stability, and a more constructive use of American power abroad. Consequently, since the Vietnam conflict, legislators have echoed the demand that Senator Vandenberg once directed at the Truman administration: Legislators want to be in on the "take-offs" as well as the "crash landings" in foreign affairs.[64] At a minimum—as in congressional insistence that the Reagan administration rethink the production and deployment of the MX missile system and growing legislative opposition to Star Wars—such legislative assertiveness can require executive policy makers to create a basic consensus *before* they undertake costly and far-reaching commitments in defense and foreign policy.

Changes within Congress

Internal changes within Congress itself—and within the broader context of American public opinion and the political system—have also instigated and sustained legislative activism in foreign affairs. Three such changes have been especially important. One of these is that Congress is getting younger: the average age of legislators has declined, and the viewpoints of many of its members today tend to reflect these changes. For example, newly elected members of the House and Senate frequently are not content to serve the customary apprenticeship or to defer to the "wisdom" of more senior and experienced legislators.

A second and related change has been the movement toward procedural reforms. Traditional concepts—such as the seniority principle governing the selection of committee chairmen and the often vast powers exercised by the chairmen—have come under repeated attack. The trend toward "democratization" within both houses has given individual legislators greater opportunities to express their ideas and to exert influence on congressional decisions. In turn, this has led to a diffusion of power and responsibility in both chambers.[65]

The third significant change has been the dramatic growth of the legislative staff. In recent years, the congressional staff has grown more rapidly than the executive bureaucracy. By the early 1980s, the combined staffs of the House and Senate totaled 23,000 people. In 1987, it cost some $3.2 billion to operate Congress. This expansion has led some commentators to say that, increasingly, the activities of Congress are influenced by its "entrepreneurial staff," whose members often appear primarily interested in gaining maximum publicity for the legislators they serve.[66] Moreover, as I. M. Destler has observed, legislative staffs have increased not only in size but also "in foreign policy expertise. . . . Committed, activist staff aides were the driving force behind many [congressional] initiatives" in foreign relations, especially in the Senate. In some cases, the influence of staff aides serving congressional committees has appeared to be more decisive than that of the committee members themselves in determining the outcome of legislation.[67]

Changes in Public Opinion

Two significant forces in public opinion have also encouraged Congress to exert its influence in foreign relations. One is the increase in lobbying activities directed at Congress (and at the executive branch as well). The case studies on the Arab-Israeli conflict (Chapter 4) and on foreign economic policy (Chapter 7) illustrate this phenomenon. Pressure-group activity has always been a conspicuous feature of the American political system, but both the intensity and the skill of lobbying campaigns have increased considerably since World War II. A novel development in recent years has been the extent to which foreign governments, often in alliance with interest groups in the United States, have undertaken lobbying campaigns designed to influence the course of American foreign policy.[68]

The other salient characteristic of public opinion that has provided Congress both an opportunity and an incentive to assert its prerogatives in foreign affairs is the evident lack of consensus about the nation's external goals and the means of achieving them. This was a major outcome of the Vietnam War and of certain other diplomatic setbacks experienced by the United States in the years that followed.

From the perspective of public opinion, and at the risk of some oversimplification, we may divide the postwar history of U.S. diplomacy into three stages. First there was the period from 1945 to the late 1960s, in which a national consensus existed on two ideas: that communist expansionism threatened the security of the United States and other independent nations, and that it had to be resisted by the strategy of containment. The period from then until the late 1970s was characterized by disillusionment with U.S. involvement in the Vietnam conflict and by the diplomatic retrenchment that followed that episode. During this period, many citizens and political leaders came to doubt the ability of the United States to achieve any worthwhile foreign policy objective; the public was extremely apprehensive about committing the nation's power overseas.

Third, by the late 1970s several events overseas—such as the collapse of the Iranian monarchy, the ensuing seizure of U.S. hostages in Tehran, and the Soviet incursion into Afghanistan—led to a pervasive impression that the diplomatic credibility of the United States was being steadily eroded. To a significant degree, President Jimmy Carter was defeated in 1980 because of a public perception that he was an indecisive chief executive who had allowed U.S. power and influence abroad to deteriorate. By contrast, one of Ronald Reagan's promises that most appealed to voters was that he would "make America great again."

Yet, like many presidents in the past—especially when the nation was experiencing economic adversity—President Reagan found it extremely difficult to create and maintain a consensus on his foreign policy goals. The apprehensions that had led to his victory did not necessarily translate into a set of clear and consistent diplomatic *objectives* having broad support among the people and their representatives on Capitol Hill. Public opinion polls, for example, indicated that the people remained apprehensive about Soviet military strength and about Moscow's diplomatic intentions; citizens were also concerned about "another Vietnam" if the United States intervened in foreign crises. Public opinion usually supported President Reagan's diplomatic moves, but many Americans also wanted to reduce the defense budget and the foreign aid program. They favored closer cooperation with the NATO allies, but there was no overwhelming public sentiment in favor of giving them a larger voice in shaping Washington's diplomatic and military strategy. In brief, during the 1980s public and congressional attitudes on foreign policy issues were more than ordinarily marked by anomalies, contradictions, and mutually exclusive objectives.[69]

In the light of the Vietnam War and events since the early 1970s, what kind of balance should the United States endeavor to maintain between interventionism and isolationism? How useful is the slogan, "No more Vietnams," as a guide for the nation's diplomatic moves in Latin America, sub-Saharan Africa, the Persian Gulf, and other regions in which the United States has major overseas commitments? How would the expanded and modernized military establishment created during the Reagan presidency actually be *used* to achieve foreign policy goals? Where is the line to be drawn between permissible and unacceptable intelligence activities abroad? Such questions are likely to be issues in the foreign policy debate for many years in the future. In the search for answers, Congress will almost certainly play a leading role in trying to forge a new bipartisan consensus as a foundation for the nation's diplomatic activities.

Notes

1. Dispatches by Nathaniel C. Nash and Elaine Sciolino, *New York Times,* October 12, 1987.
2. Detailed studies highlighting congressional activism in foreign policy in

recent years are Alan Platt and Lawrence D. Weiler, *Congress and Arms Control* (Boulder, Colo.: Westview, 1978); I. M. Destler. "Congress as Boss," *Foreign Policy* 42 (Spring 1981): 167-181; Robert A. Pastor, *Congress and the Politics of U.S. Foreign Economic Policy: 1929-1976* (Berkeley and Los Angeles: University of California Press, 1980); Thomas M. Franck and Edward Weisband, *Foreign Policy by Congress* (New York: Oxford University Press, 1979); Loch Johnson, *The Making of International Agreements: Congress Confronts the Executive* (New York: New York University Press, 1984); Douglas C. Waller, *Congress and the Nuclear Freeze* (Amherst: University of Massachusetts Press, 1987).

3. Holbert N. Carroll, *The House of Representatives and Foreign Affairs* (Pittsburgh: University of Pittsburgh Press, 1958), 3.

4. Paul A. Varg, *Foreign Policies of the Founding Fathers* (East Lansing: Michigan State University Press, 1963), 46-66; and Albert C. V. Westphal, *The House Committee on Foreign Affairs* (New York: Columbia University Press, 1942), 14-15.

5. For detailed examinations of the problems impeding Congress's role as an effective legislative body, see Richard Bolling, *House Out of Order* (New York: E. P. Dutton, 1965); Joseph Clark, ed., *Congress: The Sapless Branch* (New York: Harper and Row, 1964); Joseph Clark, ed., *Congressional Reform: Problems and Prospects* (New York: Thomas Y. Crowell, 1965); and Roger H. Davidson et al., *Congress in Crisis: Politics and Congressional Reform* (Belmont, Calif.: Wadsworth, 1966).

6. *Congressional Quarterly Weekly Report,* January 3, 1987, 3-4.

7. See the dispatches by John W. Finney, *New York Times,* November 16, 1965, and February 26, 1967; and Marvin Kalb, "Doves, Hawks, and Flutters in the Foreign Relations Committee," *New York Times Magazine,* November 19, 1967.

8. *Congressional Quarterly Almanac,* 1977, 319.

9. *Congressional Quarterly Almanac, 1985,* 18G-34G; Sen. Daniel J. Evans, D-Wash., as quoted in a dispatch by Steven V. Roberts, *New York Times,* February 26, 1986.

10. *Congressional Quarterly Weekly Report,* May 24, 1986, 1154.

11. *Congressional Quarterly's Guide to Congress,* 3d ed. (Washington, D.C.: CQ Press, 1982), 451, 471.

12. For diverse interpretations of the cost, effectiveness, and other implications of the Star Wars proposal, see Zbigniew Brzezinski, ed., *Promise or Peril: The Strategic Defense Initiative* (Washington, D.C.: Ethics and Public Policy Center, 1986); Aspen Strategy Group, *The Strategic Defense Initiative and American Security* (Lanham, Md.: University Press of America, 1987); Larry Pressler, *Star Wars: The Strategic Defense Initiative Debates in Congress* (Westport, Conn.: Greenwood, 1986); Samuel F. Wells, Jr., and Robert S. Litwak, eds., *Strategic Defenses and Soviet-American Relations* (Cambridge, Mass.: Ballinger, 1987); "Star Wars: Pros and Cons," *Foreign Affairs* 62 (Spring 1984): 820-857; and Paul B. Stares, *Space and National Security* (Washington, D.C.: Brookings Institution, 1987).

13. For more detailed discussion of recent U.S. policy toward Central America, see the speech by Secretary of State Shultz on March 3, 1986, "Nicaragua and Central America," *Current Policy,* No. 801, March 3, 1986; Clifford Krauss, "Revolution in Central America," *Foreign Affairs* 65 (special issue, 1986): 564-582; Jack Child, *Conflict in Central America: Approaches to Peace and Security* (New York: St. Martin's, 1986); John N. Moore, *The Secret War in Central America* (Lanham, Md.: University Press of Amer-

ica, 1986); Thomas J. Farer, *The Grand Strategy of the United States in Latin America* (New Brunswick, N.J.: Transaction Books, 1987); Thomas W. Walker, *Reagan versus the Sandinistas* (Boulder, Colo.: Westview, 1987); and Harold Molineu, *U.S. Policy toward Latin America: From Regionalism to Globalism* (Boulder, Colo.: Westview, 1986).

14. See *Congressional Quarterly Almanac, 1984,* 71-72.

15. In *United States v. Curtiss-Wright Export Corp.,* 299 U.S. 304 (1936), the Supreme Court made a fundamental distinction between the powers of the executive in domestic and foreign affairs, emphasizing that they were vastly greater in the latter than in the former.

16. Francis O. Wilcox, *Congress, the Executive, and Foreign Policy* (New York: Harper and Row, 1971), 146.

17. Julius W. Pratt, *A History of United States Foreign Policy* (Englewood Cliffs, N.J.: Prentice-Hall, 1955), 79-80.

18. Dexter Perkins, *The American Approach to Foreign Policy* (New York: Atheneum, 1968), 191.

19. Sometimes even legislators themselves become confused on this point. Thus, in 1987, Sen. Robert C. Byrd, D-W.Va., asserted that "the last word in this [process of approving treaties] is ratification of the treaty by the Senate."

20. *Guide to Congress,* 291-292. For historical background on senatorial action on treaties, see W. Stull Holt, *Treaties Defeated by the Senate* (Baltimore: Johns Hopkins University Press, 1933).

21. The senatorial contribution to U.S. foreign policy during this period is described in Arthur H. Vandenberg, Jr., ed., *The Private Papers of Senator Vandenberg* (Boston: Houghton Mifflin, 1952).

22. This was the view of Rep. Thomas E. Morgan, as cited in Wilcox, *Congress, the Executive, and Foreign Policy,* 6.

23. *U.S. News & World Report,* March 19, 1979, 46. For a detailed discussion of efforts by the House to compel the Reagan White House to undertake negotiations with rebel groups in Central America, see the dispatches by Martin Tolchin, *New York Times,* May 12 and May 13, 1983.

24. See the dispatches by Steven V. Roberts, *New York Times,* June 11, 1986 and October 1, 1987, and by Michael R. Gordon, *New York Times,* February 7, 1987.

25. Quoted in Loch Johnson and James M. McCormick, "Foreign Policy by Executive Fiat," *Foreign Policy* 28 (Fall 1977): 133.

26. See the study prepared by the Library of Congress for the Senate Foreign Relations Committee, *The Senate Role in Foreign Affairs Appointments,* 92d Cong., 1st sess., 1971, 3-10.

27. *Guide to Congress,* 207.

28. Ibid., 210.

29. *Congressional Quarterly Weekly Report,* March 7, 1987, 418-419.

30. *Newsweek,* July 7, 1986, 20-22.

31. See the dispatch by Bernard Gwertzman, *New York Times,* May 12, 1986.

32. Dispatch by Jonathan Fuerbringer, *New York Times,* September 12, 1987.

33. See the Associated Press dispatch by Tim Ahern, *Baton Rouge Morning Advocate,* October 2, 1987.

34. Dispatch by Peter Finney, Jr., *Baton Rouge Morning Advocate,* March 3, 1979, and Elizabeth B. Drew, "Mr. Passman Meets His Match," *Reporter,* November 19, 1964, 40-43.

35. For further information on the appropriations process, see Richard F. Fenno, "The House Appropriations Committee As a Political System,"

American Political Science Review 56 (June 1962), 310-324; and Jeffrey L. Pressman, *House vs. Senate: Conflict in the Appropriations Process* (New Haven: Yale University Press, 1966).

36. See Lawrence C. Dodd and Bruce Oppenheimer, eds., *Congress Reconsidered* (New York: Praeger, 1977), 163-192. The right of the chief executive to impound funds appropriated by Congress is examined in detail in "Controversy over the Presidential Impoundment of Appropriated Funds," *Congressional Digest* 52 (April 1973), 65-96. More recent commentaries are: John W. Sewell and Christine E. Contee, "Foreign Aid and Gramm-Rudman," *Foreign Affairs* 65 (Summer 1987): 1015-1037; Allen Schick, *Making Economic Policy in Congress* (Washington, D.C.: American Enterprise Institute, 1983); and Howard Shuman, *Politics and the Budget* (Englewood Cliffs, N.J.: Prentice-Hall, 1984).

37. The *Prize Cases,* 67 U.S. (2 Black) 635 (1863).

38. For the views of some presidents concerning their authority over the armed forces, see Senate Foreign Relations Committee, *Hearings on War Powers Legislation,* 93d Cong., 1st sess., 1973, 167-172.

39. Sen. Jacob K. Javits, R-N.Y., said that it would have been "most unfortunate" if Congress had declared war in the Vietnam conflict, for such an act would have had "unforeseeable consequences." See Jacob K. Javits, "The Congressional Presence in Foreign Relations," *Foreign Affairs* 48 (January 1970): 226.

40. Recent studies of efforts by Congress to influence the nation's military policy are Douglas C. Waller, *Congress and the Nuclear Force* (Amherst: University of Massachusetts Press, 1987); and Michel Barnhart, ed., *Congress and United States Foreign Policy: Controlling the Use of Force in the Nuclear Age* (Albany: University of New York Press, 1987).

41. The background of the resolution is discussed in Gerald R. Ford, *A Time to Heal* (New York: Harper and Row, and the Reader's Digest Association, 1979), 249-252, 280-283. See also Pat M. Holt, *The War Powers Resolution: The Role of Congress in U.S. Armed Intervention* (Washington, D.C.: American Enterprise Institute, 1978).

42. President Ford's views on the War Powers Resolution are contained in Ford, *A Time to Heal,* 251-253, 279-283. President Carter's account of the Iranian hostage crisis indicates little or no concern about the provisions of the War Powers Resolution; for example, late in 1979 Carter decided to "make a direct military attack" against Iran if the hostages were harmed. See Jimmy Carter, *Keeping Faith: Memoirs of a President* (New York: Bantam Books, 1982), 466.

43. Sen. Thomas F. Eagleton, D-Mo., declared that President Reagan effectively nullified the provisions of the War Powers Resolution when he ordered the marines into Lebanon, yet even he conceded that if the president had asked for congressional approval of this step, it would have been granted. See *New York Times,* November 17, 1982. For a discussion of congressional viewpoints on the Lebanese crisis, see *Congressional Quarterly Weekly Report,* April 23, 1983, 777.

44. This was the approach, for example, of Senator Fulbright. He contended that the nation's diplomatic success depended "on the strength and character of our society, which in turn depend on our success in resolving the great social and economic issues of American life." See his *Old Myths and New Realities* (New York: Random House, 1964), 109, 138. A more detailed analysis of this point of view, sometimes referred to as "neo-isolationism," is provided in Cecil V. Crabb, Jr., *Policy-Makers and Critics: Conflicting*

Theories of American Foreign Policy, 2d ed. (New York: Praeger, 1986), 67-111.

45. See the discussion in "How Not to Write a Trade Law," *U.S. News & World Report,* October 5, 1987, 48-50; and the analysis of congressional viewpoints on a new trade bill in *Congressional Quarterly Weekly Report,* April 25, 1987, 765-771. More detailed treatment of legislative behavior on trade questions may be found in I. M. Destler, *American Trade Politics: System under Stress* (Washington, D.C.: Institute for International Economics, 1986). See also Benjamin I. Cohen, *In Whose Interest? International Banking and American Foreign Policy* (New Haven: Yale University Press, 1986).

46. On the activities of IT&T in Chile, see Senate Foreign Relations Committee, *Multinational Corporations and United States Foreign Policy,* 93d Cong., 1st sess., March 20-April 2, 1973, pts. 1 and 2.

47. For an informative discussion of Congress's use of its economic powers in the foreign policy field, see Richard H. Ullman, "Human Rights and Economic Power: the United States versus Idi Amin," *Foreign Affairs* 56 (April 1978): 528-543. Congress's economic actions in connection with South Africa are discussed in *Congressional Quarterly Almanac, 1985,* 83-90.

48. Ralph K. Huitt, "Congress, the Durable Partner," in Sidney Wise and Richard F. Schiers, eds., *Studies on Congress* (New York: Thomas Y. Crowell, 1969), 45.

49. Wayne S. Cole, *Senator Gerald P. Nye and American Foreign Relations* (Minneapolis: University of Minnesota Press, 1962).

50. Donald H. Riddle, *The Truman Committee: A Study in Congressional Responsibility* (New Brunswick, N.J.: Rutgers University Press, 1964), and Wilfred E. Binkley, *President and Congress* (New York: Alfred A. Knopf, 1947), 268-269.

51. A useful source on congressional investigations is Arthur M. Schlesinger, Jr., and Roger Burns, eds., *Congress Investigates: A Documented History, 1792-1974,* 5 vols. (New York: Chelsea House, 1975). For a discussion of and documentary materials on Congress's investigation of Communist influences on the State Department and other executive agencies during the early 1950s, see ibid., 5:3729-3923.

52. These investigations are summarized in the annual editions of *Congressional Quarterly Almanac* for the period from 1983 to 1988. For detailed examination of one specific investigation by Congress, see Loch Johnson, *A Season of Inquiry: Congress and Intelligence* (Chicago: Dorsey, 1988).

53. *Congressional Quarterly Weekly Report,* May 7, 1983, 868-869. For another instance, see the discussion of the resolution passed by the Senate Foreign Relations Committee limiting U.S. troops in Honduras, in the dispatch by Philip Taubman, *New York Times,* May 27, 1983.

54. UPI dispatch by Ira R. Allen, *Baton Rouge Morning Advocate,* May 30, 1983. See also Senate Foreign Relations Committee, *Congress and United States-Soviet Relations,* 94th Cong., 1st sess., 1975, for a summary of a conference between members of the Senate and of the Supreme Soviet, at which a variety of diplomatic issues were discussed.

55. A discussion of efforts of this kind by President Anwar al-Sadat of Egypt is available in Stanley F. Reed, "Dateline Cairo: Shaken Pillar," *Foreign Policy* 45 (Winter 1981-1982): 176. For more recent examples, see *New York Times,* August 14, 1984.

56. *Congressional Quarterly Weekly Report,* September 19, 1987, 2230-2231.

57. *Congressional Record,* 89th Cong., 1st sess., 1965, S23855-S23865.

58. See the dispatches by Phil Gailey, *New York Times*, May 14, 1986, and Steven V. Roberts, August 4, 1986; and *Newsweek*, August 4, 1986, 15.
59. Norman A. Graebner, "Isolationism," *International Encyclopedia of the Social Sciences* (New York: Crowell, Collier and Macmillan, 1968); and Vandenberg, *Private Papers*, 1.
60. For the text of Truman's address, see *Public Papers of the Presidents of the United States: Harry S Truman, 1947* (Washington, D.C.: Government Printing Office, 1963), 176-180.
61. Donald F. McHenry and Kai Bird, "Food Bungle in Bangladesh," *Foreign Policy* 27 (Summer 1977): 83-85.
62. Douglas L. Bennet, Jr., "Congress in Foreign Policy: Who Needs It?" *Foreign Affairs* 57 (Fall 1978): 43.
63. An extremely critical account of the Johnson administration's relations with Congress during the crisis is provided in J. William Fulbright, *The Arrogance of Power* (New York: Random House, 1966), 50-53.
64. Dispatch by James Reston, in *New York Times*, March 14, 1947.
65. The decline of the seniority system in Congress is discussed in *New York Times*, November 13, 1979, and *Congressional Quarterly Weekly Report*, January 27, 1979, 154. See also the data on the 100th Congress in *New York Times*, January 5, 1987.
66. *Guide to Congress*, 477; and dispatch by Barbara Gamarekian, *New York Times*, May 12, 1986.
67. See Thomas E. Mann and Norman J. Ornstein, eds., *The New Congress* (Washington, D.C.: American Enterprise Institute, 1981). Detailed treatments of relevant changes in Congress in recent years are Charles W. Whalen, Jr., *The House and Foreign Policy: The Irony of Congressional Reform* (Chapel Hill, N.C.: University of North Carolina Press, 1982); and Leroy Rieselbach, *Congressional Reform* (Washington, D.C.: CQ Press, 1986).
68. Detailed studies of interest-group activity in the United States are Ross Y. Koen, *The China Lobby in American Politics* (New York: Harper and Row, 1974); Kay L. Schlozman and John T. Tierney, *Organized Interests and American Democracy* (New York: Harper and Row, 1985); Jeffrey M. Berry, *The Interest Group Society* (Boston: Little, Brown, 1984); David Osborne, "Lobbying for Japan, Inc.," *New York Times Magazine*, December 5, 1983, 133-139; Larry J. Sabato, *PAC Power* (New York: W. W. Norton, 1984); Robert D. Schultzinger, *The Wise Men of Foreign Affairs: The History of the Council on Foreign Relations* (New York: Columbia University Press, 1984); Edward Tirnan, *The Lobby: Jewish Political Power and American Foreign Policy* (New York: Simon and Schuster, 1987); and Laurence Halley, *Ancient Affections: Ethnic Groups and Foreign Policy* (New York: Praeger, 1985).
69. Useful studies of U.S. public opinion are William S. Maddox and Stuart A. Lilie, *Beyond Liberal and Conservative* (Washington, D.C.: Cato Institute, 1984); John C. Pierie, Kathleen M. Beatty, and Paul R. Hagner, *The Dynamics of American Public Opinion* (Glenview, Ill.: Scott, Foresman, 1982); H. Schuyler Foster, *Activism Replaces Isolationism: U.S. Public Attitudes, 1940-1975* (Washington, D.C.: Foxhall, 1983).

PART II

Congress Confronts
the Issues

We now turn our attention from the general pattern of interaction between Congress and the president in the foreign policy process to five case studies of policy making. The concrete issues selected for examination illustrate Congress's changing perceptions of its role in foreign policy making and how the executive branch and public opinion shape these perceptions.

Chapter 3 examines legislative action on the Soviet-American Anti-Ballistic Missile Treaty of 1972. This case study shows how the Senate deals with an important international agreement, how it exercises its constitutional responsibilities in the treaty-making process, and where some of the possibilities of conflict with the executive lie.

Chapter 4 deals with one aspect of the Arab-Israeli conflict, focusing upon the Reagan administration's effort to supply advanced military equipment to the government of Saudi Arabia. The case provides an illuminating example of congressional reliance upon the power of the purse to influence foreign policy. It also highlights the role and activities of pressure groups in U.S. foreign relations.

Chapter 5, "The Armed Forces," recounts ways in which Congress has attempted to draw the line between the constitutional power of the president as commander in chief and the constitutional power of Congress to declare war and to make the rules that govern the armed forces. The chapter emphasizes the essential pragmatism of the congressional approach.

In Chapter 6, the legislative oversight role of Congress is considered in reference to the intelligence community. Perhaps nothing better illustrates the evolving attitudes in Congress toward its role in foreign policy than the change in its relationship to the intelligence community. The congressional approach went from almost total neglect to item-by-item scrutiny of the intelligence budget. But as the Iran-contra affair was to indicate, legislative controls achieved only partial effectiveness.

Finally, Chapter 7 examines one of Congress's increasingly important prerogatives in the foreign policy field: its economic powers—specifically, the legislative role in dealing with trade issues. In many respects, the economic powers of Congress are among its most potent for influencing the course of external policy.

CHAPTER 3

The Anti-Ballistic
Missile Treaty

The Anti-Ballistic Missile Treaty combines in one issue several aspects of Congress's involvement in foreign policy. First, it is an example of the Senate's constitutional role in the treaty-making process—that is, the giving of its advice and consent to ratification. Second, it shows how both the Senate and the House fulfill their constitutional role of helping to determine the national defense posture and strategy. In this case, the basic question was—and is—whether to defend the country against nuclear attack by destroying the enemy's weapons before they can land or whether to rely instead on the capability to deliver an overwhelming retaliatory blow after an attack has taken place. Third, the treaty is unusual in that, long after it was ratified, it provoked a new struggle between the executive and legislative branches. The dispute was over whether the president can reinterpret an existing treaty without reference to the Senate, a question that involves the basic institutional relationships between the president and the Senate in the process of reaching and maintaining agreements with other countries.

Background

The nuclear age, which began so dramatically with the bombing of Hiroshima in 1945, confronted military strategists with wholly new problems. This new weapon seemed to be as close as the human race could come to ultimate destruction—a weapon, moreover, against which there was perhaps no defense. There is a long military history of improvements in offense leading to improvements in defense, but the atom bomb made reasonable people wonder if that was any longer possible. Other people, equally reasonable, have thought that it might be, or that the effort to find a defense against nuclear weapons should at least be made.

Another facet of the nuclear age was that it called into question the traditional way of planning force structure. For millennia, it had been taken as a given that more was better: If the enemy had a thousand spears, you needed more than that. This principle was now called into question. If you could destroy the enemy with x number of bombs, it did not matter if the enemy had $2x$ and you certainly did not need $3x$. This new principle came to be called the *doctrine of sufficiency.*

Finally, there was the problem of the relationship between nuclear and conventional weapons. In the late 1940s and early 1950s, as the cold war changed the United States and the Soviet Union from allies to adversaries, U.S. military planners had to contend with an overwhelming Soviet conventional superiority. It had initially been expected that the newly organized United Nations would deal with global conflicts, but this expectation was short-lived. In the United States, it was politically unacceptable to maintain the World War II level of mobilization, and the Soviet Union had a bigger population, anyway. The solution that was adopted was to offset Soviet conventional superiority with nuclear weapons.

Soon, however, the Soviet Union acquired nuclear weapons, too. The premise of Western strategy was that the Soviets knew that if they attacked the West, the United States would launch a devastating nuclear counterblow. It did not take long before the Soviet Union became capable of carrying out a similar retaliation against a U.S. attack. Thus, there developed what was at first called the *balance of terror* and later became formalized in the arcane language of nuclear strategy as Mutual Assured Destruction, with the ominous acronym MAD. This doctrine held that each side was able to wreak an unacceptable level of destruction on the other even after absorbing a first strike. As greater numbers of new and more powerful weapons, with new and longer-range delivery systems, were added to inventories on both sides, the assurance seemed to increase.

The strategy of Mutual Assured Destruction was also based on the premise that there was no effective defense against nuclear weapons. Even bombs dropped from airplanes, such as those that destroyed Hiroshima and Nagasaki in 1945, were so powerful that if only one penetrated an antiaircraft defense, the battle was lost. If the bombs were delivered by missiles traveling at speeds of thousands of miles an hour, defense did indeed appear hopeless. The only deterrence then became certain knowledge of instant "massive retaliation," in Secretary of State John Foster Dulles's phrase.

Nuclear Arms Control Efforts

In the immediate aftermath of World War II, the United States, which then held a monopoly on nuclear weapons, proposed in the United Nations that an international authority be created to control production of fissionable material, that there be international licensing and inspection of peaceful nuclear facilities, and that no nation be allowed to possess nuclear weapons or production facilities. This was the Baruch Plan, named for its principal author, Bernard Baruch, a financier and adviser to presidents. The Soviet Union at the time was well on the way to developing its own nuclear weapons (it produced its first in 1949) and was also at the peak of the paranoia that gripped it during the Stalin era. It rejected the U.S. proposal.

Throughout the 1950s, arms control conferences followed one after the other without significant result. The 1960s, however, saw a series of modest accomplishments. In 1963, the Limited Test Ban Treaty entered into force, prohibiting nuclear tests in the atmosphere, in outer space, and under water. Underground tests were also banned if they would vent radioactive debris beyond the national borders. The treaty was aimed not so much at controlling nuclear weapons as at protecting the environment from the radioactive fallout of tests, but it was widely hailed as a useful first step.

This treaty was followed in 1967 by a treaty banning nuclear weapons from outer space; in 1968 by the non-proliferation treaty, in which nuclear states agreed not to transfer weapons to non-nuclear states and non-nuclear states agreed not to acquire such weapons; and in 1971 by the seabed arms control treaty, banning nuclear weapons from the ocean floor. (The Antarctic Treaty of 1959, the principal purpose of which was to internationalize the Antarctic, also banned nuclear weapons from that continent, along with military bases in general.)

Thus, a quarter-century after the Baruch Plan had been put forward, the nations of the world had done no more than nibble around the edges of the problem of controlling nuclear weapons. Sen. Eugene J. McCarthy, D-Minn., observed that the weapons had been banned from outer space, from the ocean floor, and from the Antarctic, where nobody intended to put them anyway; why not, he asked, ban them from places where they might hurt somebody? The stage was set for the Strategic Arms Limitation Talks, generally known by the acronym SALT. This is where nuclear weapons and the effort to build defenses against them would come together.

President Lyndon B. Johnson had been ready to hold a summit meeting with Soviet General Secretary Leonid Brezhnev in 1968, but he canceled it when Soviet troops invaded Czechoslovakia. In 1971, the Nixon administration was embattled over Vietnam both at home and in

Asia, but Watergate was still in the future, the president was preparing an opening to China, and he wanted détente with the Soviet Union.

Beginnings of the Anti-Ballistic Missile

Despite the general assumption that there was no reasonable prospect of an effective defense against nuclear weapons, the army began a research program on anti-ballistic missile (ABM) defenses in 1954, initially as an extension of its work on antiaircraft defense. That was at a time when missiles had relatively short ranges; intercontinental missiles did not yet exist.

Presidents Dwight D. Eisenhower, John F. Kennedy, and Lyndon B. Johnson all resisted the army's anti-missile research program, mainly on the ground that it took budgetary and other resources away from more pressing needs. But, curiously in the light of subsequent events, the program found friends in Congress. In 1957, the year in which the Soviet Union acquired intercontinental ballistic missiles, Congress approved $137 million more than had been requested for ABM research.

The framework within which the ABM program was being considered changed in the middle 1960s, when it was learned that the Soviet Union was installing an ABM system of its own around Moscow. The question at once arose as to what the U.S. response should be. President Johnson stated the problem for both superpowers in a letter to Soviet Premier Aleksei Kosygin on January 21, 1967:

> I think you must realize that following the deployment by you of an anti-ballistic missile system I face great pressures from the Members of Congress and from public opinion not only to deploy defensive systems in this country, but also to increase greatly our capabilities to penetrate any defensive systems which you might establish.
>
> If we should feel compelled to make such major increases in our strategic weapons capabilities, I have no doubt that you would in turn feel under compulsion to do likewise. We would thus have incurred on both sides colossal costs without substantially enhancing the security of our own peoples or contributing to the prospects for a stable peace in the world.[1]

It may be noted that, in this letter, President Johnson made the point about a Soviet ABM that Moscow was later to make about a U.S. ABM—namely, that it would provoke an increase in offensive capabilities and thereby ratchet the arms race up another notch.

The U.S. Debate over Deployment

As Johnson had warned Kosygin, the Soviet ABM system increased pressures to deploy a similar system in the United States. The Johnson administration met these pressures with a curious in-between kind of policy. In September 1967, Defense Secretary Robert S. McNamara announced that the United States would begin to deploy a limited ABM system (which he said would cost $5 billion), not against the Soviet Union, but against China.[2] The Chinese had had nuclear weapons since 1964, but it was not expected that they would achieve an intercontinental missile capability before the mid-1970s.

In the view of its sponsors, the McNamara proposal, which was called "Sentinel," had several advantages. It avoided the prohibitive expense of a nationwide system; it avoided the appearance of building toward a first-strike capability, something which would certainly have been provocative to the Soviet Union; and yet it gave the impression that the United States was "doing something." On the other hand, as critics pointed out, what the United States was doing was defending against a threat (from China) that did not yet exist, while ignoring a threat (from the Soviet Union) that did exist.

Sentinel was initially welcomed by those members of Congress who had been pressing the Johnson administration to respond to the Soviet anti-missile defense of Moscow. In its report on the military construction authorization bill in 1968, the House Armed Services Committee said it "fully supports the Sentinel program," but also declared its "intense interest in the antiballistic missile defense of the United States"[3]—something that seemed to go far beyond Sentinel. Indeed, the Johnson administration had apparently created Sentinel as a buffer precisely against such a broader system. In announcing the decision to proceed with Sentinel, McNamara had warned against "the kind of mad momentum intrinsic to the development of all nuclear weaponry." The U.S. ABM, he said, should remain a "Chinese-oriented" light deployment and should not be expanded into a "heavy Soviet-oriented" system. The latter would provide "no adequate shield at all against a Soviet attack" and would merely induce the Soviet Union to increase its offensive capability. Clark Clifford, McNamara's successor as secretary of defense in the last year of the Johnson administration, continued to stress Mutual Assured Destruction over defense.

A major fight began in Congress. On one side were those who wanted to use Sentinel as a building block for a full-blown ABM system. On the other were those who wanted no ABM at all. Virtually nobody supported, on its own merits, the concept of an ABM limited to defense against Chinese missiles or accidental launches of other missiles.

When the Nixon administration came to office in 1969, it renamed Sentinel "Safeguard" and gave it an expanded mission: to protect U.S. missile sites against Soviet or Chinese attacks. Defense Secretary Melvin R. Laird said that protection of cities was not feasible and that it was more important to protect the nation's retaliatory capacity. The first deployments of Safeguard were to be at Grand Forks Air Force Base in North Dakota and Malmstrom Air Force Base in Montana.

The Subcommittee on International Organization and Disarmament Affairs of the Senate Foreign Relations Committee, headed by Sen. Albert Gore, Sr., D-Tenn., held hearings on the ABM from March 6 to July 16, 1969. The witnesses were mainly scientists and academic experts who argued that the ABM would not work, that it was too expensive, and that it would give the Soviet Union the impression that the United States was seeking a first-strike capability. The administration found these arguments inconsistent: if the system would not work, it could not be provocative. Laird argued that it was the Soviet Union which was building a first-strike capability. Gore, in turn, declared Safeguard to be "a weapons system searching for a mission." [4]

The Senate debated the question of funds for the ABM from July 8 to August 6, 1969, in an atmosphere of tense emotion. On August 6, it divided 50-50 on an amendment by Margaret Chase Smith, R-Maine, to kill Safeguard. Under Senate rules, a proposition loses if the vote on it is tied, so Safeguard survived. In addition, Vice President Spiro T. Agnew voted against the amendment in exercise of his constitutional right to break a tie; the final vote was therefore 50 to kill Safeguard and 51 to keep it alive. This was the high-water mark of congressional opposition to the ABM, though opponents continued to attack the program in both the House and Senate, usually through efforts to limit or deny appropriations.

SALT I and II

In 1970, the SALT negotiations with the Soviet Union were proceeding, and a new argument crept into the debate over the ABM: whether it should be kept alive to be used as a "bargaining chip" in the negotiations. If it could be given up in return for a concession the United States wanted from the Soviet Union, some people said, it should not be unilaterally abandoned. This reasoning had been used before to keep weapons programs alive in the face of congressional opposition. It might indeed give the United States greater leverage in negotiations, but acquiring something for the principal purpose of giving it away is expensive; and if the other side recognizes that something is being used as a bargaining chip, the chip's value may substantially decrease, or the other side may come up with a bargaining chip of its own for which it will demand more concessions.

In fact, ABM did become the crucial element—or bargaining chip, some would say—in the SALT agreements that were signed in Moscow by President Richard M. Nixon and General Secretary Brezhnev on May 26, 1972. Henry Kissinger, then Nixon's national security adviser, said it explicitly: "The trade-off of Soviet willingness to limit offensive forces in exchange for our willingness to limit ABMs was the essential balance of incentives that produced the first SALT agreements." [5] Similarly, Nixon, in an address to Congress on his return from Moscow, said the negotiations had been successful because "over the past three years we have consistently refused proposals for unilaterally abandoning the ABM, unilaterally pulling back our forces from Europe, and drastically cutting the defense budget." [6] Fifteen years later, in 1987, President Reagan used the same reasoning to explain the success of his meeting with Soviet General Secretary Mikhail Gorbachev that led to the treaty eliminating intermediate-range nuclear forces.

The Nixon administration's willingness to limit ABMs in negotiations with the Soviet Union was largely induced by congressional and public opposition to the system. Ironically, it seemed at times that the SALT negotiators were rushing to give the ABM away before Congress killed it. If Congress had ended the program, it might not have been possible to extract the Soviet concessions that went into the SALT I treaty (as it came to be called when a second round of negotiations—SALT II—began). On the other hand, if Congress had not threatened to kill it, the Nixon administration might not have been willing to give it up—or might have gotten more in return for it. The administration itself was divided over the issue. The State Department and the Arms Control and Disarmament Agency vacillated between being lukewarm toward the ABM and being actively opposed to it. The Joint Chiefs of Staff were more enthusiastic for it than the civilians in the Pentagon. The intelligence community could not quite make up its mind as to the extent of the Soviet program.

Treaty Provisions

The SALT I or ABM treaty limited each party to two ABM systems, one for the national capital and one for a missile base (Article III).[7] These limitations did not apply to ABM systems or their components used for development or testing and located within recognized test ranges (Article IV), but in other respects, the treaty imposed severe limitations on testing or development. These activities were prohibited for systems or components that were sea-based, air-based, space-based, or mobile land-based. This language, by implication, permitted testing or development for systems that were fixed land-based, and for their components. In addition, the treaty prohibited testing and development of launchers capable of handling more than one interceptor missile at a time or those with automatic or other rapid-reload capabilities (Article V). The parties agreed not to convert non-ABM components to ABM uses or to test such components "in an ABM mode." Finally, they agreed not to deploy early warning radars "except at locations along the periphery of [the] national territory and oriented outward" (Article VI). The purpose of this last provision, which would later figure prominently in charges of Soviet treaty violations, was to ensure that such radars were intended only to provide warning of incoming missiles and were not part of an ABM system covering the whole of the national territory. A Standing Consultative Commission was established to consider questions arising out of the treaty's provisions (Article XIII).

The treaty was of unlimited duration, but it was to be reviewed at five-year intervals, and either party had the right to withdraw on six months' notice "if it decides that extraordinary events related to the subject matter of this treaty have jeopardized its supreme interests." A notice of withdrawal was to include a statement of these events (Article XV).

Accompanying the treaty were seven "initialed statements"—that is, explanatory statements initialed by Nixon and Brezhnev (although technically not part of the treaty, these statements carry great weight); six "common understandings," statements agreed to during the negotiations that are less weighty than those initialed by the heads of state but recognized as controlling by both sides; and four unilateral statements by the U.S. negotiating delegation, elaborating its position but without any agreement or comment from the Soviet side. Most of these ancillary statements are highly technical (for example, dealing with the emitted power of phased-array radars), but some of them have been important in subsequent developments.

Initialed Statement [E] provided that if "ABM systems based on other physical principles and including components capable of substituting for ABM interceptor missiles, ABM launchers, or ABM radars are created in the future, specific limitations on such systems and their components would be subject to discussion" in the Standing Consultative Commission and to agreement pursuant to provisions for amending the treaty. For reasons that are not clear, the order of the statements was subsequently revised, and this one became [D]. Also, what had at first been called "Initialed Statements" became "Agreed Statements." What thus ended as Agreed Statement [D] later became one of the points of contention in the argument over whether the Reagan Strategic Defense Initiative threatened violation of the ABM treaty.

Common Understanding D (which later became C) was an agreement that the prohibition on mobile land-based ABM systems and components "would rule out the deployment of ABM launchers and radars which were not permanent fixed types." This also became the subject of a dispute over interpretation of the treaty.

An Interim Agreement on Strategic Offensive Arms was signed in Moscow at the same time as the ABM treaty proper. It was essentially a freeze on each country's strategic offensive missiles. No new fixed land-based intercontinental ballistic missile (ICBM) launchers were to be started, nor were old ones to be improved. Submarine-launched ballistic missile (SLBM) launchers were limited to those in being or under construction. A protocol dealt with specific numbers. It was stated to be the objective of the parties to conclude a further agreement with "more complete" measures within five years, the lifetime of the interim agreement. Meanwhile, following the pattern of the ABM treaty, each party reserved "the right to withdraw from this Interim Agreement if it decides that extraordinary events related to the subject matter of this Interim Agreement have jeopardized its supreme interests." Furthermore, in Unilateral Statement A, the United States declared that failure to achieve a further agreement within the stipulated five-year period "would constitute a basis for withdrawal from the ABM Treaty."

Congressional Action

President Nixon sent the ABM treaty to the Senate on June 13, 1972, with a request for its advice and consent to ratification. There was little controversy. The Senate gave its approval on August 3 by a vote of 88 to 2. In the defense appropriation bill for fiscal year 1973, passed in 1972, Congress even denied funds for the ABM site allowed by the treaty to protect Washington. The other site which the treaty allowed, and which the United States had chosen to put at the Safeguard site in North Dakota, was about 90 percent complete when the treaty was signed.

On the same day on which the president sent the ABM treaty to the Senate, he transmitted the Interim Agreement to both houses with a request for approval. In earlier times, the Interim Agreement might have been considered to be an executive agreement, signed under the president's constitutional powers to conduct foreign affairs and requiring no congressional action (see Chapter 1). Indeed, the president could unilaterally have done what the agreement required simply by not requesting, or by not spending, appropriations for further strategic missiles. However, when Congress created the Arms Control and Disarmament Agency in 1961, it provided in the authorizing legislation that "no action shall be taken under this or any other law that will obligate the United States to disarm or to reduce or to limit the Armed Forces or armaments of the United States, except pursuant to the treaty-making power of the President under the Constitution or unless authorized by further affirmative legislation by the Congress." [8]

The House was as enthusiastic about the Interim Agreement as the Senate had been about the treaty. A joint resolution approving it was passed August 28 by a vote of 329 to 7.

But controversy arose in the Senate. The debate revealed profound differences among senators in the way they viewed the U.S.-Soviet strategic balance and U.S.-Soviet relations in general. The argument was essentially over nuclear sufficiency versus nuclear parity or even

superiority. In its report on the Interim Agreement, the Senate Foreign
Relations Committee commented:

> The United States and the Soviet Union have at last reached a point at
> which sufficiency of weapons, rather than attempted superiority on
> both sides, can be the guiding principle in the quest for viable relation-
> ships. Each side now possesses such a plethora of strategic weaponry
> that each can now feel itself securely able to deter attack but not to
> initiate strategic nuclear attack. . . .
>   Sufficiency, or parity, which has replaced the policy of numerical
> superiority, has made computation of numbers far less germane.[9]

However, an important group of senators, led by Henry M. Jackson,
D-Wash., saw the problem from a different perspective. Jackson said
the thrust of the agreements was "to confer on the Soviet Union the
authority to retain or deploy a number of weapons . . . that exceeds our
own in every category, and by a fifty percent margin." [10] With a number
of cosponsors, Jackson offered an amendment which "urges and requests the president to seek a future treaty that, inter alia, would not
limit the United States to levels of intercontinental strategic forces
inferior to the limits provided for the Soviet Union." The Nixon White
House endorsed this, or at least acquiesced in it, but the Foreign
Relations Committee rejected it by a vote of 11 to 0.

Senator J. William Fulbright offered a substitute amendment providing that, in negotiations for a permanent treaty, the United States
should seek agreement on the basis of "overall equality, parity and
sufficiency" in the number of offensive weapons. Fulbright said Jackson
was "not asking for equality between the United States and Russia."
Rather,

> he means equality in specific weapons systems. . . . This . . . is a miscon-
> ception of the whole effort . . . by both countries to bring about a degree
> of parity, or equality, in their overall strategic weapons systems, includ-
> ing not only the ICBMs, but aircraft, other forward-based nuclear
> weapons and . . . the nuclear submarines of our allies.

The kind of equality Jackson was talking about, Fulbright said, was
"superiority—equality in one area [while] we are clearly superior in the
others." [11]

On the floor of the Senate, the Fulbright substitute was rejected, 38
to 48, and the Jackson amendment was agreed to, 56 to 35. Both houses
then approved the Interim Agreement, with this amendment included.[12]

Further Negotiations

At the end of the five-year period specified in the Interim Agreement, no new agreement had been signed. However, the limitations of
the Interim Agreement continued to be observed by the tacit agreement
of both sides while the SALT II negotiations proceeded. In large mea-

sure, the negotiating difficulties grew out of the asymmetries that had been at the heart of the Senate debate over the Interim Agreement. Finally, on June 18, 1979, a SALT II treaty was signed by President Jimmy Carter and General Secretary Brezhnev in Vienna. It provided a complicated system of sublimits as well as counting rules, and it included a statement of principles for SALT III. President Carter sent the treaty to the Senate, and it was the subject of extensive hearings before the Foreign Relations Committee.

The central concern over the treaty had to do with verification: Could the United States be sure of Soviet compliance? But other difficulties arose as well. In August, intelligence agencies reported the presence of a hitherto unsuspected Soviet brigade in Cuba. Later intelligence assessments concluded that the brigade had been there for many years, but in the meantime U.S. apprehension of the Soviet Union was rekindled. Then, in December 1979, Soviet troops intervened in Afghanistan. This led President Carter to ask the Senate to suspend consideration of the SALT II treaty. The Senate complied.

The ABM Protocol

President Nixon journeyed to Moscow for another summit in the summer of 1974, at a time when his administration was encumbered by the unfolding revelations concerning the Watergate break-in. In these circumstances, both the United States and the Soviet Union were uncertain of the future and unwilling or unable to make significant long-term commitments. Nevertheless, one result of this meeting was a protocol further limiting what was permitted under the ABM treaty. (A *protocol* is an addendum to a treaty, usually dealing with a single point. It is roughly analogous to a codicil of a will.)

That treaty, as noted, had allowed each side two ABM sites—one to protect its national capital and one to protect a field of missiles. Neither party had fully availed itself of this allowance. The Soviet Union had an ABM defense around Moscow, but none around any of its missile fields. The United States had an ABM defense around its missile base at Grand Forks, but none around Washington (and, as we have seen, Congress had specifically prohibited the expenditure of funds for building one around Washington). The protocol signed in 1974 recognized this state of affairs and limited each side to one site which it could choose—either its capital or a missile base.

The Senate Foreign Relations Committee held sporadic hearings over the course of a year and then approved the protocol, with the remark that "it would have been preferable for the two sides to agree to the limitation of one complex each at the start." [13] The Senate gave its advice and consent to ratification without floor debate by a vote of 63 to 15 on November 10, 1975.

The Grand Forks site had been completed a month earlier. In the fiscal 1976 defense appropriation bill, Congress voted to put it in mothballs (except for the perimeter acquisition radar), thereby effectively abandoning the one ABM site to which the United States was still entitled. By that time, the Safeguard program had cost $6 billion, and all that remained was the radar unit.

The Strategic Defense Initiative

The idea of a defense against missiles died hard. The ABM treaty had scarcely been ratified before the army in 1973 presented what it called "site defense system." This was an ABM to protect Minuteman ICBMs with short-range missiles, while Safeguard would provide areawide protection. In 1974, another system was offered called "advanced ballistic missile defense." In 1981, there was a program for research on laser-armed space satellites.

None of these programs generated congressional debates at all comparable to the earlier arguments over the ABM, but the concept remained controversial. Although one house of Congress or the other sometimes cut off funding for an ABM project, by the time the legislative process had run its course at the end of the year, something was almost always appropriated, though usually less than had been requested by the White House. This is a typical congressional response: when confronted with a program about which it is dubious, Congress gives something but not everything. Executive agencies know this and ask for more than they really need or expect.

A major new element was added to the debate when President Ronald Reagan proposed what he called the Strategic Defense Initiative (SDI) and what critics called Star Wars. The idea was to construct a kind of umbrella over the United States consisting of a network of space-based and space-launched laser and nuclear weapons with the capability of destroying hostile missiles in flight. According to one of the president's senior arms-control advisers, the idea grew from a private briefing on nuclear strategy that Reagan had received years before when he was governor of California. The point was made in the briefing that the nuclear standoff between the superpowers could be compared to two people each holding a pistol to the other's head; each was hostage to the other, and the size of the pistol did not much matter. Governor Reagan's response, as reported at a seminar in 1986, was, "Why don't we put on a helmet?" SDI was to be the nation's helmet. Indeed, it was to be everybody's helmet. If it worked (and nobody knew whether it would), Reagan offered to share the technology with the Soviet Union, though in the best of circumstances, the technology would not be available until long after he left office.

President Reagan presented the SDI concept to the country in a television speech on March 23, 1983, in which he said:

> I've become more and more deeply convinced that the human spirit must be capable of rising above dealing with other nations and human beings by threatening their existence. . . .
>
> Wouldn't it be better to save lives than to avenge them? Are we not capable of demonstrating our peaceful intentions by applying all our abilities and our ingenuity to achieving a truly lasting stability? . . . Let me share with you a vision of the future which offers hope. It is that we embark on a program to counter the awesome Soviet missile threat with measures that are defensive. . . .
>
> What if free people could live secure in the knowledge that their security did not rest upon the threat of instant U.S. retaliation to deter a Soviet attack, that we could intercept and destroy strategic ballistic missiles before they reached our own soil or that of our allies?[14]

The SDI proposal at once aroused a storm of controversy. The arguments were similar to those made years before with respect to the original ABM, but they were now raised to a higher intensity because of the escalation, both in cost and in technical sophistication, represented by the SDI. It was estimated that the first five years of research would cost $22 billion. Deployment would cost perhaps $500 billion or more. Harold Brown, a nuclear physicist who had been secretary of defense in the Carter administration, said that SDI might require a computer program of as much as 100 million lines.[15] The greater cost and complexity, it was now argued, would also be detrimental to the other components of the U.S. military establishment, in that both material and human resources would be diverted into the new project.

Otherwise, the same arguments that had been heard about the ABM were repeated. Just as it was once thought that nuclear weapons provided the ultimate offense, now SDI was said to offer promise of the ultimate defense. For precisely that reason, opponents replied, SDI could very well give the appearance of providing the United States with a first-strike capability. It would inspire the Soviet Union to seek ways to penetrate it and would therefore escalate the arms race to yet a higher level. SDI supporters argued, on the other hand, that the program was defensive and that, by definition, it threatened no one, particularly since it was accompanied by a presidential offer to share the technology.

Whatever the merits of these arguments, it soon became clear that the Soviet government was very disturbed. SDI became the sticking point on U.S.-Soviet arms control negotiations. It was the rock on which the meeting between Gorbachev and Reagan in Reykjavik foundered in October 1986. Repeatedly, Gorbachev demanded that SDI be abandoned or limited; adamantly, Reagan refused. SDI, he said, was not a bargaining chip; he would not negotiate it away.

Treaty Ratification

Before the debate in the United States could be fully developed over the question of the SDI on its own merits, two new and highly contentious issues were added—namely, at what point would SDI be constrained by the ABM treaty, and where in the government would that decision be made?

The first hint of these issues came from National Security Adviser Robert C. McFarlane on the "Meet the Press" television program October 6, 1985. McFarlane remarked that testing and development of ABM systems based on "new physical concepts" was "approved and authorized" by the SALT I treaty.[16] Before then, it had been taken for granted that SDI laboratory research was not covered by the treaty, but that when the SDI proceeded to testing, development, or deployment, the treaty did apply. It was not even certain in the early stages that SDI involved "new physical concepts"—nor, for that matter, what "new physical concepts" were.

The ABM treaty proper does not mention "new physical concepts." Agreed Statement [D] refers to "other physical principles" (without defining them) and says that if ABM systems involving such principles are created, then "specific limitations [on them] . . . would be subject to discussion . . . and agreement." The treaty itself is very clear in its prohibition of the development, testing, or deployment of other than fixed land-based systems (Article V).

One possible element of SDI was the use of space-based lasers to disarm enemy missiles, and this could be called a "new physical concept" or "other physical principle." Another possible element was the deployment of so-called kinetic kill vehicles—missiles which would disable enemy missiles by physically hitting them. These involved no new concepts or principles and were thus clearly prohibited by the ABM treaty, but they could also be in place earlier than the more exotic technologies using lasers or particle beams. This gave rise to a dilemma: If the United States did what could be done most quickly, it would have to deal sooner with the limitations imposed by the ABM treaty.

Administration Position

McFarlane's seemingly casual remark provoked a heated debate over a "broad" versus a "narrow" or "restrictive" or "traditional" interpretation of the ABM treaty. A few days after McFarlane's television appearance, President Reagan signed National Security Decision Directive 192, which in effect took both sides of the issue. As explained by Secretary of State Shultz in a speech two days later:

> It is our view, based on a careful analysis of the [ABM] treaty text and the negotiating record, that a broader interpretation of our authority is

fully justified. This is, however, a moot point; our SDI research program has been structured and ... will continue to be conducted in accordance with a restrictive interpretation of the treaty's obligations.[17]

Actually, the administration had been considering this question internally for some time. On October 3, 1985, the legal adviser of the State Department, Abraham D. Sofaer, a former federal judge, produced a memorandum supporting the broad interpretation based on, among other things, the *negotiating record* of the treaty—that is, the collection of all the documents involved in the negotiations.[18] For the preparation of this memorandum, he relied mainly on some young lawyers new to his staff. He later disavowed this memo and wrote another one which, however, reached the same conclusion.

Congressional Reaction

The issue prompted hearings on both sides of Capitol Hill, first by a House Foreign Affairs subcommittee and then by a Senate Armed Services subcommittee. The administration was represented by Sofaer and by Paul Nitze, who had been one of the treaty's negotiators—the only one still serving in the government. On the other side, the subcommittees heard from Gerard C. Smith, who had been head of the Arms Control and Disarmament Agency in the Nixon administration and who had been chief of the ABM treaty negotiating team. Smith was supported by John B. Rhinelander, who had been the team's legal adviser.

The issue gradually went beyond the question of the legally correct interpretation. SDI opponents wondered why, if the issue was indeed "moot," as Shultz had said, the administration was so insistent about it. Was it seeking to establish the validity of the broad interpretation against the day when it would want to conduct tests that were prohibited by the narrow interpretation? Some supporters of SDI wanted to move quickly to make the broad interpretation irreversible, so that it could not be abandoned by the new administration that would take office in 1989. The system probably could not be tested and certainly could not be deployed before then, but if the right to do so under the ABM treaty could be firmly established, SDI's political survivability would be improved.

This argument, in turn, affected the annual debate over appropriations. How fast should Congress allow the SDI program to go? On this point, Congress once again compromised. For fiscal 1986, the administration requested $3.7 billion for SDI development; the House appropriated $2.5 billion, the Senate $2.96 billion, and the final figure was $2.75 billion.

The fundamental argument provoked by the Sofaer memorandum,

however, had to do with what Congress, and particularly the Senate, perceived to be their institutional prerogatives. Few issues arouse more fervor on Capitol Hill, and it was even greater in this case because Reagan, more than most presidents, was jealous of the prerogatives of his office. Sofaer had based his reinterpretation largely on the negotiating record, but senatorial requests to see that record were resisted. Finally, it was supplied, or at least enough of it to satisfy the Senate, but only after repeated delays had sorely tried senatorial patience. (The Shultz State Department thereby demonstrated that it had failed to learn the lesson that had also eluded the State Department under every other secretary at least since Dean Acheson: The department's relations with Congress would be greatly improved if it would supply promptly and graciously what it is eventually going to supply tardily and grudgingly.)

Administration officials insisted that the interpretation of a treaty was the prerogative of the president alone. Some senators, notably the minority leader, Robert J. Dole, R-Kan., supported this view, but others vigorously dissented. Senator Sam Nunn, D-Ga., said it would amount to having "the Senate of the United States declare itself a potted plant ... an ornament in the foreign policy arena, adorning but having no influence." [19] The Foreign Relations Committee called the reinterpretation "the most flagrant abuse of the Constitution's treaty power in 200 years." [20]

Confrontation

How some senators felt about reinterpreting the treaty depended on how they felt about SDI: Those favoring SDI favored the reinterpretation; those opposing SDI opposed the reinterpretation. But there was another group, epitomized by Nunn, which thought that, regardless of SDI, reinterpretation amounted to a unilateral changing of the rules of treaty making. The Senate had thought the treaty meant one thing when it had approved it; now the Senate was being told that the treaty really meant something else. Further, the Senate was being told, in effect, that it did not even have a voice in the matter. This sounded to some not simply like reinterpretation by the president but like amendment by the president. Moreover, they said, the matter was without precedent. The Foreign Relations Committee declared that it was "aware of *no* instance in which a treaty was reasonably supposed by the Senate, when it consented to ratification, to mean one thing, and it was argued later by the Executive to mean something altogether different." [21] In this view, any reinterpretation of a treaty, like the treaty itself, should result from joint action by the president and the Senate. Nunn had warned the president about the potential consequences of acting unilaterally. In a letter of February 6, 1987, he wrote:

I am concerned that absent due consultation, a unilateral Executive Branch decision to disregard the interpretation of the Treaty which the Senate believed it had approved when the accord was ratified in 1972 would provoke a Constitutional confrontation of profound dimensions.[22]

The administration held to the reinterpretation (though without actually doing anything to violate the old interpretation), and the constitutional confrontation that Nunn had predicted began to take form. First, Nunn made a major speech in the Senate, which extended over three days (March 11, 12, and 13, 1987). He exhaustively analyzed the negotiating record he had been supplied, the record of Senate consideration, and the Sofaer memorandum. His conclusion was that, although there were some ambiguities in the negotiating record, they were not

of sufficient magnitude to demonstrate that the Nixon administration reached one agreement with the Soviets and then presented a different one to the Senate. The preponderance of evidence in the negotiating record supports the Senate's original understanding of the treaty, that is, the traditional interpretation.[23]

Nunn's speech was followed by joint hearings by the Senate Foreign Relations and Judiciary committees. The purpose of the hearings was to consider a resolution on the subject by Sen. Joseph R. Biden, Jr., D-Del., chairman of Judiciary and the second-ranking Democrat on Foreign Relations. The Biden resolution set forth the legislative history of the ABM treaty in great detail and concluded that the broad interpretation "would be inconsistent with the provisions of the Treaty and would require an amendment to the Treaty." Further, the resolution declared, "no amendment to the ABM Treaty may occur without the agreement of the Parties and the advice and consent of the Senate." [24]

Biden assailed the administration view as being "a purposeful act of revisionist distortion." [25] On the other hand, Sen. Gordon J. Humphrey, R-N.H., said the president should withdraw from the ABM treaty altogether and carry the battle for anti-missile defenses to the public. Sen. Ernest F. Hollings, D-S.C., also consulted the negotiating record and announced his agreement with Sofaer.[26]

Despite the joint hearings, the Foreign Relations Committee had sole jurisdiction over the resolution and approved it on May 19, 1987, by a vote of 11 to 8. Nancy Landon Kassebaum of Kansas was the only Republican to vote for it, a fact that suggested there would be difficulty in bringing it to a vote in the Senate as a whole. The resolution was reported in September, but was not further considered in 1987. Other business was clogging the Senate calendar as the session moved to a close, and administration supporters made it plain they would mount a major fight against any effort to bring the resolution to a vote.

The Battle over Funding

The question of reinterpreting a treaty is an issue between the Senate and the president, and this particular reinterpretation involved a major issue of national defense as well. On this latter issue, the House joined the Senate in resorting to the congressional power of the purse. Members of the House generally approached the matter on the basis of the merits of SDI and thought that the issue of treaty reinterpretation was secondary. House opponents of SDI welcomed the reinterpretation issue as a further roadblock and House proponents deplored it for the same reason, but generally the House did not feel so institutionally involved as the Senate.

The first action came in the House Armed Services Committee in connection with the defense authorization bill. (For the distinction between authorization and appropriation, see Chapter 2.) The committee voted to require continued observance of the ABM treaty's traditional interpretation. The House passed the bill with the committee's restriction intact. The strength of feeling in the House was shown by a vote of 159 to 262 against a proposal to delete the restriction.

The Senate Armed Services Committee went further. It approved a provision, offered by Nunn and Sen. Carl Levin, D-Mich., prohibiting tests of anti-missile devices that were based in space or on aircraft, ships, or mobile ground vehicles unless the tests were approved by Congress. This prohibition was strongly opposed by the administration and set off a Republican filibuster, which went on throughout the summer of 1987.

The Senate spent a great deal of time in parliamentary skirmishing over the filibuster. Nunn served notice on the president that if the administration insisted on reinterpreting the ABM, he would insist that the Senate be given the negotiating record of the treaty eliminating intermediate-range nuclear forces (INF), which was then close to being completed. (It was signed by Reagan and Gorbachev in Washington in December 1987.) "In effect," Nunn wrote to the president, "the Sofaer doctrine holds that if the Senate is misinformed by Executive Branch officials as to the meaning of a proposed treaty, that is simply too bad.... If Congress relies upon the testimony of your administration as to the meaning of an INF treaty, it will be at its own risk." [27] Claiborne Pell, D-R.I., chairman of the Foreign Relations Committee, went further. He demanded the negotiating records for twenty treaties that were already pending before the committee.

Nunn finally broke the filibuster by threatening to keep the Senate from taking up the nomination of Robert Bork to the Supreme Court until after it had disposed of the defense bill. (The president had nominated Bork to fill a vacancy on the Court during the summer and had made Senate confirmation one of his highest priorities. The nomination became bitterly controversial and was eventually rejected by the Senate, but of course that was not foreseen at the time of Nunn's threat.) The Senate then voted 58 to 38 to table a motion to delete the Nunn-Levin amendment. To "table" a motion technically means only to set it aside, but in practice it is the functional equivalent of rejection; hence, when a motion to delete an amendment is tabled, the amendment remains intact.

Sen. Pete Wilson, R-Calif., called the Nunn-Levin amendment "the most glaring unilateral concession in the history of arms control." [28] Nunn, on the other hand, said that what he called the "Sofaer doctrine" was "the boldest assertion of executive power at the expense of the Senate as an institution that I've ever seen." Unless the administration repudiated Sofaer, Nunn continued, the Senate would have to review the entire negotiating record on all future treaties. Thus, he concluded, "in an effort to temporarily strengthen this president on the ABM treaty [the administration has] weakened the presidency as an institution." [29] Meanwhile, in the background was the threat of a veto if the president believed his powers were unduly limited.

In the end, the matter was compromised, and the basic issue was left unresolved. The bill that was sent to the president in late November replaced the Nunn-Levin amendment with a provision limiting anti-missile tests to those which the administration had previously announced would take place during the year ending September 30, 1988. All of these fell within the traditional or narrow interpretation of the ABM treaty. Both the president and Congress had made their points for another year. Congress achieved what it wanted—namely, limiting SDI tests to those permitted under the narrow interpretation. The president avoided a congressional restriction on his prerogatives; the limitation he accepted permitted him to do all that he had intended to do, anyway. It was a classic example of how the legislative process works.

The Issue Recurs

President Reagan and General Secretary Gorbachev had also in effect postponed their dispute about the ABM treaty. They had failed to reach any agreement at their meeting in Reykjavik because of that dispute, but they finally resolved their differences in order to be able to sign the INF treaty in December 1987. The result was a wordy paragraph in their joint statement which said that they would observe the ABM treaty "as signed . . . while conducting their research, development and testing as required." [30] It was a piece of what Henry Kissinger called "constructive ambiguity."

But within a week, each leader made it clear that he continued to hold to his earlier position. In January 1988, the United States submitted a new draft treaty in the continuing arms negotiations in Geneva, in which it insisted on the broad interpretation. Georgi M. Kornienko, a senior Soviet official visiting Washington, accused the United States of "disrespect" for the December Gorbachev-Reagan statement.[31]

This dispute affected Senate consideration of the INF treaty. After considerable negotiation with a number of senators, Secretary of State Shultz provided a letter that satisfied Nunn. In it, the secretary gave assurances that executive-branch testimony could be regarded as authoritative without being incorporated in the Senate resolution of ratification. Shultz also promised that the Reagan administration would not adopt a different meaning for the treaty without the approval of the Senate.

On March 30, 1988, the Foreign Relations Committee voted 17-2 to report the treaty favorably to the Senate. By a vote of 12-7, the committee added the substance of Shultz's letter to Nunn as a condition in the resolution of ratification. The committee then went on to say in the resolution that any departure from this understanding would require "Senate advice and consent to a subsequent treaty or protocol, or the enactment of a statute." [32]

This became a major issue during Senate debate on the INF treaty in May 1988. The issue was still viewed as an institutional one involving the respective prerogatives of the president and the Senate, but a group of Republican senators argued that the Foreign Relations Committee's proposals would undermine the president and enhance the Senate at his expense.

Majority Leader Robert Byrd proposed a somewhat diluted compromise that attracted some Republican support, including that of Minority Leader Dole. The Byrd substitute contained a provision that the United States would not depart from the "common understanding" of the treaty's meaning except with the advice and consent of the Senate or through enactment of a law by both houses of Congress.[33]

The Senate agreed to the Byrd substitute, 72-27, on May 26, 1988. The following day, it tabled (that is, in effect rejected) two final efforts by Sen. Arlen Specter, R-Pa., to dilute the provision further. One of these would have defined "common understanding" as a "shared interpretation" that the Senate clearly relied on. It was tabled 67-30. The other disclaimed any intent by the Senate to change "the heretofore accepted constitutional law." [34] It was tabled, 64-33. The Senate then gave its advice and consent to the INF treaty, 93-5.

The Issue of Soviet Violations

While Congress and the executive branch were quarreling over what the ABM treaty permitted the United States to do, both of them were concerned over what the Soviet Union might be doing in its own antiballistic missile program. The first Soviet activity to attract attention was a large phased-array radar at Krasnoyarsk in southern Siberia. The radar's antennas were first observed in 1983, and by mid-1984 most people in the United States who were knowledgeable about arms control (including those outside as well as in the government) were in agreement that the Krasnoyarsk radar was probably a violation of the ABM treaty. The pertinent provision is Article VI(b), which prohibits deployment of "radars for early warning of strategic ballistic missile attack except at locations along the periphery of its national territory and oriented outward." In 1987, both houses of Congress voted unanimously to declare that the Krasnoyarsk radar violated this provision (Krasnoyarsk is more than three hundred miles north of the Soviet border with Outer Mongolia), and the administration supported this assessment.

However, in September 1987, in a display of the new Soviet policy of *glasnost* (openness), three members of the House and a staff member of the House Armed Services Committee were permitted to visit Krasnoyarsk and to photograph the radar. The staff member, Anthony R. Battista, was a technical specialist, and he concluded that, although the radar might technically violate the treaty, it could not provide battle management for anti-missile defenses.

The second Soviet action to arouse concern was the movement of two radars from the test range near Sary Shagan in Kazakhstan to Gomel, a city about 350 miles southwest of Moscow. The treaty permitted the radars on the test range, but it prohibited their relocation elsewhere. The Soviet Union said that the equipment had not been moved but dismantled, or partially so, and invited the United States to inspect it. The United States sent a team of radar experts in December 1987; in April 1988, they had still not announced their conclusions.

In a report to Congress required by law, the administration, through the Arms Control and Disarmament Agency, listed these and several other instances of alleged Soviet "noncompliance" with arms-control agreements. The agency said that the Krasnoyarsk and Gomel radars were violations of the ABM treaty, but in the other cases—the development of mobile land-based ABM systems, concurrent testing of ABM and air defense components, the development of an ABM capability in surface-to-air missile (SAM) systems, and the development of a rapid-reload mechanism for ABM launchers—it said the evidence was "insufficient" or the Soviet actions were "ambiguous." [35]

At about the same time, the House Intelligence Committee issued a report reaching substantially the same conclusion, calling the evidence of violations "inconclusive," but it—or at least its Democratic majority—implied that the charges of Soviet noncompliance were not always objective. "In cases where U.S. intelligence could not provide evidence that was conclusive," the committee said, "considerations leading to a particular compliance assessment were at times found to be as much judgmental as they were analytic." [36] The committee's Republican members dissented, claiming that the majority's "main ambition was to discredit" the administration's judgments and to minimize problems of verification in future treaties.[37] Thus, to oversimplify matters somewhat, in the Democratic view, charges of violations were sometimes based more on skepticism than on hard analysis; in the Republican view, the Democrats simply wanted to ignore the verification issue.

Conclusion

Taken by themselves, the ABM treaty of 1972 and its protocol of 1974 are routine examples of the way in which the president and the Senate share power in the treaty-making process. But there is far more to them than that. These agreements are at the heart of two issues that, in one form or another, have agitated U.S. defense policy since 1945.

On the one hand, there are the more or less technological questions. Is there any point in trying to construct a defense against nuclear weapons? Conversely, is there any justification for not trying? If a serious effort were made to provide effective defense, either through SDI or some other means, would it in fact lead to security? Or would it merely stimulate an adversary's search for more, and more powerful, offensive weapons? With or without a defense, how many nuclear missiles are enough? Finally, when the United States and the Soviet Union agreed in the ABM treaty not to construct nationwide ABM defenses, they agreed in effect to put their populations mutually at risk. Is this morally or strategically acceptable?

On the other hand, there are the constitutional issues. The Constitution gives Congress the power to "provide for the common defense" and "to raise and support armies," and therefore Congress must have a role in searching for the answers to all these questions—but it also designates the president as commander in chief. Similarly, the Constitution gives the president the power to make treaties, but only with the approval of the Senate by a two-thirds vote. The issue of anti-missile defense, as it evolved into the SDI, raised the question of how much flexibility the president has in interpreting a treaty after it has been made. The Reagan administration implied that the president's flexibility is virtually unlimited, while a majority of the Senate (and the House, too, for that matter) said it is constrained by the Senate's powers. Senator Nunn warned that Reagan's unyielding insistence on upholding what he saw as the powers of the presidency might be counterproductive, in that it would ultimately weaken the office. Something of the same thing occurred as a consequence of President Johnson's persistence in the face of congressional opposition to his Vietnam policy.

One of the advantages of the U.S. political system is that it usually finds a way—perhaps unsatisfactory to many people, but nonetheless workable—to compromise differences or, if that is not possible, to make them look compromised, or to postpone them. That is what was done in 1987 with the issues raised by the ABM. But the issues came to the fore again in 1988, and they are still there for future presidents and future Congresses.

Notes

1. Lyndon Baines Johnson, *The Vantage Point: Perspectives of the Presidency, 1963-1969* (New York: Holt, Rinehart and Winston, 1971), 479-480.
2. The text of McNamara's speech is in *New York Times,* September 18, 1967.
3. House Armed Services Committee, *Military Construction Authorization.* 90th Cong., 2d sess., 1968, H. Rept. 90-1296 (H.R. 16703), 5.
4. *CQ Almanac* 25 (1969), 260.
5. Henry Kissinger, *White House Years* (Boston: Little, Brown, 1979), 208.
6. *Congressional Record,* 92d Cong., 2d sess., June 1, 1972, 19516.
7. 23 UST 3435; TIAS 7503. The texts of the treaty, the Interim Agreement, the agreed interpretations, and the unilateral statements, as well as useful related documents, are in House Committee on Foreign Affairs and Senate Committee on Foreign Relations, *Legislation on Foreign Relations through 1985,* vol. 3, *Treaties and Related Material* (Washington, D.C.: Government Printing Office, 1986), 80-87.
8. Arms Control and Disarmament Act of 1961, as amended, sec. 33 (22 USC 2573).
9. Senate Committee on Foreign Relations, *Agreement on Limitation of Strategic Offensive Weapons,* 92d Cong., 2d sess., 1972, S. Rept. 92-979, pp. 5, 8.
10. U.S. Congress, Senate, *Congressional Record,* 92d Cong., 2d sess., August 11, 1972, 27935.
11. Ibid., September 7, 1972, 29725.
12. The Jackson Amendment is in sec. 3 of the joint resolution on the agreement, P.L. 92-448, approved September 30, 1972.
13. *Congressional Record,* 94th Cong., 1st sess., November 6, 1975, 35363.
14. *Weekly Compilation of Presidential Documents,* vol. 19, no. 12 (March 28, 1983): 447.
15. Harold Brown, "Is SDI Technically Feasible?" *Foreign Affairs* 64 (*America and the World, 1985*): 444.
16. *Department of State Bulletin* 85 (December 1985): 33.
17. Ibid., 23.
18. The negotiating record includes summaries of the negotiating sessions, memoranda of conversations with representatives of the other government and of communications between the U.S. negotiators and the government in Washington, summaries of telephone conversations, and even travel vouchers and hotel bills. These records are, obviously, voluminous. Along with a great deal of dross, they also contain some very sensitive material and are very tightly held by the State Department. Nevertheless, they are usually viewed as being of no more than historical interest. The ABM treaty is the only instance since World War II when they have been an important subject of controversy or source of interpretation.

19. Dispatch by Helen Dewar, *Washington Post,* September 16, 1987.
20. Dispatch by R. Jeffrey Smith, *Washington Post,* September 21, 1987.
21. Senate Committee on Foreign Relations, *The ABM Treaty Interpretation Resolution,* 100th Cong., 1st sess., 1987, S. Rept. 100-164, p. 48 (italics in the original).
22. The full text of Nunn's letter is in *Congressional Quarterly Weekly Report,* February 14, 1987, 274.
23. U.S. Congress, Senate, *Congressional Record,* daily ed., 100th Cong., 1st sess., March 13, 1987, S3172. The full text of Nunn's speech is in ibid., March 11, 1987, S2967-S2986; March 12, 1987, S3090-S3095; and March 13, 1987, S3171-S3173.
24. S. Res. 167, 100th Cong., 1st sess.
25. Senate Committee on Foreign Relations and Committee on the Judiciary, *The ABM Treaty and the Constitution, Joint Hearings,* 1987, 118.
26. Ibid., 109-112, 442-470.
27. *Congressional Quarterly Weekly Report,* September 5, 1967, 2127.
28. *Congressional Record,* daily ed., 100th Cong., 1st sess., September 16, 1987, S12142.
29. *Congressional Quarterly Weekly Report,* September 19, 1987, 2232.
30. Text in *Washington Post,* December 11, 1987.
31. Dispatch by Don Oberdorfer and R. Jeffrey Smith, *Washington Post,* January 30, 1988. A5.
32. Senate Committee on Foreign Relations, *The INF Treaty,* 100th Cong., 2d sess., Exec. Rept. 100-15 (April 14, 1988), 436 (resolution of ratification), 442 (Shultz's letter to Nunn). This report also contains much other useful material on treaty interpretation.
33. *Congressional Record,* daily ed., 100th Cong., 2d sess., May 26, 1988, S6724.
34. *Congressional Record,* daily ed., 100th Cong., 2d sess., May 27, 1988, S6884 and S6890.
35. Arms Control and Disarmament Agency, "The President's Unclassified Report on Soviet Noncompliance with Arms Control Agreements," December 2, 1987, 4-7, 10-13.
36. House Permanent Select Committee on Intelligence, *Intelligence Support to Arms Control,* 100th Cong., 1st sess., November 19, 1987, H. Rept. 100-450, p. 2.
37. Ibid., 32.

CHAPTER 4

The Arab-Israeli Conflict and Arms Sales to Saudi Arabia

U.S. Diplomacy in the Middle East

One of the most intractable problems of the post-World War II era has been the Arab-Israeli conflict. It has been particularly difficult for the United States because of contradictory interests—on the one hand, a deep commitment to the idea and the reality of a Jewish state; on the other, the importance of the Arab states because of their geography, their leadership of the Moslem world, American fears of Soviet influence, Arab oil reserves, and the strategic importance of the Persian Gulf area.

The foreign policy of the United States toward the Arab-Israeli conflict may be conveniently envisioned in four stages.[1] In the first, from the founding of the Zionist movement in the late nineteenth century until World War II, the United States had no official involvement in the Arab-Israeli controversy. Yet private citizens and groups—whose views were often supported by resolutions passed by the state legislatures and Congress—were active in behalf of Zionist goals.

In the second stage—during and after World War II, until the creation of the state of Israel on May 14, 1948—the Roosevelt and Truman administrations supported the establishment of a Jewish state in the ancient land of Palestine, and they endorsed other Zionist goals, such as expanded Jewish immigration to Palestine after the war.

For almost twenty years after Israel came into existence, American foreign policy in its third stage was overtly pro-Israeli. Economic and technical aid by the United States, along with military assistance and arms sales (often on highly advantageous terms for the Israelis), enabled

Israel to survive, to absorb a steady stream of Jewish refugees, and to create a high standard of living for its citizens. Governmental aid and loans to Israel were supplemented by a high level of private donations, loans, and other forms of assistance to Israel by Jewish groups and other supporters in the United States.

Some time after the third round of military hostilities between Israel and the Arab states in 1967, American policy toward the controversy entered the fourth stage. The transition did not become evident perhaps until the period of the Nixon administration, beginning in 1969; it was accelerated by the events of the fourth round in the Arab-Israeli conflict, which erupted in 1973. While by no means abandoning its longstanding ties of friendship with Israel, the United States did endeavor to assume a more even-handed or impartial position toward the Arab-Israeli disagreement. More than at any time in the past, U.S. policy reflected awareness among policy makers and informed citizens that "the Arab case" deserved more sympathetic consideration and that a number of Arab grievances against Israel were well founded. By the mid-1970s, even Israeli officials had become aware of, and disturbed by, this change in official and public attitudes in the United States.

Two developments symbolized this transition in the direction of American diplomacy. One was the close rapport that developed between officials in Washington (President Jimmy Carter was a notable example) and President Anwar Sadat of Egypt. More than any other single Arab leader, Sadat was responsible for engendering good will and sympathy in the United States for the Arab position. One of the Carter administration's leading diplomatic accomplishments, the Camp David peace agreements between Israel and Egypt in 1979, epitomized America's role as a peacemaker in the Arab-Israeli imbroglio. This goal was continued by the Reagan administration, which endeavored (unsuccessfully) to pacify strife-torn Lebanon and repeatedly sought to discover some basis for peace between the other Arab states and Israel. Yet the Reagan White House was unable to persuade other Arab governments to join Egypt in entering into peace talks with Israel.

The other development was the event that has been selected as a case study in this chapter: the Reagan administration's attempts over a period of several years to sell AWACS aircraft and other modern weapons to the government of Saudi Arabia. As with all other aspects of the Arab-Israeli conflict, this step proved to be highly controversial in Washington. It also illustrated several key problems and issues related to executive-legislative relations in the foreign policy field.

Background

The state of Israel is the fulfillment of Zionism, or the idea of a Jewish state. Zionism as a political idea was developed and elaborated by Theodor Herzl at the end of the nineteenth century in his influential book *The Jewish State* (1896). For Herzl, a native of Hungary who spent most of his life in Austria and France, Zionism was the answer to the pervasive anti-Semitism that, in his view, made the assimilation of Jews in Europe impossible.[2]

The World Zionist Organization, with Herzl as its president, was established by a conference he organized in Switzerland in 1897. Herzl entered into unsuccessful negotiations with the Turkish government for lands in Palestine and with the British for lands in the Sinai Peninsula. Britain instead offered some territory in Uganda, which Herzl favored accepting but which the Zionist Congress of 1903 turned down.

World War I gave momentum to Zionism, and World War II gave it fulfillment. In 1917, Lord Balfour, the British foreign minister, issued the now famous Balfour Declaration:

> His Majesty's Government view with favour the establishment in Palestine of a national home for the Jewish people, and will use their best endeavors to facilitate the achievement of this object, it being clearly understood that nothing shall be done which may prejudice the civil and religious rights of existing non-Jewish communities in Palestine, or the rights and political status enjoyed by Jews in any other country.[3]

A similar statement was adopted by the U.S. Congress as a joint resolution in 1922. Two points are to be noted. First, the reference in the Balfour Declaration was to a "national home for the Jewish people"— which was not necessarily the same thing as a Jewish state. Second, there was also a proviso against prejudicing the rights of the Arabs in Palestine, who comprised a substantial majority of the population.

The Balfour Declaration was also incorporated into the British mandate for Palestine under the League of Nations. Resistance from the Arab population of Palestine (which had previously been part of the Ottoman Empire) was almost immediate, and the British government soon became involved in a continuing conflict over the levels of Jewish immigration into Palestine that would be permitted in the years ahead and over other issues that engendered controversy between the Zionists and the Arabs. As the mandatory authority administering Palestine on behalf of the League of Nations, Great Britain was increasingly caught in the crossfire between the Zionists, who wanted to create a Jewish state in the country, and the Arabs, who opposed the Zionist goal. As time passed, officials in London became increasingly preoccupied with the approach of World War II; they had neither the incentive nor the power to resolve the Palestinian problem. The Palestinian question became acute in the aftermath of World War II. The Zionists exerted pressure on London to enable survivors of the Holocaust—Nazi Germany's campaign to exterminate the Jews—not only to immigrate into Palestine, but also to establish a Jewish state there. On November 29,

1947, the United Nations General Assembly voted for a plan to partition an independent Palestine into separate Jewish and Arab states, tied together in an economic union, with the city of Jerusalem under direct U.N. trusteeship. While the Arabs rejected the partition proposal, the Zionists reluctantly accepted it, since the plan did grant them the long-awaited Jewish state.

On December 3, 1947, the British announced that they would consider their mandate from the League of Nations terminated on May 15, 1948. Both Jews and Arabs prepared for a war that, in fact, did not wait until May. The state of Israel was proclaimed in Palestine at midnight, May 14. President Truman recognized it eleven minutes later.[4]

Throughout this period, in energetically supporting Zionist objectives, Truman acted largely on his own, although he received encouragement from many legislators. Truman accorded increased Jewish immigration into Palestine priority over establishment of a Jewish state. The State Department—viewed by Truman as dominated by "Arabists" who were under British influence—advised against his policy. Dean Acheson, undersecretary of state at the time, frankly stated in his memoirs, "I did not share the President's views on the Palestine solution." [5] Pro-Zionist pressures were coming from Capitol Hill, notably from Sen. Robert F. Wagner and Rep. Emanuel Celler, both prominent New York Democrats. Secretary of Defense James V. Forrestal, concerned even then over access to Arab oil, supported the State Department. Postmaster General Robert Hannegan, charged with arranging Truman's reelection, supported the Zionists—who were themselves extraordinarily active. "I do not think I ever had as much pressure and propaganda aimed at the White House as I had in this instance," Truman wrote later.[6]

For whatever reason or combination of reasons, the deed was done; the state of Israel was created. Then began the continuing effort by the United States to balance its diverse interests in the Middle East.

The Actors

Israel. In many respects, it is remarkable that Israel even exists, and it is perhaps even more remarkable that it came into being only half a century after Herzl articulated modern Zionism. For many Israelis and other Jews as well, the state of Israel is the fulfillment of an ancient dream, one that has been present since biblical times.

The dream has been made a reality only after a long and torturous history, which culminated in the horror of Hitler's Holocaust. Since its creation, Israel has engaged in four wars with the Arabs—the War of Independence (1948-1949), the Suez War (1956), the Six-Day War (1967), and the Yom Kippur War (1973). Since 1973, hardly a day has passed in which Israelis have not been subject to some kind of violent opposition or attack by their adversaries. Throughout its short existence, Israel has been surrounded by hostile neighbors. On a map of the Middle East, it is a tiny blip; until it occupied the West Bank of the Jordan River in 1967, it was only eight miles wide at its narrowest point. By the late 1980s, Israel had a population of just over 4 million people, vis-à-vis upwards of 160 million Arabs. Furthermore, Israel is almost totally lacking in natural resources. In view of these facts, private and official American aid has been vital to Israel's survival.

Israel's defense strategy, which has paid off in the four wars against the Arabs, has been based on mobility, a high state of readiness, and superiority of weapons and training to offset Arab superiority in numbers. Nevertheless, Israel's military victories have not brought the country security, which remains as elusive today as in the late 1940s. Israel's extraordinarily high level of military expenditures (on a per capita basis, the highest in the world); its determination to acquire the latest and best military equipment; its insistence on retaining control of Jerusalem, the West Bank territories, and the Golan Heights in Syria—these provide tangible evidence of Israel's continuing sense of military vulnerability and isolation. Adding to the nation's predicament is a formidable array of internal problems, despite a high standard of living. In contrast to the biblical depiction of Palestine as a "land flowing with milk and honey," in reality it is largely desert or semidesert, with few mineral resources. Since 1948, Israel has consistently incurred a growing foreign trade deficit; high levels of inflation have been endemic; and Israel remains dependent upon a high volume of official and private aid from the United States, a condition which shows no sign of changing in the years ahead.[7]

The Arabs. While the Israelis, despite their nation's insecurity, are today brimming with pride over their accomplishments, the Arabs have long felt a sense of humiliation, outrage, and injustice. First of all, to their minds, foreigners took over lands in Palestine that Arabs viewed as rightfully theirs, driving the inhabitants into a wretched existence as refugees. Secondly, despite their overwhelming numbers, the Arabs have suffered four crushing military defeats.

On top of all this, there has been a feeling of hopelessness. In the Arab view, for many years Israel had the unflinching, unquestioning support of the United States for whatever it wanted. As Arabs saw it, the Israeli government, through the pro-Israeli lobby in the United States, controlled American foreign policy in the Middle East.

Yet it is unwise to generalize about the Arabs. Nine different countries are considered "Arab" (Egypt, Syria, Jordan, Lebanon, Iraq, Saudi Arabia, the Yemen Arab Republic, South Yemen, and Kuwait), as are a series of tiny sheikdoms along the Persian Gulf and four North

African states known collectively as the Maghreb (Algeria, Morocco, Tunisia, and Libya). There are other distinctions to be made among the Arab states: between rich (those with oil) and poor (those without oil); between those adjacent to Israel and those that are not; and among conservative, moderate, and radical regimes.

Most Arabs do, of course, share a common religion (Islam) and a common language (Arabic), but this common ground has resulted in no more unity than Roman Catholicism and the Spanish language have produced in Latin America. Divisions within the Islamic faith itself were never more apparent than in November 1979, when Moslem fanatics took over the Grand Mosque in Mecca; the move was forcefully suppressed by the government of Saudi Arabia, whose actions were approved by the religious authorities.

Throughout most of the period since 1948, opposition to Israel has been the principal unifying force throughout the Middle East, to the extent that there has been unity at all. Yet differences have also existed, ranging from intransigent radicalism to cautious moderation, even with respect to Israel. Indeed, one of the most serious splits in the Arab world since 1948 came about in 1979, when the other Arab states joined to ostracize Egypt because it had signed a peace treaty with Israel. A crucial economic difference has existed between the Arab nations (such as Saudi Arabia, Kuwait, Libya, and Iraq) that possess substantial oil resources and those (such as Lebanon and Jordan) that do not. With the exception of the major oil-producing states of the Middle East, the Arab nations continue to suffer from pervasive poverty, a high incidence of disease and malnutrition, widening income disparities, and high levels of population growth that offer little hope of significant improvement in their standard of living. The war between Iran and Iraq has also aggravated intra-Arab differences, with most Arab nations supporting Iraq, while Syria aided a non-Arab state, Iran, against its Arab neighbor, Iraq. For Americans, another pivotal difference between Israel and its Arab neighbors has been that the latter have usually been governed by authoritarian (sometimes fanatically anti-American) regimes, whereas Israel has a democratic system.[8]

The United States. In their approach to the Arab-Israeli conflict, American policy makers have exemplified three different points of view toward the issue. The bureaucracy of the executive branch—represented principally by the State and Defense departments—has tended to favor either a pro-Arab or an evenhanded approach to the question. State Department specialists on the Middle East tend to view the area primarily in terms of international, rather than domestic, politics. They envision the Middle East as mainly an Arab region, whose political systems are unstable and often subject to Soviet influence. Since 1973 especially, they have been concerned about the continued access of the United States and its allies to the region's oil reserves; and since 1979, after the Iranian revolution and the Soviet thrust into Afghanistan, Defense Department officials have been apprehensive about the security of the Middle East.

The orientation of the White House has reflected the fact that the president is elected by the entire nation. Inevitably, perhaps, White House viewpoints have been more sensitive to domestic political considerations than have attitudes in the State or Defense departments. Yet since the early 1970s, incumbent presidents have also seen the necessity to maintain a more balanced approach to the Arab-Israeli problem and to preserve at least minimally cooperative relations with most Arab governments. President Ronald Reagan's proposal to sell sophisticated aircraft to Saudi Arabia—in the face of vocal opposition by Israel and its supporters—illustrated this transition in White House attitudes.

Congress has been, and remains, the most pro-Israeli actor of all in the American foreign policy process. This derives from several factors: the strength of the pro-Israeli lobby in the United States; the deep and sincere convictions of many legislators on the Palestine question; the impact of American public opinion, which has as a rule been overwhelmingly sympathetic to the Israeli position; and the general ineffectiveness of Arab attempts to influence American public opinion favorably.

In attempting to understand the Arab-Israeli conflict, it is essential to bear in mind that not all Jews are Zionists, and, of course, not all supporters of the Zionist cause are Jewish. Although the Zionist movement has its roots in the Jewish religious tradition, Zionism is essentially a political movement: its dominant goal has been the creation and (after 1948) the support and protection of the state of Israel. In the United States and other countries, Zionism has drawn support from people of many religious backgrounds. Nevertheless, the basic strength of the pro-Israeli lobby rests in the American Jewish community, whose continuing support of Israel has been vital to that country's survival as an independent nation.

Although the Jewish community in the United States numbers only some 6 million people (less than 3 percent of the American population), its political influence—especially on Capitol Hill—is greatly disproportionate to its numbers. By many criteria, the pro-Israeli lobby has been one of the most conspicuously successful pressure groups in the postwar American political system, serving as a model of effective lobbying. Many Arabs and their supporters in the United States believe that America's consistent support of, and identification with, Israel for over a generation has been "dictated" by the influence of the Zionist lobby on the news media, public opinion, and Washington generally, particularly Capitol Hill.[9]

In reality, the relationship between the activities of the Zionist lobby and American diplomacy in the Middle East is a highly complex one, involving a number of diverse elements. One of these is unquestionably the fact that Jewish individuals and groups in the United States tend to be especially active and involved politically. Furthermore, their interest is frequently translated into tangible and financial support for candidates who favor Israel's position. Morris Amitay, the former executive director of the American-Israel Public Affairs Committee (AIPAC) and principal spokesman for the lobby, has put it this way:

> A lot of these [uncommitted] Senators are from the Midwest, West, down South, and these [Jews] are some of the elite types of people that these Senators like to be with and talk to, besides the pull of actual contributions. I do not think anyone ever likes to be approached on the very gut political level. You look around at who the Jewish constituents are from sparsely inhabited states. They are teachers, they are doctors, they have invariably been involved some way in politics. They are usually respected people in the community, so you do not have to pitch it at the level of, "I contributed ten thousand dollars to your campaign—unless you do this you will make me unhappy and I will contribute to your opponent next time." At most it's implicit, and it is not even implicit a large percentage of the time.[10]

As a rule, politicians get elected and reelected less by pleasing people than by not offending them. It follows that a vocal, dedicated, and well-organized minority has more influence politically than an apathetic or indifferent majority. The success of the pro-Israeli lobby provides a striking illustration of the emergence and growing importance of single-issue politics in the United States.

The strength of the Zionist lobby also illustrates the role of ethnicity in the American political system. In demanding support for Israel, Jewish groups in the United States have followed the path taken by Polish-Americans, Greek-Americans, Irish-Americans, and other ethnic minorities in seeking to influence governmental policy toward the "old country."

In addition to these factors, the success achieved by the pro-Israeli lobby in the United States can be in part accounted for by an old axiom with which students of propaganda have long been familiar: the most effective propaganda motivates those toward whom it is directed (the target) to believe and act as they are already inclined to do. In propaganda strategy, this concept is known as *reinforcement*. In the case of American attitudes toward the Arab-Israeli conflict, this concept means that the pro-Israeli lobby has operated in an environment highly congenial to the achievement of its objectives. The values and norms of American society, for example, are derived from the Judeo-Christian tradition (there is no comparable "Islamic-Christian" tradition).

As the only Western-style democracy in the Middle East, Israel draws many of its political traditions and practices from the United States and Europe. The pioneers who founded the state of Israel (the Ashkenazim, or Jews of European origin) came from the West and believed in maintaining close ties with the United States and other Western nations. The accomplishments of Israeli society since 1948 in "making the desert bloom" also seem to many Americans a reenactment of their own frontier experience in the face of great odds and dangers. If Israel has received billions of dollars in official and private aid from the United States, the Israelis for their part have used this assistance effectively to achieve a high standard of living, to improve agricultural output dramatically, to raise industrial productivity, and to achieve other goals favored by Americans.

Moreover, as Israeli officials have reiterated many times since 1948, Israel is one of the few nations in the Middle East that has not at some stage developed close ties with the Soviet Union—another key factor that enhances Israel's appeal to the United States. Except for an interest in Israel—and, since the 1973 war in the Middle East, for concern about the price and availability of petroleum products—most Americans have little knowledge of the Middle East and minimal interest in it. For over three decades, these factors have combined to create a milieu in the United States considerably more favorable to the Israeli than to the Arab cause.

Through its embassy in Washington, as well as directly from Jerusalem, the Israeli government maintains close contacts with Congress and with pro-Israeli lobbying groups, principally AIPAC and an umbrella organization called the Conference of Presidents of Major American Jewish Organizations (Conference of Presidents, for short). Israeli prime ministers, foreign ministers, defense ministers, and other officials visit Washington frequently; Capitol Hill is a routine stop on their rounds, for informal meetings with key committees or with the House and Senate membership in general. These visiting officials almost always confer, as well, with the Conference of Presidents and with other prominent Jewish leaders. During a particularly tense period in the negotiations for the Israeli-Egyptian peace treaty, Prime Minister Menachem Begin met with two thousand Jewish leaders in New York on his way back to Jerusalem from Washington. Begin said to his audience, "You have great influence. Do not hesitate to use that influence." [11] It should also be noted that the American Jewish community has sometimes served as a voice of moderation in endeavoring to get the government of Israel to modify its policies.

The Arab-Israeli conflict has been a singular episode in American postwar foreign policy in another respect: in illustrating the phenomenon of lobbying *by foreign governments* to influence the diplomacy of the United States. Historically, American policy making toward the issue has followed a familiar and often predictable pattern. The president overrules the executive bureaucracy; then Congress overrules the White House, compelling the president to call for more aid or otherwise be more generous toward Israel; in some cases, Congress has tried to prevent the chief executive from putting pressure on Israel to change its internal or external policies. Israeli officials have known that they could often successfully "appeal" the decisions of executive officials to Congress. Visits by the Israeli prime minister and other high-level officials to the United States have frequently had this objective as a primary goal. As the case study of arms for Saudi Arabia will illustrate, in some instances these appeals to Congress have been directed at preventing or circumscribing diplomatic and military moves by the United States deemed favorable to the Arabs.

The Context of the AWACS Proposal

A few weeks after he entered the Oval Office in 1981, President Ronald Reagan proposed to Congress that the United States sell five Airborne Warning and Control System, or AWACS, aircraft to Saudi Arabia. Reagan's request, which precipitated one of the most intense debates over American policy toward the Middle East witnessed since World War II, must be understood against a background of major tendencies and developments in the region, as these affected Washington's diplomatic interests.[12]

Since the late 1940s, Israel had been involved in four major military conflicts with the Arab states. The first round of fighting grew out of the establishment of the state of Israel in 1948. Miraculously, the outnumbered Israelis defeated several Arab military forces, successfully founded the state of Israel, and greatly enlarged its borders. In the process, some nine hundred thousand Arabs were displaced from Palestine—a group which remained intensely antagonistic toward Israel and which in later years supplied many of the recruits for the Palestine Liberation Organization (PLO) and other groups that forcibly opposed Israel's existence.[13]

The Suez crisis of 1956 was the second round in the Arab-Israeli contest. British, French, and Israeli troops invaded Egypt, quickly defeated its armed forces, and sought to depose President Gamal Abdel Nasser's government. Owing to the firm opposition of the Eisenhower administration, however, in time these foreign troops were withdrawn from Egyptian soil, and Israel was compelled to relinquish the territory occupied by its armed forces in the Sinai area.[14]

Animosity between Israel and the Arab states continued; it reached a new level of violence in the third round of hostilities, which erupted on June 5, 1967. The ensuing Six-Day War was an overwhelming military triumph for Israel. Relying upon a preemptive strike, Israel's air force largely wiped out the Egyptian air fleet on the ground, leaving Egyptian armored forces in the Sinai defenseless against Israeli air and ground attacks. Israeli military superiority also defeated the smaller armed forces of Syria and Jordan.[15]

The Six-Day War had far-reaching consequences for nations inside and outside the Middle East. As a result of the conflict, Israel greatly expanded its borders, extending them to the Suez Canal and to the strategic Golan Heights in the north. Another outcome of this conflict was that the Arab enemies of Israel—after sustaining three defeats in orthodox military engagements—now relied increasingly upon guerrilla warfare, carried out particularly by the PLO, to achieve their goals.[16]

Two other developments growing out of the Six-Day War directly involved Saudi Arabia and its relations with the United States. As a result of its spectacular military victory, the government of Israel officially annexed the city of Jerusalem (from 1948 until 1967 the Old City had been under Jordanian authority). In the months that followed, Israeli officials asserted that the annexation of the Old City was a *fait accompli* that was nonnegotiable. Later, Israel went further and proclaimed Jerusalem its capital. While Arabs generally were incensed by Israel's action, it was especially offensive to Saudi Arabia. Controlled by the rigidly orthodox Wahhabi sect of Sunni Islam, its government has long served as the custodian of the religious shrines most sacred to Sunni Moslems. Next to Mecca and Medina, Jerusalem (according to Sunni tradition, the site from which Mohammed ascended into heaven) is the third holiest shrine in Islam. Following the 1967 war, therefore, Saudi Arabia became actively involved in the Arab-Israeli conflict for the first time. Saudi Arabia does not directly border Israel, and its relatively small military establishment would be no match for the armed might of Israel. After 1967, the Saudi contribution to the Arab campaign against Israel consisted mainly of subsidies provided to the PLO and certain Arab governments (such as Jordan, and, during some periods, Syria).[17]

Another far-reaching consequence of the Six-Day War was the discovery of what came to be called "oil power" and reliance upon it to achieve Arab diplomatic objectives. Although Arab oil producers ceased production during the 1967 war in an attempt to bring pressure to bear on the United States and other Western nations viewed as sympathetic to Israel, this initial reliance upon oil power had only very limited success. The United States (along with Venezuela and Indonesia) increased its production to supply the petroleum needs of its principal allies. Yet the discovery of oil power in 1967 was important for two reasons: it established a precedent that the oil-producing states of the Middle East were to use with telling effect in their next confrontation with Israel (1973); and it underscored the mounting vulnerability of the United States, Western Europe, Japan, and other advanced nations to an oil embargo.

After the 1967 conflict, tensions between Israel and its Arab adversaries continued to engender instability, violence, and the prospect of a fourth round of direct military hostilities in the Middle East. Despite its decisive military victories, Israel still found the peace and security it sought elusive. Arab governments showed no inclination to accept Israel or to arrive at a resolution of outstanding differences with it. The PLO and other anti-Israeli political movements continued to rely on guerrilla attacks and terrorist incidents to express their militant opposition to Israel. The Soviet Union found new opportunities for expanding its ties and influence with the Arab states. By the early 1970s, for example, it was estimated that upward of fifteen thousand Soviet officials, technicians, and advisers were resident in Egypt (although this large Soviet presence was expelled from Egypt by President Sadat in 1972). Countries like Syria and Iraq had become heavily dependent on Soviet arms aid to rebuild and modernize their military establishments.[18]

As time passed, most informed observers predicted that a new wave of hostilities would engulf the Middle East. It came on October 6, 1973, when the fourth round (called by Israelis and Americans the Yom Kippur War and by Arabs the Ramadan War) in the Arab-Israeli conflict erupted. In well-executed surprise attacks, Egyptian forces struck the Bar Lev Israeli defense line in the Sinai region, while Syrian troops attacked Israeli defense forces in the Golan Heights; in these initial thrusts, the Arabs inflicted heavy losses on the Israeli military establishment. After their tank losses were replaced by a massive American airlift, Israeli troops ultimately reversed the tide of battle. In the final stage, Israeli officials were restrained by Washington from threatening the Syrian capital, Damascus, and from mounting attacks aimed at Egyptian territory west of the Suez Canal.[19]

In the sense that Israeli forces were ultimately victorious on the battlefield, the Yom Kippur War again demonstrated Israel's military superiority over its Arab enemies. Yet in several respects the conflict was a highly traumatic episode for Israel and its supporters in the United States. The war had shattered several myths: that Arab troops would not fight; that Arab governments were incapable of planning a surprise attack that would escape early detection by Israel's vaunted intelligence service; and that Israeli forces were invincible on the battlefield. For Arabs, the 1973 war immensely bolstered their self-confidence and morale. Most fundamentally perhaps, the 1973 war highlighted the facts that Arab opposition to Israel remained intense and that with each passing year the Arabs were improving their military capabilities.

For the United States, perhaps the most far-reaching consequence of the Yom Kippur War was that the Arab states had effectively employed oil power against it and other industrialized nations.[20] After hostilities erupted in 1973, the oil-exporting states of the Middle East— which collectively produced over one-third of the oil needed by the noncommunist world—imposed an embargo on oil shipments. Saudi Arabia alone accounted for nearly half (42 percent) of the region's output; the Saudi government's decision to join in the embargo was a crucial factor in its success. The five-month oil embargo cost the United States between $10 and $20 billion in income lost because of decreased production, which led to the loss of some five hundred thousand jobs. Western Europe and Japan—which derived 75 percent or more of their oil from the Middle East—were even more adversely affected by the embargo. If it had continued for several more months, the embargo would have produced severe economic dislocations in these regions, possibly engendering political crises and seriously impairing the defense efforts of America's principal allies. Shortly after the 1973 war, the price of oil on the world market reached a new high of $20 per barrel; and in the years that followed, it moved steadily upward, reaching $36 per barrel by the early 1980s before dropping back to $14 by 1986. The Yom Kippur War served as a pointed reminder to the United States of its growing dependence on oil imports and of the key role of Saudi Arabia in the Arab states' decision to use oil power as a diplomatic weapon.

The Elusive Search for Peace

The 1973 war in the Middle East did little to remove the underlying sources of tension between Israel and the Arab states. In retrospect, the conflict did, however, have three results that induced officials in Washington to try again to resolve Arab-Israeli differences. In the first place, its victory was extremely costly for Israel in terms of casualties sustained and the financial burden of the war. Israeli officials might well have recalled Napoleon's observation after one of his triumphs on the battlefield: "Many more victories like that, and I am undone!"

In the second place, some Arab governments—Anwar Sadat's Egypt was the leading example—concluded on the basis of the 1973 war that another direct military encounter with superior Israeli military power was futile and irrational. As the leader of the Arab nation that had borne the brunt of the military effort, President Sadat concluded that Egypt and Israel must resolve their differences so that the Egyptian government could devote its attention primarily to internal needs.

In the third place, the Yom Kippur War unquestionably affected official and popular attitudes in the United States toward the Israeli and Arab positions—a change induced in no small degree by the embargo imposed on Middle East oil exports during this conflict. By the mid-1970s, as even the Israelis and some Arabs acknowledged, American opinion had become less overtly pro-Israeli, more critical of specific Israeli policies and behavior, and more inclined to demand flexibility from Israel's leaders in efforts to stabilize the Middle East.[21]

These developments created an environment conducive to intensive peace-making efforts by the United States in the Middle East. Under the Nixon and Ford administrations, Secretary of State Henry Kissinger engaged in a prolonged series of negotiations—known as "shuttle diplomacy"—in an effort to discover a basis for a peaceful resolution of Arab-Israeli differences. Except for Egypt, Kissinger's efforts failed. Sadat alone among Arab leaders was prepared to enter into peace talks with Israel.[22]

Prospects for peace in the Middle East were greatly enhanced by President Sadat's historic visit to Jerusalem on November 19, 1977. This meeting was followed by bilateral discussions between Israeli and Egyptian officials and by Prime Minister Menachem Begin's visit to Egypt at the end of 1977. In mid-1978, President Jimmy Carter invited Sadat and Begin to the presidential retreat at Camp David to resume the peace talks under American auspices.

For almost two weeks—in some of the most complex and difficult diplomatic negotiations in modern history—Sadat, Begin, and Carter, with their aides, endeavored to resolve Israeli-Egyptian disagreements. On several occasions, the Camp David conference seemed on the verge of failure; it was saved largely by President Carter's determination to make it succeed. Time and again, Carter reminded Sadat and Begin of the possibly dire consequences of failing to reach a peaceful settlement. Finally, Sadat and Begin signed two draft accords on September 17, 1978, but not until March 26, 1979, was a treaty signed, inaugurating an era of peaceful relations between the two countries.

Although the Camp David talks made considerable progress toward stabilizing the Middle East, events soon made it clear that the Arab-Israeli conflict had by no means ended. Two things were memorable about President Sadat's role in the discussions. First was his courage in being the first Arab leader to join Israel in formal peace negotiations. Second, as quickly became apparent—and was dramatically highlighted by his assassination on October 6, 1981, by Moslem extremist elements—Sadat had become isolated from the other Arab states; they were unwilling to be associated with his peace-making activities.[23]

Despite high hopes by Israel and the United States, other Arab states showed no inclination to make peace with Israel. Arab enmity toward Israel—often graphically expressed by PLO attacks—continued. Meanwhile, Lebanon was engulfed in civil war, while the stability of the Persian Gulf area was endangered by the Iran-Iraq war and the Soviet Union's effort to dominate Afghanistan. Overall, by the early 1980s, the influence of the United States in the Middle East was at low ebb.

The Saudi-American Diplomatic Connection

By the 1980s, three major segments of Arab opinion toward Israel and toward what Arabs viewed as its sponsor, the United States, could be identified. As we have already observed, one point of view was exemplified by Egypt—the only Arab nation willing to sign a peace treaty with Israel. After Camp David, Egypt's influence within the Middle East dropped sharply, although by the late 1980s Cairo had begun to regain its former position among the Arab states. A second group comprised the Rejectionist Front, which consisted of the Arabs who remained implacably opposed to Israel. Led by Syria, Iraq, Libya, and several factions within the PLO, this group tended to be overtly anti-American; often they were recipients of massive Soviet economic, military, and other forms of assistance.

The third group consisted of moderate Arab opinion, illustrated by the position of Saudi Arabia on the Arab-Israeli conflict and related regional issues. This attitude envisioned the ultimate possibility of peace with Israel, provided that the government of Israel made a number of fundamental concessions designed to satisfy Arab grievances and to guarantee Arab rights. (It was of course highly questionable whether Israeli authorities would ever make the kind of concessions demanded by this segment of Arab opinion.) From this point of view, the key questions related to Israel's readiness to grant true political autonomy to the Arab inhabitants of the occupied West Bank; to return the Old City of Jerusalem to Arab jurisdiction; and, above all, to accept a Palestinian homeland whose territory would include some Israeli territory. American officials had long been aware that moderate Arab opinion held the key to peace in the Middle East.

The central role of Saudi Arabia in achieving American diplomatic objectives in the Middle East was emphasized by another climactic event: the collapse of the Iranian monarchy in January 1979. This event ranks as one of the most serious American diplomatic reverses in the postwar period; it was followed by the emergence of an outspokenly anti-American regime in Iran, headed by the Ayatollah Ruhollah Khomeini, whose power base was the Shi'ite clergy. Viewing the United States as the "Great Satan," Khomeini and his followers were determined to eliminate Western influence from the Persian Gulf area and to overthrow governments (such as Saudi Arabia's) that were friendly with the United States.[24] Shi'ites believe that the successor to Mohammed (called the Imam) must be a lineal descendant of the Prophet himself. Shi'ism has also always reflected a non-Arab influence within Islam.

Under Khomeini, Iran lapsed into a prolonged period of internal upheaval and repression. In foreign relations, the Islam-based government called for revolution in other states throughout the Persian Gulf

area; supported the PLO and other enemies of Israel (while concurrently selling oil to the Israeli government); denounced Soviet intervention in Afghanistan and Communist machinations within Iran; and
fought an exhausting war against Iraq, whose forces invaded Iran in
September 1980. Prolonged political turbulence in Iran, coupled with
the Soviet invasion of Afghanistan at the end of 1979, called into
question the future stability of the entire Persian Gulf area and of
Western access to its vital oil reserves.

Confronted with this new danger, President Jimmy Carter issued a
"Carter Doctrine" in his State of the Union message to Congress on
January 23, 1980. This pronouncement declared the defense of the
Persian Gulf area vital to the security and well-being of the United
States, and it pledged America to defend the area from forces that
might endanger its security. While the Carter Doctrine was directed
specifically at the Soviet Union—it was an explicit warning to Moscow
not to extend its hegemony in Afghanistan to adjacent countries—
informed students of the Middle East were aware of two other forces
that might jeopardize the security of the Persian Gulf area.[25] One of
these was the revolutionary movements (such as those sponsored by
Iran and the Ba'ath party in Iraq) aimed at radicalizing the governments adjoining the Persian Gulf. The other potential threat was the
possibility of a fifth round in the Arab-Israeli conflict.

Washington's ties with Saudi Arabia of course antedated the Iranian revolution and the issuance of the Carter Doctrine. Before 1932,
when the Kingdom of Saudi Arabia was proclaimed under its first ruler,
Ibn Saud I, the traditional homeland of the Arabs was little more than a
collection of primitive Bedouin tribes, whose main pursuits appeared to
be nomadism and warfare.[26] Ibn Saud succeeded in uniting the tribes
under his leadership and in defeating his rivals (such as the Hashemites,
who governed Jordan and Iraq after World War I). Throughout his long
rule (Ibn Saud died in 1953), the kingdom was largely governed according to tribal customs and traditions and in accordance with the fundamentalist Wahhabi religious principles professed by its leaders and the
vast majority of its people.*

---

* The Wahhabi sect of the Sunni branch of Islam (with the Shiite branch, one of the two
great divisions of Islam) derived from the life and thought of Mohammed ibn Abd al-
Wahhab (1703-1791). His movement represented a reaction against the corruption and
adulteration of the pure and revealed Islamic faith by foreign religious ideas and philosophical concepts, and even by Islamic movements (like Sufism) deemed at variance with
the Koran. Thus, Wahhabism demanded a return to the original and literal tenets of
Islam; Wahhabis have been called the Puritans of Islam and the custodians of religious
fundamentalism. In practice, as it has evolved in Saudi Arabia, Wahhabism calls for literal
adherence to Koranic requirements in such spheres as religious rites, treatment of crimi-
nals, and the status of women. See Bayly Winder, *Saudi Arabia in the Nineteenth
Century* (New York: St. Martin's, 1965), 8-15, and John B. Christopher, *The Islamic
Tradition* (New York: Harper and Row, 1972), 158-162.

The most crucial development during Ibn Saud's reign was the discovery of oil in Saudi Arabia in the early 1930s and the development of this oil by the Arabian American Oil Company (Aramco). Saudi Arabia was officially neutral in World War II, although it did assist the Allied cause during that conflict. From the end of the war through the early 1960s, U.S. air bases in Saudi Arabia contributed to the defense of the Middle East; then, mindful of adverse Arab reaction, the Saudi government requested that the bases be closed. When Ibn Saud I died, he was succeeded by his son, Ibn Saud II. The new king's extravagances and lack of interest in the welfare of the country finally led the Saudi royal family to depose him late in 1964, in favor of Crown Prince Faisal, who ruled until his assassination early in 1975.

King Faisal was a devout Moslem and was devoted to his country's modernization and welfare. Under his rule, the bulk of the oil income was allocated to national development. After Faisal's death, the infirm King Khalid ruled until his death in June 1982. His successor was the present ruler of Saudi Arabia, King Fahd.

Among the governments of the Middle East, Saudi Arabia is the epitome of oil power. Its oil reserves are estimated as high as 500 billion barrels (three times those of the United States). At full production, Saudi Arabia can ship upwards of 10 million barrels of oil daily into the world market, although in recent years its actual production has sometimes been no more than one-third of that amount. For many years, Saudi Arabia was the most influential member of the Organization of Petroleum Exporting Countries (OPEC).[27] In the deliberations of OPEC, Saudi Arabia has acquired a reputation for moderation and restraint. In contrast to some other members, for example, Saudi officials appeared to understand that using oil power to precipitate economic chaos in the West would in the end also engender severe economic and political problems in the Middle East. By the period of the Reagan administration, Saudi Arabia also cooperated with the United States in containing Iranian influence in the Persian Gulf area.[28]

The AWACS Proposal

In what was to become the first major test of his authority in the foreign policy field, President Ronald Reagan in April 1981 disclosed his administration's intention of selling five advanced AWACS aircraft,*

---

* Officially known as Airborne Warning and Control System aircraft, AWACS planes were advanced aircraft equipped with several forms of modern radar, designed to provide early warning of approaching enemy aircraft and missiles. As the Iraqi-Iranian war spread to the Persian Gulf area, these aircraft played a crucial role in defending Kuwait and Saudi Arabia, along with American and other neutral shipping, from attack, chiefly by Iranian aircraft and missiles. From 1981 until 1986, these AWACS planes were under the direct control of the United States.

valued at $5.8 billion, to the government of Saudi Arabia. Under the terms of the Arms Export Control Act (P.L. 90-629), Congress had thirty days within which to disapprove of (or veto) foreign arms sales through resolutions passed by majority votes in both the House and the Senate. Following established custom, the Reagan administration had provided Congress with informal notification of the proposed AWACS sale, but formal notification of this intention was not sent to Capitol Hill until October 1. Congress, therefore, had until October 30 to disapprove the transaction or the president would be free to complete it. In addition to the AWACS planes, the White House proposed to sell Saudi Arabia equipment for F-15 fighter aircraft that would improve their capability; several KC-707 tanker aircraft, valued at some $2.4 billion; and 1,177 AIM-9L air-to-air missiles, costing approximately $200 million. Another item in the package (devices for improving the offensive striking power of the F-15s) was dropped after the government of Israel expressed outspoken opposition to it.[29]

In justifying the AWACs transaction, the president and his advisers emphasized its importance in promoting the diplomatic and security goals of the United States in the Persian Gulf area. On August 5, for example, President Reagan in a letter to Congress called the AWACS transaction one of the "essential elements" in his Middle Eastern policy.[30] A few days later, Under Secretary of State James Buckley referred to such recent developments as the Iranian revolution, the Iraqi-Iranian war, the Soviet invasion of Afghanistan, and Moscow's reliance upon proxies (such as South Yemen) to promote its objectives in the Middle East. In the State Department's view, the AWACS transaction would contribute to achieving four major American goals in the Persian Gulf region. First, it would help preserve the nation's continued access to Middle East oil. Second, it would serve as a deterrent to Soviet influence in the area. Third, it would enhance the security of nations friendly to the United States, including Israel. Fourth, it would demonstrate America's "constancy" and "resolve" in protecting the security of nations bordering the Persian Gulf. In brief, the secretary argued, this arms sale package would make "a major contribution to Saudi security and to our vital regional security objectives." [31] Quoting President Sadat, Secretary of State Alexander Haig said that a congressional veto of the AWACS deal would raise "a huge question mark" about the reliability of the nation's foreign policy.[32]

Lobbying Activities

The AWACS case precipitated some of the most intense lobbying activities witnessed on a foreign policy question since World War II. Major participants in this campaign included the government of Israel and its supporters within the United States, the government of Saudi

Arabia and those groups favoring its position, and officials of the Reagan administration.

Predictably, the response of the pro-Israeli lobby to the AWACS proposal was vociferously adverse. Prime Minister Menachem Begin informed State Department officials that making AWACS aircraft available to Saudi Arabia would "present a very serious threat" to the security of his nation. Secretary Haig's offer to increase American assistance to Israel did little to reassure Begin's government and its supporters in the United States.[33]

As the weeks passed, blocking the AWACS transaction became the primary goal of the Israeli lobby in the United States. Spearheaded by the American Israel Public Affairs Committee (AIPAC), the pro-Israeli lobby undertook a grass-roots campaign to rally public opinion against the sale and to direct popular sentiment against it to executive and legislative officials in Washington. Initially, opponents sought to prevent the Reagan White House from submitting the AWACS proposal to Congress. Failing to achieve that objective, the Israeli lobby concentrated on convincing members of the House and Senate that the AWACS sale was in neither America's nor Israel's interests. At a minimum, Israel and its supporters called for the imposition of numerous conditions and restrictions upon the sale (some of which were clearly unacceptable to Saudi Arabia and might induce its government to withdraw the request); they also advocated a public pledge by the White House that the military superiority of Israel would be maintained.[34]

Arguments advanced against the AWACS sale included the following: (1) in view of the political instability of the Persian Gulf area, the aircraft might fall into the hands of governments or political groups that would use them against Israel or the United States; (2) Saudi Arabia, with its limited armed forces, did not need sophisticated weapons like AWACS and the other advanced military hardware it had requested from the United States; (3) the provision of these weapons to Saudi Arabia could well add to its political instability, leading to the kind of domestic opposition that had toppled the Iranian monarchy; and (4) to match Saudi Arabia's intensified defense efforts, Israel would be required to embark on a new round of military spending that would further damage its economy.

A noteworthy feature of the AWACS case was that—perhaps for the first time in the history of the Arab-Israeli conflict—the pro-Israeli lobby found itself pitted against a skillful and effective pressure campaign conducted by the Arab lobby in support of the AWACS transaction. By the 1970s, moreover, American attitudes toward the Arab-Israeli dispute had clearly begun to change. After four military victories since 1948, Israel no longer appeared to many Americans as the underdog in the Arab-Israeli contest. Arab imposition of the oil embargo during the 1973 war and the consequent rapid increases in the price of oil imports from the Middle East served as forceful reminders to Americans of their vulnerability and dependence upon the oil reserves of the region. By the end of the decade, Soviet gains in the vicinity of the Persian Gulf and on its western flank (as in eastern Africa) focused American attention once more on the region's strategic importance. Moreover, many Americans in time concluded that Arab viewpoints, as articulated by Arab leaders such as King Hussein of Jordan and President Sadat of Egypt, were often more reasonable, persuasive, and entitled to serious consideration than they had earlier believed. In this new environment, foreign governments and organizations in the United States that advocated the AWACS sale found conditions favorable for their activities.

For many years, pro-Arab groups in the United States had found their lobbying activities hindered by several factors that diminished their political impact. Among these were the overall American ignorance of the Middle East and of important forces (such as modern Arab nationalism and the Islamic religion) that affected the region's political development; the continuing schisms that perpetuated suspicions and rivalries among Arab governments and political movements; the negative feelings of many Americans toward oil corporations and their links with Arab states; and the relative smallness of the Arab-American community (some 2 million people, most of Lebanese extraction).

Yet the Arab lobby also possessed strengths that had slowly enhanced its effectiveness as a pressure group. Led by the National Association of Arab Americans (NAAA), the Arab lobby had unquestionably become more skillful in its public relations and media campaigns designed to make Americans more receptive to Arab viewpoints. The NAAA's mailing list was growing steadily and its budget was increasing. Several Arab governments retained former legislators, such as J. William Fulbright, to represent their interests in the United States. Saudi Arabia was represented by Frederick Dutton, who had been a State Department official during the Kennedy administration. For several years, a few legislators, such as Sen. James Abourezk, D-S.D. (who was of Lebanese background), had been willing to champion the Arab cause on Capitol Hill. Even so, developments such as the internecine strife among various Arab groups in Lebanon remained a serious obstacle to unified Arab lobbying activities in the United States.[35]

For several months, the Arab lobby undertook a public relations and media campaign emphasizing the importance of the AWACS sale for cooperative Saudi-American relations. Certain actions by the government of Israel—such as its bombing attack against a nuclear installation in Iraq in the summer of 1981 and its intensive bombing of the city of Beirut several weeks later (in which some three hundred people were

killed)—reinforced the Arab contention that the Saudi military establishment needed the AWACS planes and related military equipment.

Congress Considers the AWACS Proposal

From the beginning, it was evident that the AWACS proposal faced
formidable opposition in the House and Senate. As expected, opposition
to the AWACS sale was especially intense in the Democratic-controlled
House of Representatives, where pervasive fears existed that the move
would endanger Israel's security. On October 14, 1981, by a vote of 301-
111, the House passed a resolution (H. Con. Res. 194) disapproving the
AWACS transaction. (In order to block the sale, it must be remembered,
majorities in both the House and Senate had to vote against it; otherwise, the president was free to conclude the transaction.) Although
prospects did not initially appear encouraging, the White House now
turned to the Senate for the support it needed to complete the AWACS
transaction.[36]

On October 15, the Senate Foreign Relations Committee voted 9-8
against approving the proposed AWACS sale. It is illustrative of the
divisions within Congress on foreign policy issues that on the same day
the Senate Armed Services Committee voted 10-5 in favor of providing
the AWACS aircraft and other military equipment to Saudi Arabia. As
events proved, sentiment in the full Senate on the AWACS question was
closely divided. Before the issue reached the Senate floor, President
Reagan and his aides renewed their efforts to gain the support of
wavering senators. A presidential promise to provide Israel with radar-
jamming equipment reassured several senators that the AWACS planes
would not jeopardize Israel's security. The White House also pledged
that providing the AWACS planes to Saudi Arabia would not be followed by a large-scale military buildup in the Persian Gulf area. At the
administration's initiative, three former chief executives—Presidents
Nixon, Ford, and Carter—endorsed the AWACS proposal as a move
that would promote American diplomatic interests in the Middle East
and pose no threat to Israel's security.[37]

The climax came on October 28, when after prolonged and heated
debate the Senate voted on the AWACS transaction. Ultimately, the
outcome was an impressive, if narrow, victory for the Reagan administration, for the Senate failed, by a vote of 48-52, to join the House in
disapproving the AWACS transaction. Crucial to the outcome was the
fact that President Reagan and his aides had persuaded seven new
Republican senators to change their positions and to support the White
House proposal. In the end, President Reagan was granted the authority
he requested to provide an $8.5 billion arms sale package, including the
AWACS aircraft and related military equipment, to the government of
Saudi Arabia.[38]

Other Arms-Sale Proposals

As events indicated, the AWACS case proved to be not the last in a series of instances in which the president and Congress were required to face the issue of American arms sales to Arab countries. As tension mounted in the Persian Gulf area—with the clerically dominated Islamic Republic of Iran advocating revolution in neighboring countries—the Reagan administration became increasingly concerned about the security of Saudi Arabia, Kuwait, and the smaller nations within the region.

During the first half of 1984, the Reagan White House authorized the shipment of four hundred Stinger antiaircraft missiles to the Saudi government, primarily for defense against the growing Iranian threat. Predictably, the government of Israel vocally opposed this transaction, viewing it as inimical to Israel's security. Yet in this instance President Reagan got his way, since by law the president was permitted for reasons of national security to "waive" the usual thirty-day waiting period for such sales, during which time Congress would have an opportunity to disapprove of the transaction.[39]

In mid-June 1986, the Reagan White House informed Congress that it proposed to transfer ownership to Saudi Arabia of five AWACS aircraft (planes actually purchased by the Saudi government in 1981). Concurrently, President Reagan gave assurances that certain preconditions governing the transaction (such as Saudi steps to protect the security of AWACS technology) had been fulfilled. The president commended past Saudi efforts to promote peace in the Middle East; he took note of Saudi subsidies to the pro-Western government of Jordan; and he called attention to Riyadh's major role in efforts to aid the Afghan rebels who were resisting Soviet rule. In addition, President Reagan emphasized that American military teams would supervise the security measures required to guarantee that secret AWACS technology would not be compromised. In contrast to the earlier AWACS case, in 1986 the Israeli lobby in the United States did not actively oppose the White House proposal.[40]

Although the Reagan White House gained its immediate objective, executive officials were compelled by their legislative critics to delete Stinger missiles from the Saudi arms package; opponents feared that, in the wrong hands, these missiles could be used against Israeli or even American planes. Legislative opposition also forced the administration to abandon a plan to provide F-15 fighter aircraft, along with the new M-1 tanks, to Saudi Arabia. In the end, the Saudi arms deal was reduced to approximately one-third of its original size.

During this same period also, the State Department informed Congress that it was postponing indefinitely a proposal to sell modern arms, valued at between $1.5 and $2 billion, to the government of Jordan, long regarded as one of the most pro-Western regimes in the Middle East. Faced with widespread congressional opposition to this step—along with anticipated objections by the government of Israel—executive officials conceded that the proposal had no chance of obtaining legislative approval. Secretary of State George Shultz promised Congress that it would be given thirty days advance notice before the Jordanian arms sale plan was renewed. At the same time, Shultz was outspoken in blaming opposition in Congress to the sale of arms to Jordan for Amman's failure to play a more active role in peace negotiations with Israel.

As in 1981, the Reagan White House had won an extremely narrow victory over legislative opponents on the Saudi arms deal. Once again, an intensive lobbying campaign by the president and his supporters was required before victory was achieved. Proponents of the arms sale contended that the ability of the White House to conduct foreign affairs successfully was at stake in the willingness of Congress to support the president's diplomatic efforts in the Middle East.[41]

Arms for Riyadh in 1987

The issue of arms sales to Saudi Arabia has become a "perennial" in recent American diplomacy. In June 1987 the Reagan administration once again proposed a new arms package for Saudi Arabia. Immediate and massive opposition to the step on Capitol Hill, however, persuaded the White House to withdraw the measure, at least temporarily.[42] Yet, as the war between Iran and Iraq continued unabated, and as the revolutionary government of Iran continued to sponsor violence and subversive actions against other governments within the region, President Reagan and his advisers concluded that a new effort was needed to bolster Saudi Arabia's military capability.

Accordingly, late in September 1987 the Reagan White House formulated and proposed to Congress a $1.4 billion arms sale package for Saudi Arabia. Specifically, this new measure contemplated the sale of American F-15 fighter planes, some 1,600 Maverick antitank missiles, and electronic equipment designed to "upgrade" aircraft and tanks already in the Saudi arsenal. Almost immediately, some sixty-four supporters of Israel in the Senate sent a letter to President Reagan opposing the transaction.[43] Meanwhile, reflecting the Arab belief that American foreign policy was strongly biased in favor of Israel, the government of Kuwait conspicuously refused to invite Secretary of Defense Caspar Weinberger to visit the country during a tour of the Middle East.[44] Pro-Israeli spokesmen in Washington and abroad argued that transfer of modern arms to Saudi Arabia would threaten Israeli security, that weapons like the Maverick missile might fall into the hands of terrorist groups, and that, in reality, the arms would do little to enhance security in the Persian Gulf area. The bill was ultimately amended and allowed to languish in the Congress.

Arms to Saudi Arabia in Perspective

Our detailed treatment of the issue of arms sales to Saudi Arabia leads to certain general conclusions regarding executive-legislative relations in the foreign policy field.

First, the evidence in this case study indicates clearly that support for Israel is still a "constant" in American foreign policy toward the Middle East. Israel's position on arms sales to Arab nations, and toward other major Middle Eastern issues, continues to have a potent impact upon public and official opinion in the United States.

Second, pro-Israeli sentiment remains strong on Capitol Hill. Perhaps even more today than in the past, executive officials are more prepared than most legislators to think in terms of the overall diplomatic and strategic interests of the United States in the Middle East. While they are not indifferent to America's close ties with Israel, the president and his advisers are equally aware that the United States has important links with key Arab states and that these ties must be preserved and strengthened. In the executive view, American foreign policy in the Middle East must reflect both of these concerns. Even though the attitudes of the principal executive officials involved in formulating and carrying out national policy toward Israel may reflect such objectives, sentiment in Congress remains highly supportive of Israel. In fact, many members of the House and Senate agree with Israeli officials that the level of aid by the United States government to Israel should be increased.

Third, while public opinion in the United States remains predominantly pro-Israel, some change in attitudes has occurred since the 1973 war. While public and official opinion in the United States remains markedly sympathetic to Israel, American support for Israel is less "automatic" and uncritical than in the past. Sometimes even the extremely influential pro-Israeli lobby has been compelled to conclude that it cannot win every battle in which it engages; or that, even if it does win in the end, the cost to the Israeli cause may prove excessively high.

Fourth, the case study examined here provides interesting data calling attention to the changes that have occurred in lobbying in recent years. Today, some of the most intensive and successful lobbying activity is that carried out by executive officials, sometimes in collaboration with private interest groups. Such coalitions between official and private interests have become commonplace in the foreign policy field.

Fifth, there can be no doubt that, as long as no peace treaty exists between Israel and its Arab adversaries, any proposal by the White House to make modern weapons available to Arab states will evoke a strong negative reaction on Capitol Hill. Yet it is noteworthy that Congress has not formally invoked its power to prohibit the White House from supplying arms to Saudi Arabia. (This statement takes no account of the fact that, faced with congressional opposition to an arms transaction, executive officials have sometimes deferred the sale or significantly changed its terms to accommodate the views of legislative critics.) In the end, the White House has usually gotten substantially what it wanted and, in the process, has been able to preserve the close ties traditionally existing between the United States and Saudi Arabia. (Even in the case of Jordan, King Hussein's government remains one of the most overtly pro-Western in the Middle East.)

Sixth, the fact that Congress has not used the power of the purse to block the provision of modern arms to Saudi Arabia highlights an interesting and recurrent characteristic of legislative behavior in the diplomatic sphere. In some instances since the question of a Saudi-American arms deal first arose in 1981, the possibility at least exists that much of the militant and vocal legislative opposition has been political posturing by members of the House and Senate—a fact that is widely recognized by executive and legislative officials alike. To some degree, legislators are "making points" with domestic constituents. In doing so, they are aware that they may do so safely: Eventually Congress will approve the arms deal, although perhaps in modified form, and close ties will be preserved between the United States and Saudi Arabia.

Seventh, from the experience of the Saudi arms deal an important truth emerges about the "invitation to struggle" in the contemporary era. The struggle between the president and Congress for control of the foreign policy process is real; it continues to take place—weekly and monthly—in Washington. As our earlier discussion emphasized, since the end of the Vietnam War particularly, Congress has forcefully asserted its foreign policy prerogatives, and there is no reason to doubt that this process will continue into the future.

Yet the material presented in this case study indicates that, as a general rule, Congress does not want to assume the ultimate responsibility for managing the nation's foreign policy. If it wished, Congress could have used the power of the purse to deny the White House the funds needed to provide modern weapons to Saudi Arabia. Yet time after time, Congress has refrained from doing so. It is a reasonable conclusion, therefore, that in the final analysis, legislators do not wish to assume the responsibility for risking a possible major diplomatic failure or setback by the United States in the volatile Middle East.

Notes

1. Background on the evolution of American diplomacy in the Middle East is available in William R. Polk, *The United States and the Arab World* (Cambridge, Mass.: Harvard University Press, 1965); John S. Badeau, *The American Approach to the Arab World* (New York: Harper and Row, 1968); and Georgiana Stevens, ed., *The United States and the Middle East* (Englewood Cliffs, N.J.: Prentice-Hall, 1964).
2. The establishment, growth, and goals of the Zionist movement are discussed more fully in Soloman Grayzel, *A History of the Jews,* rev. ed. (New York: New American Library, 1968); Arthur Hertzberg, *The Zionist Idea* (Garden City, N.Y.: Doubleday, 1959); and Oscar I. Janowsky, ed., *Foundations of Israel* (Princeton, N.J.: D. Van Nostrand, 1959).
3. The background and text of the Balfour Declaration may be found in Polk, *The United States and the Arab World,* 108-112.
4. See Janowsky, *Foundations of Israel,* 81-88, 157-173; and Grayzel, *A History of the Jews,* 669-727.
5. Dean Acheson, *Present at the Creation: My Years in the State Department* (New York: W. W. Norton, 1969), 169.
6. Harry S Truman, *Years of Trial and Hope,* vol. 2 of *Memoirs* (Garden City, N.Y.: Doubleday, 1956), 158.
7. Recent treatments of Israel are Bernard Reich and Gershon R. Kieval, eds., *Israel Faces the Future* (New York: Praeger, 1986); Eric Silver, *Begin: The Haunted Prophet* (New York: Random House, 1984); Peter Grose, *A Changing Israel* (New York: Vintage Books, 1985); Ilan Peleg, *Begin's Foreign Policy, 1977-1983* (Westport, Conn.: Greenwood, 1987); and Yoram Ben-Porath, *The Israeli Economy: Maturing through Crisis* (Cambridge, Mass.: Harvard University Press, 1986).
8. Comprehensive information on the contemporary Middle East is available in *The Middle East,* 6th ed. (Washington, D.C.: Congressional Quarterly, 1986), and William Spencer, ed., *The Middle East* (Guilford, Conn.: Dushkin, 1986). For more specialized studies of specific countries and problems in the region, see Phebe Marr, *The Modern History of Iraq* (Boulder, Colo.: Westview, 1986); Cardri (pseudonym), ed., *Saddam's Iraq: Revolution or Reaction?* (London: Zed, 1986); Moshe Maoz and Avner Yanir, eds., *Syria under Assad* (New York: St. Martin's, 1986); Lillian C. Harris, *Libya: Qadhafi's Revolution and the Modern State* (Boulder, Colo.: Westview, 1986); Robert O. Freedman, ed., *The Middle East since Camp David* (Boulder, Colo.: Westview, 1984); Shamir Khalaf, *Lebanon's Predicament: Dynamics of Conflict* (Totowa, N.J.: Zed, 1985); Robert O. Freedman, ed., *The Middle East after the Israeli Invasion of Lebanon* (Syracuse, N.Y.: Syracuse University Press, 1986); Peter Gubser, *Jordan: Crossroads of Middle Eastern Events* (Boulder, Colo.: Westview, 1983); and Tareq Y. Ismael, *International Relations of the Contemporary Middle East* (Syracuse, N.Y.: Syracuse University Press, 1986).
9. The course of Israeli-U.S. relations in recent years is examined in greater detail in Harry S. Allen and Ivan Volgyes, eds., *Israel, the Middle East, and U.S. Interests* (New York: Praeger, 1983); Bernard Reich, *The United States and Israel: Influence in the Special Relationship* (New York: Praeger, 1984); Hyman Bookbinder and James G. Abourezk, *Through Different Eyes* (Washington, D.C.: Adler and Adler, 1987); Stephen L. Spiegel, *The Other Arab-Israeli Conflict: Making America's Middle East Policy*

from Truman to Reagan (Chicago: University of Chicago Press, 1985); Wolf Blitzer, *Between Washington and Jerusalem* (New York: Oxford University Press, 1985); and Cheryl A. Rubenberg, *Israel and the American National Interest* (Champaign: University of Illinois Press, 1986).

10. Quoted in Stephen D. Isaacs, *Jews and American Politics* (Garden City, N.Y.: Doubleday, 1974), 264-265.

11. Marquis Childs, "Stirrings against Carter," *Washington Post,* March 13, 1979.

12. For historical background, see Haim Shaked and Itamar Rabinovic, eds., *The Middle East and the United States* (New Brunswick, N.J.: Transaction Books, 1980). More detailed discussion of recent U.S. policy toward the Middle East is available in Emile A. Nakhleh, *The Persian Gulf and American Policy* (New York: Praeger, 1982); Robert E. Hunter, "The Reagan Administration and the Middle East," *Current History* 86 (February 1987): 49-53; Nimrod Novik, *Encounter with Reality: Reagan and the Middle East* (Boulder, Colo.: Westview, 1986); Marvin G. Weinbaum, *Egypt and the Politics of U.S. Economic Aid* (Boulder, Colo.: Westview, 1986); and Robert G. Darius, John W. Amos II, and Ralph H. Magnus, *Gulf Security into the 1980s* (Stanford, Calif.: Hoover Institution Press, 1984).

13. The 1948 war in Palestine and the resulting refugee problem are analyzed more fully in Fred J. Khouri, *The Arab-Israeli Dilemma* (Syracuse, N.Y.: Syracuse University Press, 1968), 68-102. See also Don Peretz, *Israel and the Palestine Arabs* (Washington, D.C.: Middle East Institute, 1958).

14. The origins, developments, and principal consequences of the Suez Crisis of 1956 are examined in Dwight D. Eisenhower, *Waging Peace* (Garden City, N.Y.: Doubleday, 1965), 20-58; Anthony Eden, *The Suez Crisis of 1956* (Boston: Beacon, 1960); and Peter Calvocoressi, ed., *Suez: Ten Years Later* (New York: Random House, 1967).

15. Informative treatments of the Six-Day War are Khouri, *The Arab-Israeli Dilemma*, 242-292; and Trevor N. Dupuy, *Elusive Victory: The Arab-Israeli Wars, 1947-1974* (New York: Harper and Row, 1978), 221-343.

16. The goals, organization, and membership of the PLO are examined more extensively in Gerard Chaliand, *The Palestine Resistance* (Baltimore: Penguin, 1972). More contemporary information is available in *The Middle East.*

17. *The Middle East,* 140-142; and see the more extended discussion in Nadav Safran, *From War to War: The Arab-Israeli Confrontation, 1948-1967* (New York: Pegasus, 1969), 317-417.

18. Soviet diplomacy in the Middle East is analyzed more fully in R. D. McLaurin, *The Middle East in Soviet Diplomacy* (Lexington, Mass.: D. C. Heath, 1975); Robert O. Freedman, *Soviet Policy Toward the Middle East since 1970* (New York: Praeger, 1975); and Alvin Z. Rubinstein, *Red Star on the Nile* (Princeton, N.J.: Princeton University Press, 1977).

19. The outbreak of the 1973 war, its principal stages, and its consequences are examined in *The Middle East,* 20-26; Dupuy, *Elusive Victory,* 387-603; and Nadav Safran, "The War and the Future of the Arab-Israeli Conflict," *Foreign Affairs* 52 (January 1974): 215-237.

20. The concept of oil power and its implications for U.S. policy in the Middle East are appraised in Dankwart A. Rustow, "Who Won the Yom Kippur and Oil Wars?" *Foreign Policy* 17 (Winter 1974-1975): 166-176; the symposium on OPEC in *Foreign Policy* 13 (Winter 1973-1974): 123-139; and James Akins, "The Oil Crisis: This Time the Wolf Is Here," *Foreign Affairs* 51 (April 1973): 462-491.

124   Invitation to Struggle

21. See, for example, the views of President Carter about President Sadat in his *Keeping Faith: Memoirs of a President* (New York: Bantam Books, 1982); and his more extensive views on Middle Eastern questions in *The Blood of Abraham* (Boston: Houghton Mifflin, 1985). See also Juliana S. Peck, *The Reagan Administration and the Palestinian Question: The First Thousand Days* (Washington, D.C.: Institute for Palestinian Studies, 1984); Ian S. Lustick, "Israeli Politics and American Foreign Policy," *Foreign Affairs* 61 (Winter 1982-83); 379-399; Paul Findley, *They Dare to Speak Out: People and Institutions Confront Israel's Lobby* (Westport, Conn.: Lawrence Hill, 1985); George W. Ball, *Error and Betrayal in Lebanon* (Washington, D.C.: Foundation for Middle East Peace, 1984); James L. Ray, *The Future of American-Israeli Relations: A Parting of the Ways?* (Lexington: University of Kentucky Press, 1985); and Eytan Gilboa, *American Public Opinion toward Israel and the Arab-Israeli Conflict* (Lexington, Mass.: D. C. Heath, 1986).

22. Detailed accounts of Kissinger's shuttle diplomacy are provided in Edward R. F. Sheehan, *The Arabs, Israelis, and Kissinger* (New York: Reader's Digest Press, 1976); and Kissinger's memoirs, *Years of Upheaval* (Boston: Little, Brown, 1982).

23. The Camp David peace negotiations are described at length in Carter, *Keeping Faith;* and in William B. Quandt, *Camp David: Peacemaking and Politics* (Washington, D.C.: Brookings Institution, 1986). For an Arab perspective, see Ismail Fahmy, *Negotiating for Peace in the Middle East* (Baltimore: The Johns Hopkins University Press, 1983).

24. Studies of Iran since the revolution of 1979 are R. K. Ramazani, *Revolutionary Iran: Challenge and Response in the Middle East* (Baltimore: The Johns Hopkins University Press, 1987); Nikki R. Keddie and Eric Hooglund, eds., *The Iranian Revolution and the Islamic Republic* (Syracuse, N.Y.: Syracuse University Press, 1986); Cheryl Bernard and Zalmay Khalilzad, *The Government of God: Iran's Islamic Republic* (New York: Columbia University Press, 1984); and Shaul Bakhash, *The Reign of the Ayatollahs* (New York: Basic Books, 1984).

25. For an analysis of the origins, meaning, and implications of the Carter Doctrine, see Cecil V. Crabb, Jr., *The Doctrines of American Foreign Policy: Their Meaning, Role, and Future* (Baton Rouge: Louisiana State University Press, 1982), 325-371. More recent discussions of U.S. security interests in the Persian Gulf region are available in Lenore G. Martin, *The Unstable Gulf: Threats from Within* (Lexington, Mass.: D. C. Heath, 1984); William J. Olson, *U.S. Strategic Interests in the Gulf Region* (Boulder, Colo.: Westview, 1987); and Aryeh Yodfat, *The Soviet Union and the Arabian Peninsula: Soviet Policy towards the Persian Gulf and Arabia* (New York: St. Martin's, 1983).

26. Historical background on the emergence of Saudi Arabia is available in R. Bayly Winder, *Saudi Arabia in the Nineteenth Century* (New York: St. Martin's, 1965), and Fred Halliday, *Arabia Without Sultans: A Survey of Political Instability in the Arab World* (New York: Random House, 1975).

27. For more extensive discussion of Saudi Arabia's behavior as a leading member of OPEC, see William B. Quandt, "Riyadh Between the Superpowers," *Foreign Policy* 44 (Fall 1981): 37-57; and Dankwart A. Rustow, *Oil and Turmoil: America Faces OPEC and the Middle East* (New York: W. W. Norton, 1982).

28. For analyses of Saudi domestic and foreign policy in the recent period, see Nadav Safran, *Saudi Arabia: The Ceaseless Quest for Security* (Cambridge,

Mass.: Harvard University Press, Belknap Press, 1985); Christine M. Helms, *The Cohesion of Saudi Arabia* (Baltimore: The Johns Hopkins University Press, 1981); Robert Lacey, *The Kingdom* (New York: Avon Books, 1983); and A. R. S. Islami and Rostam M. Kavoussi, *The Political Economy of Saudi Arabia* (Seattle: University of Washington Press, 1984).

29. *The Middle East,* 61. American assistance in helping the government of Saudi Arabia strengthen its air defense system had initially been extended late in 1973. In the months that followed, Riyadh purchased 115 fighter planes; subsequently, Washington sold Hawk missiles to Jordan and transport aircraft to Egypt as well. Early in 1978, the Carter administration proposed a "package" aircraft sale to Egypt, Saudi Arabia, and Israel. Early in 1980, Saudi officials asked Washington for AWACS aircraft and other modern equipment. See the dispatch by Charles Mohr, *New York Times,* November 1, 1981.

30. President Reagan's letter is reproduced in *Department of State Bulletin* 81 (October 1981): 52.

31. Ibid., 52-57.

32. Testimony to the Senate Foreign Relations Committee, in *Department of State Bulletin* 81 (November 1981): 60-67.

33. *Congressional Quarterly Weekly Report,* April 11, 1981, 632; *The Middle East,* 61-62; dispatch by Charles Mohr, *New York Times,* November 1, 1981.

34. *The Middle East,* 61-63.

35. Fuller discussion of the emergence, organization, and techniques utilized by the Arab lobby may be found in ibid., 63-70, and *Congressional Quarterly Weekly Report,* April 22, 1981, 1523-1530.

36. See *Congressional Quarterly Weekly Report,* October 10, 1981, 1942, and December 26, 1981, 2573.

37. The Reagan administration's lobbying activities in behalf of the AWACS proposal are described in *Congressional Quarterly Weekly Report,* April 11, 1981, 632; September 26, 1981, 1868; October 10, 1981, 1942; October 31, 1981, 2095; and December 26, 1981, 2577-2578; and in a dispatch by Phil Gailey, *New York Times,* October 1, 1981.

38. See *Congressional Quarterly Weekly Report,* September 26, 1981, 1868; October 31, 1981, 2095; and December 19, 1981, 2514; and *Newsweek,* November 9, 1981, 30-33.

39. Dispatch by Leslie H. Gelb, *New York Times,* May 29, 1984; and *Congressional Quarterly Almanac, 1984,* 117.

40. *Congressional Quarterly Almanac, 1986,* 376.

41. *Congressional Quarterly Almanac, 1986,* 373-377; and dispatches by Steven V. Roberts, *New York Times,* April 18, 1986, May 7, 1986, and May 22, 1986. See also *U.S. News & World Report,* May 19, 1986, 14.

42. Associated Press dispatch in *Baton Rouge Morning Advocate,* October 9, 1987.

43. Dispatch by Elaine Sciolino, *New York Times,* September 29, 1987.

44. Dispatch by Youssef M. Ibrahim, *New York Times,* October 4, 1987.

CHAPTER 5

The Armed Forces

Where to draw the line between the power of Congress to declare war (Article I, Section 8) and the power of the president as commander in chief (Article II, Section 2) is one of the most controversial issues relating to the Constitution. How far may the president go in ordering troops into combat, or into situations where combat is likely, in the absence of a declaration of war by Congress? How far may Congress go in restraining the president? How far may, or should, Congress go in determining where the armed forces are to be deployed, even in nonhostile environments?

These questions have been the subject of scholarly and inconclusive exegesis, and it is not our purpose to review that voluminous literature here. Nor shall we review the long history of dispute over these questions, during which the pendulum has swung between the two ends of Pennsylvania Avenue. Rather, we shall look at examples of the use of the armed forces since World War II and examine some of the problems that have arisen. What becomes clear from the post-World War II practice is that Congress pays much less attention to constitutional niceties or consistency than it does to pragmatic considerations. When Congress has agreed with the general thrust of a presidential policy, it has acquiesced in the use or even the enlargement of presidential power. When it has disagreed, it has asserted its own prerogatives.

Korea

American troops in Korea provide a good illustration of how Congress's attitudes toward its own powers change over time. In 1950,

Congress was content to let the president act on his own authority in sending U.S. troops to Korea. In 1977, Congress insisted on having a voice in deciding whether to bring them home.

Getting In

Korea emerged from World War II a divided country. Installed by the Soviet Union, a Communist regime (the Democratic People's Republic of Korea, or North Korea) governed north of the thirty-eighth parallel. Below that line, the Republic of Korea (or South Korea) developed close ties with the United States. Growing tension characterized relations between the two Koreas.

On Sunday, June 25, 1950, North Korean troops crossed the thirty-eighth parallel in an evident attempt to overrun South Korea. In the week of frantic decision making that followed, Congress played no significant role, nor did it give much indication of wanting to. In large part, this was because most members of Congress supported, initially anyway, the administration's response to the crisis. Such disagreement as developed was over whether Congress should formally bestow its blessing on the administration's Korea policy and whether such a blessing was constitutionally necessary or politically desirable.

The first U.S. response to the North Korean invasion was to call for an emergency meeting of the UN Security Council. On Sunday, with the Soviets absent, the Security Council voted 9-0 to order North Korea to cease the invasion and withdraw. That night, following a meeting with executive officials, President Truman ordered Gen. Douglas MacArthur, the U.S. commander in the Far East, to evacuate Americans from Korea and to get ammunition and other supplies to South Korea, by airdrop if necessary. MacArthur was authorized to use air and naval power, but was cautioned to keep it south of the thirty-eighth parallel. This precaution becomes more significant in light of later events.

As the meeting broke up, Truman directed the State Department to prepare a statement for him to make on Tuesday, perhaps to Congress, although that was left undecided. He emphasized that no other statement was to be made in the meantime, not even by Secretary of State Dean Acheson or Secretary of Defense Louis Johnson, both of whom had previously been scheduled to appear the next day before the Senate Appropriations Committee in connection with the mutual defense assistance program.

Truman's injunction of silence reflected a typical and traditional executive-branch preference—namely, to arrive at a finished policy before involving Congress in the decision-making process. The extent to which Congress was willing to acquiesce in this procedure is shown by Acheson's remark that the appropriations committee hearing, which was held in executive session, "went off without too much trouble." [1]

On that Monday, Truman himself talked to the chairman of the Senate Foreign Relations Committee, Tom Connally, D-Texas. The president inquired whether the senator thought a declaration of war would be necessary "if I decide to send American forces into Korea." Connally replied:

> If a burglar breaks into your house, you can shoot at him without going down to the police station and getting permission. You might run into a long debate by Congress, which would tie your hands completely. You have the right to do it as commander in chief and under the U.N. Charter.[2]

On Monday night, Truman authorized MacArthur to use air and naval power in direct support of South Korea and again cautioned him to stay south of the thirty-eighth parallel. On Tuesday, June 27, the UN Security Council met again and called on all members of the United Nations to give assistance to the Republic of Korea. This was later used to give an added color of legitimacy to U.S. actions.

The morning of that same day, Truman met with a bipartisan group of fourteen members of Congress from both houses. Acheson summarized the situation in Korea. Truman read a press release (the statement he had asked on Sunday night to have prepared), announcing U.S. air and naval support for South Korea. The president then requested the views of the congressional leaders; Truman later reported in his memoirs that they "approved of my action."[3] According to Acheson, "Senator [Alexander] Wiley [R-Wis.] seemed to express the consensus by saying that it was enough for him to know that we were in there with force and that the President thought the force adequate."[4] (It was not.) Connally recalls that he and others stressed the importance of the UN action and that "a few wondered if Congress should approve."[5]

Sen. Robert A. Taft, R-Ohio, who was not in the group invited to the White House, did not wonder; he was convinced. In a speech in the Senate on Wednesday, June 28, Taft noted that the congressional leaders had had no opportunity to change the president's statement and that "there has been no pretense of consulting the Congress." There was, he said, no legal authority for what the president had done, yet he added that "if a joint resolution were introduced asking for approval of the use of our Armed Forces already sent to Korea and full support of them in their present venture, I would vote for it."[6]

On Thursday, June 29, Truman expanded the involvement of U.S. air and naval forces to include military targets in North Korea, but not beyond. He also authorized the use of ground forces to secure the port, airfield, and communications facilities at Pusan on the southeast coast. On the morning of Friday, June 30, Truman gave MacArthur authority to use the ground forces under his command. The United States was then fully committed to the conflict.

That same day, a second White House meeting was held with members of Congress. Perhaps twice as many were present as on Tuesday. Truman reported to the legislators the orders he had issued about ground troops. There was, says Acheson, "a general chorus of approval," and Rep. Dewey Short, R-Mo., declared that "Congress was practically unanimous in its appreciation of the President's leadership." [7] But Senate Republican leader Kenneth Wherry of Nebraska questioned the president's legal authority. Sen. H. Alexander Smith, R-N.J., suggested a resolution approving the action. The president said he would consider this and asked Acheson to prepare a recommendation.

Acheson recommended against the resolution at a meeting with the president July 3, by which time Congress, incredibly, had recessed for a week over the Fourth of July. Senate Majority Leader Scott Lucas, D-Ill., was the only member of Congress present at the meeting, and he agreed with Acheson. Lucas argued that the vast majority of Congress was satisfied and the minority could not be won over but could keep debating and delaying a resolution so as to dilute much of its public effect.[8]

Getting in Deeper

During July and August, the North Koreans swept down the peninsula and the UN forces, principally Americans, were hard pressed to hold a beachhead around Pusan. Then, in September, MacArthur made a surprise amphibious landing at Inchon on the northwest coast, cutting off the bulk of the North Korean forces to the south and rapidly driving the remainder north of the thirty-eighth parallel. This totally changed the military situation and led to a rethinking, both in Washington and in the UN, of U.S. and UN objectives. The ultimate objective of U.S. policy in Korea since World War II had been the political reunification of the country under a democratic system.

As a consequence, what had started in June as a defensive operation aimed at restoring the status quo ante became in September and October an offensive operation aimed at achieving a united, independent, and democratic Korea. In June, MacArthur had been instructed not to cross the thirty-eighth parallel; now he was authorized to do so. The UN General Assembly went further on October 7 in a resolution looking toward UN-sponsored elections in a unified Korea.

This was a radical expansion of military goals, and it led to disastrous consequences, but Congress had almost nothing to do with it. Two members of the Senate Foreign Relations Committee—Henry Cabot Lodge, Jr., R-Mass., and John Sparkman, D-Ala.—were serving as delegates to the General Assembly that year. Sparkman later confessed to doubts about the wisdom of the offensive operation; but if he expressed those doubts at the time, he certainly did so quietly.

That the doubts were well founded became apparent in late November, when massive Chinese forces poured across the Yalu River boundary between China and Korea and drove the UN troops southward. In the course of the bitter winter of retreat, a long-simmering dispute erupted between MacArthur on the one hand and the Joint Chiefs of Staff, the president, and the State Department on the other. In brief, MacArthur wanted to widen the war by air attacks on China; the government in Washington, fearful of possible Soviet intervention and of becoming inextricably entangled on the mainland of China, wanted to fight a limited war in Korea.

MacArthur steadily became more strident in his criticism of the administration's policy, and on April 10, 1951, Truman relieved him of all his commands. This led Congress to inject itself into the Korean conflict for the first time in a major way. Two separate but related issues were involved: civilian control of the military (one of the bedrock principles of the U.S. government) and the conduct of the war itself or, more broadly, the grand design of America's global strategy.

As has repeatedly occurred in connection with other cases, Congress involved itself in the controversy over MacArthur's dismissal on pragmatic grounds of policy, not on grounds of constitutional principle or procedure. Nobody questioned Truman's authority as president and commander in chief to relieve a general, but many people questioned his wisdom in doing so. At the bottom of this dispute was a fundamental difference over whether the United States should pursue a defensive or an offensive global strategy; in other words, the United States could attempt either to contain the Communist world or to put unrelenting pressure on it at all available points. This difference was epitomized in Korea. On one side, General MacArthur and his supporters wanted to pursue the offensive strategy—that is, to expand the war by carrying it to China. On the other side, President Truman, his principal advisers, and their supporters wanted to follow the defensive strategy—that is, to confine hostilities to Korea.

In the context of the recall of MacArthur, the debate over this broader issue took the form of a series of narrow, essentially tactical questions, such as whether to bomb north of the Yalu River. It was a classic example of the problem of where to draw the line between the day-to-day *conduct* of the war (which was the prerogative of the president as commander in chief) and the long-range *policy* of the war itself (in the determination of which Congress had a major role). The policy choice would obviously affect the way the war was to be conducted: a defensive policy to drive the Communists out of South Korea implied one kind of war; an offensive policy to unify both parts of Korea implied quite a different kind of war; and a policy to carry the war to China would require even more markedly different military operations. The converse was also true, though in a more subtle way: the manner in which the war was conducted could gradually, perhaps imperceptibly, lead to a policy different from the one with which the country started. Aggressive tactics, repeated over time, can change a defensive policy into an offensive policy. This is what MacArthur was trying to do and what Truman fired him to prevent. The same issue would arise in less dramatic form two decades later, in connection with the bombing of Hanoi during the Vietnam War.

The outcry that followed the firing of MacArthur was immense, both in Congress and in the public. The general returned to the United States, for the first time in fourteen years, more as a hero than an officer disgraced for insubordination. He was met everywhere by wildly enthusiastic crowds. Congress took the astonishing step of inviting him to address a joint session and greeted him with an emotional ovation.

Pursuant to action by the Senate, the committees on Armed Services and on Foreign Relations made a meticulous and exhaustive inquiry into MacArthur's dismissal under the general heading, "Military Situation in the Far East." Over forty-three days, beginning May 3 and ending June 27, 1951, the two committees took testimony from fourteen witnesses, including General MacArthur, Secretary of State Acheson, Secretary of Defense George C. Marshall, and all the members of the Joint Chiefs of Staff. The record of the proceedings covers 3,691 pages. In the end, no report was issued and no further action taken, although different members of the committees delivered themselves of different conclusions.

The hearing served the purpose—intended by the Democratic leadership of the two committees—of defusing the Truman-MacArthur controversy by talking it to death. In large part because of the prolonged public airing the controversy received in Congress, popular and legislative support for General MacArthur's position declined significantly. The result was that the conduct of the Korean War was left where the Democratic leaders of Congress wanted it: in the hands of the president. Furthermore, the policy reverted to the defense of South Korea, as distinguished from the unification of the two Koreas.

Following lengthy negotiations, an armistice in the Korean War was finally signed on July 27, 1953. No peace treaty was ever concluded, however, and relations between the two Koreas remained hostile thereafter. On October 1, 1953, the United States and South Korea concluded a mutual defense treaty, formally signifying a U.S. commitment to the preservation of South Korea's independence.

Getting Out

A quarter of a century later, Jimmy Carter campaigned for the presidency advocating, among other things, withdrawal of some of the forty-one thousand U.S. troops that remained in Korea in 1976. As Carter moved to execute this withdrawal in 1977, however, he ran into unexpected congressional opposition, opposition not unlike that encountered by President Truman in the MacArthur affair.

First, the differences over global strategy that were so noticeable in 1951 still existed in 1977, but with a significant change. In 1951, it was the doves who wanted to maintain the status quo; in 1977, it was the hawks. Second, on May 19, 1977, the *Washington Post* published an interview with Maj. Gen. John K. Singlaub, chief of staff of the U.S. military command in Korea, in which the general was quoted as saying, "If we withdraw our ground forces on the schedule suggested, it will lead to war." Singlaub was recalled and reassigned by the White House. He was given a hearing by the Investigations Subcommittee of the House Armed Services Committee. These hearings, like the MacArthur hearings, were marked by controversy and ended inconclusively.

Also in May, the Senate Foreign Relations Committee, at the instigation of Sen. George McGovern, D-S.D., added a policy statement about Korea to the bill authorizing appropriations for the State Department. The principal provision of this statement was that "the United States should seek to accomplish, in accord with the President's announced intention, a complete withdrawal of United States ground forces from the Korean peninsula within four or five years." [9]

When the bill came before the Senate in June, this provision ran into a buzz saw of opposition. The debate was directed primarily to the merits of the issue—that is, whether withdrawing some or all of the troops from Korea was a sensible thing to do—but it also marked a new assertiveness by Congress with respect to the congressional role in deciding the issue. To avoid congressional repudiation of the president's policy, and more particularly to blunt an effort to enact some kind of prohibition on troop withdrawal, the majority leader, Sen. Robert C. Byrd, D-W.V., offered a substitute amendment that watered down McGovern's support of the president. As it finally passed the Senate, the Byrd amendment had Congress declaring that "U.S. policy toward Korea should continue to be arrived at by joint decision of the President and the Congress" and that "any implementation of the foregoing policy should be done in regular consultation with the Congress." [10]

In 1973, as will be discussed later, Congress had passed, over President Richard M. Nixon's veto, the War Powers Resolution, which sharply circumscribed presidential authority to send troops abroad. Nixon had based his veto on grounds of unconstitutional interference with the president's powers as commander in chief. Now Congress was going further and attempting to limit presidential authority to bring troops home. It argued in part from the precedent of the War Powers Resolution.

"I do not think this is strictly an executive branch decision," said Sen. Sam Nunn, D-Ga., a prominent member of the Armed Services Committee. "Under the War Powers Act [sic], we talked a long time about the commitment of troops abroad. I should think that, by implication, we would have some control over the withdrawal of forces that are in a dangerous spot in the world. . . . If it works one way, it works the other." [11]

Some senators who had opposed the War Powers Resolution now also opposed the president's authority unilaterally to withdraw troops from Korea. During the hearings on war powers, the following exchange occurred:

> Senator Javits: So really you are opposed to my bill because you have less faith in the Congress than you have in the President; isn't that true?
> Senator Goldwater: To be perfectly honest with you, you are right. [12]

Goldwater argued that the president should send his requests about Korea "to the proper committees of Congress, and then we can hold hearings." [13] Sen. James Allen, D-Ala., arguing against the Carter policy, said:

> We are turning our backs completely, as I see it, on the principle that was established in the Vietnam war debates, namely, that Congress have a right to participate in decisions regarding the waging of war or foreign policy in general.
> But here, we are abdicating our role. A role that was fought for here in the Congress.
> I did not always support that. . . . I thought the President as Commander-in-Chief of our Armed Forces should have a right to dictate the other policy, but the wisdom of the Congress, in which I now concur, prevailed and Congress did assert unto itself the right to participate in foreign policy decisions. [14]

Congress returned to the subject in 1978. Various proposals to put firm limits on the withdrawal were rejected, but the military assistance bill expressed the view that "further withdrawal of ground forces of the United States from the Republic of Korea may seriously risk upsetting the military balance in that region and requires full advance consultation with Congress." The act also says that the president "should" transmit to Congress, 120 days before each phase of troop withdrawal, "a report on the viability of the withdrawal." [15] The use of the word "should" is curious; most reporting requirements use the stronger "shall."

In January 1979, new intelligence estimates showed North Korean military strength to be greater than had previously been thought. This finding increased doubts both in Congress and in the Pentagon. Finally, in July, the White House announced that further implementation of Carter's plan was being postponed until 1981. By that time there was a new president in the White House, and the issue died by common consent. The total troop reduction from 1977 to 1979 was from 41,000 to 38,000.

Europe

Getting In

As part of its strategy of containing communism, the United States joined eleven other Western nations in establishing the North Atlantic Treaty Organization (NATO) early in 1949. Then, on September 9, 1950 (less than three months after U.S. troops had been committed to the defense of South Korea with little objection from Congress), President Truman announced his approval of a "substantial increase" in U.S. forces in Europe over the two divisions already in Germany. On December 19, Truman said this increase would be carried out as soon as possible.

This latter decision provoked a great debate in the Senate, which began on January 5, 1951, with a major foreign policy speech by Sen. Robert Taft, R-Ohio, which foreshadowed arguments that would be heard fifteen years later with repect to Vietnam:

> As I see it, members of Congress, and particularly members of the Senate, have a constitutional obligation to reexamine constantly and discuss the foreign policy of the United States. If we permit appeals to unity to bring an end to that criticism, we endanger not only the constitutional liberties of the country, but even its future existence.[16]

The president, Taft asserted,

> has no power to agree to send American troops to fight in Europe between members of the Atlantic Pact and Soviet Russia. Without authority, he involved us in the Korean war. Without authority, he apparently is now attempting to adopt a similar policy in Europe.[17]

Three days later, Senate Republican leader Kenneth Wherry of Nebraska introduced a sense of the Senate resolution (a resolution voted on by the Senate but without the president's signature and not having the force of law) that no U.S. ground forces "should be assigned to duty in the European area for the purposes of the North Atlantic Treaty pending the formulation of a policy with respect thereto by the Congress."[18] This resolution was the subject of prolonged hearings by the Foreign Relations and Armed Services committees, in the course of which the administration put a figure of four divisions on its planned increase.

As had happened in the MacArthur controversy, the hearings and the Senate debate that followed were confused by the mixing of the issue of substantive policy and the issue of the proper role of Congress. Those who favored Truman's policy in Europe tended to take a broad view of the president's powers to act on his own. Those who opposed the policy tended to take a narrow view. The matter was complicated by the desire of the president's supporters to avoid any action on the part of Congress. They feared that, even if Congress approved the policy, the action might set a precedent that Congress had the right to do so. The end result was ambiguous and not wholly satisfactory to either side, though less so to those who supported a broad concept of presidential authority.

In March, following the hearings, the Foreign Relations and Armed Services committees reported two resolutions that were identical in language but different in form. One was a simple Senate resolution; the other was a concurrent resolution, that is, one requiring passage by both houses. The operative provisions of the resolutions approved the appointment of Gen. Dwight D. Eisenhower as NATO commander and a "fair share" contribution of U.S. forces to NATO; asked the president to consult with the Senate Foreign Relations and House Foreign Affairs committees and the Armed Services committees in both houses before sending the troops abroad; and asked that the Joint Chiefs of Staff certify that other NATO countries were doing their share before U.S. troops were sent.[19]

The reasons for reporting two resolutions, though complicated in a technical parliamentary sense, reflected the underlying substantive issues. A Senate resolution requires action only by the Senate; a concurrent resolution requires action by the House as well. Neither is submitted to the president for his signature and neither has the force of law. They are only formal expressions of the sense of the Senate or the Congress, as the case may be. If the Senate passes both a Senate and a concurrent resolution in the same terms, the Senate resolution can stand alone if the House fails to act. A concurrent resolution, being an expression of both houses of Congress, carries somewhat more weight, but it also ruffles a latent senatorial jealousy of the House in matters of foreign affairs. Some senators wanted the action to be taken in still another form, a joint resolution. A joint resolution goes to the president for his signature and has the force of law. Thus, in the hierarchy of these things, a joint resolution is the most binding action; a simple Senate (or House) resolution, the least binding. Those who took the broadest view of the president's powers favored a Senate resolution; those who took the narrowest view favored a joint resolution.

These crosscurrents of opinion were reflected in the Senate votes. The simple Senate resolution passed by a vote of 69-21. The concurrent resolution passed by only 45-41 in the Senate and then was not acted on in the House. The Senate rejected the idea of a joint resolution by 31-56. The Senate also adopted an amendment offered by John McClellan, D-Ark., that no more than four divisions should be sent without the Senate's approval. The McClellan amendment was first rejected by 44-46, but it was then reconsidered and agreed to, 49-43. The McClellan amendment had no force of law, but it was an assertion of Senate prerogatives that distressed the Truman administration.

Getting Out

Thereafter, discussion of the issue in Congress died out for a time. Over a period of years, U.S. troops in Europe were increased until they numbered approximately 300,000, accompanied by 225,000 dependents, most of them in Germany (which became a member of NATO in 1955). By 1966, there began to be agitation to bring some of them home. In a sense, it was a spillover of the nascent Senate disillusionment with Vietnam. More directly, it was a consequence of the French withdrawal from the military side of NATO and a generalized feeling that the U.S. contribution to NATO was more than its "fair share" (in the words of the 1951 resolution).

The chief advocate of a reduction in U.S. troops in Europe in the 1960s and 1970s was Senate Majority Leader Mike Mansfield, D-Mont. In 1971, Mansfield proposed that funds for the forces in Europe be limited to the amount necessary to support 150,000 troops. This would have meant a reduction of 50 percent, and it provoked a major debate in the Senate, during which five alternative troop-cut proposals were offered. All of them were less drastic than Mansfield's, and all were defeated by a coalition of those who thought they did too little and those who thought they did too much. In the end, the Mansfield proposal itself was also rejected by a vote of 36-61. However, sixty senators had voted for at least one of the alternatives—a clear indication that a majority of the Senate thought something should be done, even if it was unable to agree on what. The Nixon administration's opposition to troop reduction received a major assist from the Soviet Union in the form of the overture that led to the Mutual Balanced Force Reduction (MFBR) talks (which were still going on in Vienna in 1988). The prospect of these talks provided opponents of troop reduction with the argument that the troops ought to be left in Europe as bargaining chips.

After 1971, Congress let the issue drop for a decade, but returned to it in the early 1980s, as concern mounted anew over the fairness of NATO cost sharing, especially in the light of growing U.S. commitments in the Persian Gulf (to be discussed later in this chapter). The reports of congressional committees on defense legislation in the period from 1981 to 1987 are sprinkled with stern warnings about the limits of congressional tolerance. Thus, the House Appropriations Committee said in 1983, "The committee does not intend to continue to fund the unilateral buildup of U.S. forces overseas without actual commitments for similar increases from our allies." [20]

Mansfield left the Senate at the end of 1976. By 1984, his place as the leading exponent of troop withdrawals had been taken by Senator Nunn, who became chairman of the Armed Services Committee when the Democrats resumed control of the Senate in 1987. That position alone would have made Nunn a force to be reckoned with; but in addition, during his service in the Senate since 1972, he had become widely recognized as an authority on defense. Nunn's concern was less with the number of U.S. troops than with NATO strategy. He wanted more ammunition stockpiles and better maintenance facilities. He felt that NATO conventional forces were inadequate and that unless they were improved, NATO could not offer a serious non-nuclear defense against a Soviet invasion with conventional forces. Nunn sought to use the threat of withdrawal of U.S. troops to force improvements in NATO forces. However, his withdrawal proposal was tabled (i.e., killed) in 1984 by a vote of 55 to 41.

Congressional uneasiness continued to churn over fairness and cost sharing as well as over the issues raised by Nunn, but no proposal of major import survived the full congressional process. In the spring of 1987, it seemed that the wheel might have turned full circle when the House agreed by voice vote to an amendment offered by Representative Bill Richardson, D-N.M., barring any reduction in troops in Europe. But few thought this would put the issue to rest.

It is noteworthy that, ever since the debate over sending troops to Europe in the first place in 1951, members of Congress have chosen to approach the matter through limitations on money (the power of the purse). This avoided the constitutional issue that was raised by the McClellan amendment in 1951 and again in the debate on the War Powers Resolution in 1973. Eleven of the senators who voted on the McClellan amendment, including McClellan himself, were still in the Senate for the vote on Nixon's veto of the War Powers Resolution. A consistent view of the relative powers of the president and Congress over the armed forces would have required the same vote—yea for those favoring a restriction of the president's powers and nay for those opposing a restriction. Only two senators, McClellan and Milton Young, R-N.D., voted the same way both times, yea in each case.

The Senate in 1951 also included two future presidents and one future vice president—Lyndon Johnson, Richard Nixon, and Hubert Humphrey. Although Humphrey voted against the limitation on the president's powers implied in the McClellan amendment, twenty-two years later he voted for the tighter limitation contained in the War

Powers Resolution. Johnson and Nixon, each of whom as president was to assert sweeping executive powers, split on the McClellan amendment. Johnson—consistent with his later actions—voted against it. Nixon voted for it, then later vetoed the War Powers Resolution.

The other senators who voted on both the McClellan amendment and the War Powers Resolution were John Sparkman, J. William Fulbright, Russell Long, James Eastland, John Stennis, John Pastore, George Aiken, and Warren Magnuson. (Technically, Magnuson did not vote on the McClellan amendment, but he was paired against it, which for practical purposes is the same thing.) [21] All of them changed from a less to a more restrictive view of presidential power.

Vietnam

What brought about this change was the war in Vietnam, which in the late 1960s and early 1970s became the most divisive issue in the United States since the Civil War. The period was marked by a growing split between Congress and two presidents, a schism that led to the enactment of the War Powers Resolution over Nixon's veto in November 1973 and finally to use of the ultimate congressional power—the power to withhold appropriations.

The differences between Congress and the president originated in the substantive policy of U.S. involvement in Vietnam. The argument over their respective constitutional powers came later. Congress itself, like the country at large, was divided over Vietnam. The curve of opinion in Congress, like that of public opinion, progressed from acceptance of presidential policies, through opposition by a minority, to opposition by an overwhelming majority. A farsighted member of the House saw this development coming at a time when the U.S. buildup was just beginning. "We can take 1 casualty per congressional district," he said privately. "We can maybe even take 10. But if it gets to be 100, Congress will stop it." That is precisely what happened. By the time Congress stopped it, American deaths totaled somewhat more than 50,000, or a little more than 100 per congressional district.

Getting In

Congress paid strikingly little attention to the steps taken by the Johnson administration in 1965 to convert the U.S. role in Vietnam from support and advice to active participation. The first of these steps came in February, when Johnson ordered the bombing of North Vietnam in retaliation for a Viet Cong attack on an American barracks (housing military personnel who were technically still advisers). The second came in July, when Johnson, after publicly agonizing over the decision, ordered an additional 50,000 U.S. troops to Vietnam.

One reason for the almost silent congressional acquiescence was relief that those measures were not more far-reaching. Before the July decision, officials of the Johnson administration had talked about the possibility of calling up the reserves, raising taxes, and imposing controls on the economy. Compared to these proposals, sending 50,000 more regular army troops to Vietnam did not seem so drastic.

The same psychology had been at work to some extent the year before, when Congress, to its later regret, provided a statutory basis for the war through the Gulf of Tonkin Resolution. This resolution was occasioned by a reported attack August 2, 1964, on the U.S. destroyer *Maddox* while it was on what was described as a routine patrol in the Gulf of Tonkin off the North Vietnamese coast. On August 4, further attacks were reported on the *Maddox* and on the *C. Turner Joy*, which had joined it. There was no damage to the destroyers, but President Johnson ordered air strikes against North Vietnamese torpedo-boat bases. The next day, Johnson asked Congress for a joint resolution. In part, it read:

> The Congress approves and supports the determination of the President, as Commander-in-Chief, to take all necessary measures to repel any armed attack against the forces of the United States and to prevent further aggression. . . .
> The United States regards as vital to its national interest and to world peace the maintenance of international peace and security in southeast Asia. Consonant with the Constitution of the United States and the Charter of the United Nations and in accordance with its obligations under the Southeast Asia Collective Defense Treaty, the United States is, therefore, prepared, as the President determines, to take all necessary steps, including the use of armed force, to assist any member or protocol state of the Southeast Asia Collective Defense Treaty requesting assistance in defense of its freedom.[22]

This resolution passed Congress August 7—two days after Johnson had requested it—by votes of 416-0 in the House and 88-2 in the Senate. Later, Johnson was fond of carrying a tattered copy of it in his pocket and of showing it to anyone who questioned his authority, especially members of Congress who had voted for it. He and other executive officials considered the resolution the "functional equivalent" of a declaration of war.

One reason Congress passed the resolution so promptly and overwhelmingly was that the immediate military response to the incidents of August 2-4 had been limited. This made Johnson look moderate, especially when compared to Sen. Barry Goldwater, his Republican opponent in the 1964 presidential election. Later on, however, a serious question developed of whether the resolution has passed Congress under false pretenses. A review of navy documents by the Senate Foreign Relations Committee revealed that the *Maddox* had not been on a routine patrol, but rather on a sensitive and provocative intelligence mission. There was even some doubt as to whether one of the reported attacks actually occurred. Congress repealed the Gulf of Tonkin Resolution in 1971.

Getting Out

For a number of years, Congress did no more than argue, albeit with increasing stridency, the merits of presidential policies in Vietnam. It hoped to effect change through persuasion rather than through legislation. In large part, this was because until the 1970s the opposition was still not strong enough to muster a majority in Congress for legislation that would significantly restrict the scope of U.S. involvement. Many members of Congress who had doubts about the wisdom of the involvement still felt compelled to support it because troops had already been committed.

As opposition to the war increased, so did congressional frustration in trying to end it, and Congress turned to the power of the purse. A significant step in that direction was taken in 1970, when in the Cooper-Church amendment to the foreign military sales bill, Congress prohibited the expenditure of funds to support military operations in Cambodia after July 1, 1970. In a sense, this action was symbolic, inasmuch as by that cutoff date the Nixon administration had already withdrawn U.S. ground forces from the country. It did, however, have the practical effect of preventing the reintroduction of U.S. air and ground forces when the situation in Cambodia later deteriorated.

Throughout the months that followed, Congress utilized the same approach toward involvement in Indochina. In 1973 and 1974, for example, no less than seven restrictions were placed on the use of funds appropriated by Congress for military activities in the region. Typical of these restrictions was the language of the State Department Authorization Act of 1973:

> Notwithstanding any other provision of law, on or after August 15, 1973, no funds heretofore or hereafter appropriated may be obligated or expended to finance the involvement of United States military forces in hostilities in or over or from off the shores of North Vietnam, South Vietnam, Laos, or Cambodia, unless specifically authorized hereafter by the Congress.[23]

Again, as with the Cooper-Church amendment, the immediate effect of such measures was in a sense symbolic; the U.S. involvement was winding down. The question was whether the disengagement would have occurred anyway or whether it was a response to growing congressional insistence. The congressional grip on the purse strings may also have prevented a reinvolvement in the hectic days of the final withdrawal in 1975.

The War Powers Resolution

When President Nixon ordered U.S. troops into Cambodia in May 1970, his action provoked several members of Congress, prominent among them Senators Jacob Javits, R-N.Y., and Thomas Eagleton, D-Mo., joined later by Representatives Dante B. Fascell, D-Fla., and Clement J. Zablocki, D-Wis., into drafting proposals to place limits on the president's powers to deploy military forces abroad. For three years, these ideas were subjected to congressional consideration. When a proposal finally emerged from the legislative process in November 1973, it took the form of the War Powers Resolution, a complicated law in which a number of disparate strands of congressional thought were woven together. It reflected a general desire to restrain the president by ensuring a larger congressional role in war making, but the fulfillment of this desire was sought by various routes.

Some saw the resolution as a restatement of what the Founders had intended, an intent which in this view had been distorted through congressional abdication. It was a way of forcing Congress to share the responsibility for sending Americans into combat. Others viewed the resolution as a way to delineate the powers of the president as commander in chief. Some, including Senator Eagleton, ended by opposing it because in their view it expanded those powers. Still others, such as Senator Javits, viewed it as providing the basis for a compact between the president and Congress on how the totality of their combined powers would be exercised—a concept that was shattered when Nixon vetoed the resolution.

The War Powers Resolution was an effort to specify the constitutional powers of the president as commander in chief. It states (and it is still in effect) that he is permitted to introduce armed forces into hostilities "or into situations where imminent involvement in hostilities is clearly indicated by the circumstances" *only* "pursuant to (1) a declaration of war, (2) specific statutory authorization, or (3) a national emergency created by attack upon the United States, its territories or possessions, or its armed forces" [Sec. 2(c)]. Note that the resolution excludes a national emergency created some other way—for example, by an attack on U.S. civilians abroad, an attack on merchant shipping, or the perceived threat of an attack on the United States (as in the Cuban missile crisis). In any event, the resolution said, the president "shall" consult with Congress "in every possible instance beforehand (Sec. 3).

In the absence of a declaration of war, the president is to report to Congress within forty-eight hours of deploying the armed forces in three kinds of situations: when the forces are sent into hostilities or into situations where hostilities are imminent; when forces equipped for combat are sent to any foreign country (except for supply, replacement, repair, or training); and when they are sent in numbers that "substantially enlarge" combat-equipped forces already abroad (Sec. 4 [a]).

With respect to the last two of these three situations, the president's report is the end of the matter. With respect to the first, the law originally provided that Congress could order the forces withdrawn at any time by a concurrent resolution, which does not require the president's signature and is therefore not subject to his veto. However, this provision was invalidated in the summer of 1983, when the Supreme Court, in a case involving a different statute, ruled that the procedure, known as a legislative veto, is unconstitutional. The Court held that Congress instead must pass a law—that is, either a bill or a joint resolution, which must be presented to the president for his signature or veto.[24]

In any event, under the War Powers Resolution the forces are to be withdrawn at the end of sixty days—in special cases, ninety days— unless Congress in the meantime has declared war, enacted some other specific authorization, extended the sixty-day period, or is physically unable to meet (Sec. 5). There is also provision for expedited consideration of resolutions of congressional approval or disapproval under procedures which rule out filibusters or other delaying tactics.[25]

In the form in which it became law, the War Powers Resolution passed Congress in October 1973. President Nixon vetoed it on October 24, calling it "unconstitutional and dangerous to the best interests of our Nation." [26] Nixon's objections were directed less at the concurrent resolution procedure (which was later nullified by the Supreme Court decision) than at what he saw as infringement of the president's powers as commander in chief. Both houses voted to override the veto on November 7, the House by 284-135, the Senate by 75-18.

Gerald Ford shared Nixon's view that the resolution was unconstitutional, and as a member of the House he voted against it. Nevertheless, when he became president after Nixon's resignation, Ford sent Congress the reports required by the resolution on four occasions: the evacuations of Danang, Phnom Penh, and Saigon in April 1975 and the rescue of the ship *Mayaguez* from Cambodian captors the following month. These four incidents were of short duration, ranging from less than three hours to eight days.

No question was raised about the operations in Danang and Phnom Penh. The evacuation of Saigon was controversial mainly because many in Congress thought it should have been carried out sooner than it was. The rescue of the *Mayaguez* was very controversial. Critics charged that the Ford administration had overreacted, that Congress had not been consulted, and that forty-one U.S. servicemen had been killed in rescuing thirty-nine crewmen. But of course nobody complained about the fact of the rescue itself.

The Carter administration did not contest the constitutionality of the War Powers Resolution. On April 26, 1980 (within the forty-eight-hour period provided in the resolution), President Carter submitted a report to Congress on the abortive mission to rescue the hostages in Iran. The president had not, however, consulted with Congress, as required by the resolution, before launching the mission. He did at least inform, if not consult, Senator Byrd, the majority leader. Byrd apparently expressed no view as to the substance of the operation, but he did advise the president to consult more widely in Congress ("to bring Congress in as an equal partner," as Byrd later put it) and particularly to consult with the minority.[27] Carter's failure to consult was later upheld in a legal opinion by Lloyd Cutler, the president's counsel, as "a lawful exercise of his constitutional powers as President and Commander-in-Chief." [28]

The Reagan administration initially took the position that it would comply with the resolution, without committing itself as to its binding nature. However, as the administration became caught up in controversies about the presence of U.S. troops in Lebanon, Grenada, and Central America, it became more resistant to what it saw as an encroachment on the constitutional powers of the president. By the time President Ronald Reagan sent the navy to the Persian Gulf in 1987, he was so protective of his prerogatives that consultation became more difficult. It may be noted, though, that President Reagan did make two war-powers reports that did not excite controversy. One was in March 1982, in connection with the participation of up to 1,200 U.S. troops in the Multinational Force and Observers in the Sinai Peninsula under the Egyptian-Israeli peace treaty. This deployment had been previously authorized by Congress. The other was in August 1983, when Reagan responded to appeals from Chad for help in its war against Libya by sending two AWACS and eight F-15 fighter planes to stand by in Sudan. France, which had been the colonial power before Chad's independence, assumed the leading role in its defense, and the U.S. planes began leaving Sudan two weeks after they arrived.

The Resolution in Practice

Lebanon.   The dispatch of U.S. marines to Lebanon was a part of the Reagan administration's efforts to bring peace and stability to that country and thus to lessen tension in the Middle East. The Lebanese difficulties were many and complex. The population is part Christian and part Moslem (Moslems are now in the majority), with both Christians and Moslems further subdivided into disputatious factions, many with their own armies. In addition, Lebanon has received waves of Palestinian refugees from Israel, and there was an influx of Palestine Liberation Organization (PLO) fighters whom King Hussein ejected from Jordan in 1970. All of this erupted into a bitter and destructive civil war in 1975. In 1976, Syrian military intervention, carried out on behalf of the Arab League, temporarily ended the fighting, and the Syrian army remained in Lebanon. Israel subsidized a Christian militia to keep the PLO away from northern Israel, but sporadic guerrilla raids on Israeli settlements continued.

Their patience exhausted, the Israelis invaded Lebanon in the summer of 1982, driving as far as Beirut. In August, agreement was reached, with the crucial diplomatic assistance of the United States, for PLO withdrawal. A part of the agreement was that the evacuation would be observed by an international force of eight hundred Americans, eight hundred French, and four hundred Italians. U.S. marines began arriving August 25. Reagan reported his action to Congress the day before—as he put it, "consistent with the War Powers Resolution." With this phrasing he avoided recognizing the validity of the resolution (as would have been the case if he had reported "under" it or "pursuant to" it) and at the same time made it difficult to charge that he was flouting the resolution. The evacuation was carried out successfully (though subsequently, elements of the PLO began to infiltrate back), and the marines left Lebanon September 10.

They were back September 29, this time numbering twelve hundred (later increased to seventeen hundred), and again in company with the French and Italians, later joined by a small British contingent. Their new mission was to interpose themselves between the various parties to the conflict—Israelis, Syrians, Lebanese government forces, and the numerous armed factions. On September 29, Reagan reported to Congress on their return, again "consistent with the War Powers Resolution." Initially, it was hoped that the marines would stay no longer than thirty days and then that they would be gone by the end of 1982, but this hope was not realized.

Meanwhile, controversy grew over their presence and over whether the situation was one of "imminent" hostilities. If it was, then under the War Powers Resolution they could stay no more than sixty days—in exceptional circumstances, ninety days—unless Congress declared war or passed a specific statutory authorization. Congress dealt with the problem tangentially in the Lebanon Emergency Assistance Act of 1983 (P.L. 98-43, approved June 27, 1983). This law provided, among other things, that the "President shall obtain statutory authorization . . . with respect to any substantial expansion in the number or role in Lebanon of United States Armed Forces." This was a way of saying that Congress accepted, perhaps even approved, the policy thus far but was uneasy over where it might lead.

This uneasinesss increased after August 29, when the marines had their first casualties—two killed and fourteen wounded, the consequence of fighting between the Lebanese armed forces and various other factions. Two more marines were killed September 6; the French also suffered casualties. On September 8, U.S. navy guns offshore fired into the mountains, the source of the fire directed at the marines. On September 13, the White House announced that U.S. air power and artillery might be used to defend positions of the Lebanese armed forces important to the defense of the marines. On September 17, there was more U.S. naval fire, this time against guns in Syrian-held territory that were shelling the Lebanese defense ministry and the U.S. ambassador's residence. On September 19, the navy opened fire to prevent the Lebanese army's loss of a strategic town in the mountains.

Thus, in the space of three weeks there occurred a gradual, unannounced expansion of the U.S. role from providing a buffer to taking sides in a civil war. The president reported the marine casualties to Congress August 30, but he still resisted describing the U.S. forces as being engaged in hostilities.

The administration did, however, enter into negotiations with congressional leaders, principally House Speaker Thomas P. O'Neill, Jr., D-Mass., and out of these talks emerged a compromise. This compromise passed the House September 28 and the Senate September 29. Reagan signed it October 12.[29] Its key provisions were:

> United States Armed Forces ... in Lebanon are now in hostilities requiring authorization of their continued presence under the War Powers Resolution.... The requirements of section 4(a)(1) of the War Powers Resolution became operative on August 29, 1983. [This is the section applying to actual or imminent hostilities.] ... The Congress intends this joint resolution to constitute the necessary specific statutory authorization under the War Powers Resolution for continued participation by United States Armed Forces in the Multinational Force in Lebanon.... Such protective measures as may be necessary to ensure the safety of the Multinational Force in Lebanon [are not precluded].

The authorization was good for eighteen months, meaning that it would expire April 12, 1985. In signing the resolution, Reagan said:

> I do not and cannot cede any of the authority vested in me under the Constitution as President and as Commander-in-Chief of the United States Armed Forces. Nor should my signing be viewed as any acknowledgment that the President's constitutional authority can be impermissibly infringed by statute, that congressional authorization would be required if and when the period specified in ... the War Powers Resolution might be deemed to have been triggered and the period had expired, or that [the eighteen-month authorization] may be interpreted to revise the President's constitutional authority to deploy United States Armed Forces.

The vote on the resolution in the Senate, 54-46, was sharply partisan, with all but three Republicans voting for it and all but two Democrats voting against it. A Democratic alternative to hold strictly to the sixty-day limitation in the War Powers Resolution was defeated by a straight party vote of 45-55. The House passed the Lebanon resolution by a vote of 270-161. In that chamber, the Democrats were sharply divided, voting 130-134 against the resolution and against their party leadership.

The argument in Congress was not so much over whether the War Powers Resolution should be invoked (there was general agreement that it should be) as over the duration and conditions of the marine presence. Many Republicans were prevailed on to support the Lebanon resolution by appeals to their loyalty to the president and the party. Many (but not quite most) Democrats in the House voted for it out of loyalty to the Speaker, who had played a leading role in negotiating it with the White House. This role was counterproductive in the Senate, where many Democrats were irritated at being left out of the negotiations and at what semed to them to be efforts by the House to usurp the Senate's foreign policy prerogatives. Senate-House sensitivity about these matters is never far below the surface.

With respect to the substance of the resolution, many members of Congress thought that eighteen months was far too long. The House Appropriations Commitee went so far as to vote 20-16 to cut off funding for the marines in Lebanon after sixty days unless the president himself invoked the War Powers Resolution, but the committee backed down under pressure from the Speaker. On the other hand, there were two factors in favor of the longer period. It avoided a showdown with the president, who had made it clear he would not accept a shorter time; and it meant that, barring an unforeseen change in circumstances, Congress would not have to face the issue again until after the 1984 election—and maybe the marines would be home in less than eighteen months, anyway.

Many members also were uneasy about the provision for "such protective measures as may be necessary to ensure the safety of the Multinational Force in Lebanon." Even before this chilling reminder of the Gulf of Tonkin resolution, members had been comparing Lebanon to Vietnam. The provision could easily open the way to almost unlimited expansion of the marines' role. It was, said Senate Majority Leader Byrd, "a hole that you can run Amtrak through." [30] Rep. Toby Roth, R-Wis., said, "If we keep the Marines in Lebanon, we're just waiting for a tragedy to happen." [31]

It happened October 23, when a suicidal terrorist crashed a truck laden with explosives into the lobby of the marine headquarters building at the Beirut airport and blew it up, killing 241. A nearly simultaneous bombing of French paratroop quarters killed forty-seven. The incident produced yet another unsuccessful effort in the House to withdraw the marines. An amendment was offered to the defense appropriations bill by Clarence D. Long, D-Md., and Samuel S. Stratton, D-N.Y. The amendment would have cut off funding for keeping the marines in Lebanon after March 1984. The House defeated it November 2 by a vote of 153-274. In the Senate, Republicans used parliamentary maneuvers to avoid a vote in the Foreign Relations Committee on proposals to reduce from eighteen months to three the authorization for the marines to remain in Lebanon.

Congress adjourned November 18 until January 23, but the restiveness of its members increased with three developments in December. First, the fighting escalated. U.S. navy planes bombed Syrian positions in Lebanon in retaliation for Syrian antiaircraft fire against U.S. reconnaissance planes. Two of the attacking planes were shot down; one crewman was killed and one was captured. (The captive was freed by the Syrians after Democratic presidential candidate Jesse Jackson made a dramatic trip to Damascus to plead for his release.) The sixteen-inch guns of the battleship *New Jersey*—the heaviest guns in the world—were also brought into play. Second, it was revealed that the Joint Chiefs of Staff had unanimously opposed sending the marines to Lebanon in the first place. Third, a Pentagon commission investigating the October bombing issued a scathing report criticizing the marines' security arrangements.

In early 1984, both the political and the military situation in Lebanon deteriorated markedly as Moslems (with Syrian support) pressed their campaign against President Amin Gemayel. On February 7, President Reagan removed the immediate issue of the marines' presence when he ordered them withdrawn (his term was "redeployed") to ships offshore. (The previous week, he had said that withdrawal would have "a pretty disastrous result" for U.S. foreign policy, and as late as February 5, Secretary of State George Shultz had criticized Congress for even tolerating discussions about withdrawal.) [32] Total U.S. casualties had been 264 killed and 134 wounded.

Larger issues remained concerning the U.S. role in Lebanon and the application of the War Powers Resolution to the navy. Had the U.S. air and naval attacks on Moslem and Syrian positions been purely in self-defense, or were they in support of the Lebanese government? And what application, if any, did the War Powers Resolution have to warships in hostile or potentially hostile waters? The framers of the resolution had been concerned primarily with ground forces, but they wrote the law to apply to all the armed forces, including the much more mobile navy and air force. Precisely when the resolution came into play with respect to ships and planes, however, remained unanswered. It became an especially urgent question in 1987, with the involvement of U.S. naval forces in the Persian Gulf (to be discussed below).

Grenada. On October 25, 1983, two days after the terrorist attack on the marines in Lebanon, other marine detachments, accompanied by army units, invaded the tiny island of Grenada in the Caribbean. (Administration officials objected to descriptions of the action as an "invasion." Jeane Kirkpatrick, U.S. ambassador to the UN, said it was a "liberation"; President Reagan called it a "rescue mission," referring to the evacuation of U.S. students from the island.) Grenada has a land area of 133 square miles (just twice the size of the District of Columbia) and a population of 110,000. It became independent from Great Britain in 1974, contrary to the desires of many Grenadans. There was also strong opposition to the postindependence government of Prime Minister Eric Gairy. Neighboring Caribbean states boycotted the independence ceremonies and labor unions in Trinidad refused to handle cargos destined for Grenada. Gairy was overthrown in 1979 in a coup led by Maurice Bishop, whose father, a labor leader, had been killed in the disorders accompanying independence. Bishop was the head of the New Jewel Movement (Joint Endeavor for Welfare, Education, and Liberation). He set the island on a leftward course and established close relations with Cuba. His accession was not welcomed by the Carter administration, and the Reagan administration was even colder.

In October 1983, Bishop was himself deposed in a rather unclear series of events. Reporting was sketchy, because the United States did not maintain an embassy in Grenada, nor were there any foreign correspondents on the island. Bishop was at first arrested, then freed by a mob of his supporters, then rearrested and shot. The principal figures emerging in power were Gen. Hudson Austin, who had been chief of the army, and Bernard Coard, who had been Bishop's deputy prime minister. U.S. officials feared that the new leadership would follow an even more leftist course and possibly provide a military base for Cuba, the Soviet Union, or both. In light of the uncertain situation, the Reagan administration was also worried about the safety of one thousand U.S. citizens on the island, seven hundred of them students in an American-operated medical school.

Other Caribbean countries were also concerned about the course of events in Grenada, and the Reagan administration said that they had asked for U.S. assistance in occupying the island. There was, indeed, some Caribbean participation in the invasion, though by far the bulk of the force consisted of U.S. troops. Since most of the Caribbean countries involved are members of the British Commonwealth, the United States consulted with Great Britain before taking action. The British advised against it and refused to take part themselves.

Reagan reported the invasion to Congress on the same day it occurred. He had provided an advance briefing for congressional leaders the night before. There was little resistance to the U.S. action, and within a week some of the troops were already back in the United States. On October 28, the Senate voted 64-20 that the sixty-day clock of the War Powers Resolution had started running in Grenada on October 25. This stipulation was incorporated in an amendment to an unrelated bill, which was subsequently defeated, but the strong Senate vote could not be ignored. The House voted 403-23 for a similar resolution November 1. By December, only three hundred military police, technicians, and support troops remained, and they were under the aegis of the Organization of East Caribbean States.

Libya.   The 1980s were marked by increasing friction between the United States and Libya, an oil-rich desert country that had been ruled since 1969 by Colonel Muammar al-Qaddafi, the leader of a radical socialist revolution. Qaddafi was virulently anti-Israeli and anti-American. His speeches were laced with threats of terrorism. The first U.S.-Libyan armed clash, however, came over a more prosaic issue—the extent of Libyan territorial waters in the Mediterranean Sea. The Libyan coast line is sharply indented by the Gulf of Sidra. Qaddafi maintained that Libya's territorial waters were bounded by a straight line drawn twelve miles north of a line from one headland of the gulf to the other—in other words, that all of the gulf was Libyan. The United States maintained that the line marking Libyan territorial waters should follow the indentations of the coast. This was also the position taken by most of the rest of the world, but historically the question had been the subject of much international discussion.

In August 1981, U.S. naval units in the Mediterranean sailed through the gulf in what the United States said were international waters but Qaddafi said were Libyan waters. The exercise had been announced in advance as a demonstration of the U.S. right to be in the gulf. Two Libyan jets were shot down when they approached the units in what the naval officers took to be a threatening manner. The incident was over quickly, with no damage to U.S. ships or planes. Reagan made no report on it to Congress.

In March 1986, there was another, larger clash between U.S. and Libyan forces in and over the Gulf of Sidra. This time, Libya attacked U.S. planes with surface-to-air missiles launched from shore installations. The United States responded with air-to-surface missiles, which temporarily disabled the Libyan radar. At approximately the same time, Libyan patrol boats were attacked as they approached the U.S. ships. Two were damaged, one was driven off, and one was apparently sunk. Two days afterward, on March 26, Reagan reported the incident to

Congress "in accordance with my desire that the Congress be informed on this matter." He did not mention the War Powers Resolution.

On April 5, 1986, a bomb exploded in a discothèque frequented by U.S. soldiers in West Berlin, killing one of the soldiers and a Turkish woman and injuring 230, including fifty U.S. service personnel. U.S. intelligence agencies said they had established Libyan complicity from intercepted communications. On the night of April 14-15, U.S. planes attacked targets in Libya—some in Tripoli, the capital and largest city, others across the Gulf of Sidra in or near Benghazi. The planes came from U.S. bases in the United Kingdom and from two aircraft carriers in the Mediterranean. One plane was shot down with the loss of its two crewmen; Libyan casualties were estimated at 130.

Reagan told selected members of Congress about the strike three hours in advance. The planes from the British bases were then already in the air, but theoretically they could still have been called back. It has not been reported what kind of advice, if any, the members gave the president, but most of them later supported the action. House Speaker O'Neill said the consultation was adequate; House Foreign Affairs Committee Chairman Fascell said it was not; Senate Foreign Relations Committee Chairman Richard G. Lugar, R-Ind., said it was "arguable." [33]

Reagan reported the action to the full Congress on April 16, "in accordance with my desire that Congress be informed on this matter, and consistent with the War Powers Resolution." His report also contained a warning: "Should Libyan-sponsored terrorist attacks against United States citizens not cease, we will take appropriate measures necessary to protect United States citizens in the exercise of our right of self-defense." [34]

Persian Gulf. The question of the applicability of the War Powers Resolution to air and naval forces had been suggested in Lebanon; it had been raised more directly in Libya; and it was even more at issue in the Reagan administration's policy in the Persian Gulf. The forerunner of this policy was established in what came to be known as the Carter Doctrine, as enunciated in President Carter's 1980 State of the Union address to Congress: "An attempt by any outside force to gain control of the Persian Gulf region will be regarded as an assault on the vital interests of the United States of America, and such an assault will be repelled by any means necessary, including military force." [35]

This pronouncement was a response to two events in the gulf region: first, the overthrow in January 1979 of Shah Mohammed Reza Pahlavi of Iran and his replacement by the radical Moslem fundamentalist regime of Ayatollah Ruhollah Khomeini, followed in November of that year by the seizure of hostages in the U.S. embassy in

Tehran; and second, the invasion of Afghanistan by the Soviet Union in December 1979.

In the spring of 1987, the Reagan administration substantially raised the U.S. commitment in the gulf and, with it, the level of congressional concern and public controversy. The administration did this by acceding to a Kuwaiti request to protect Kuwaiti tankers in the Persian Gulf from attack by participants in the Iran-Iraq war. The tankers would be registered in the United States so that they could fly the U.S. flag and thereby come under the protection of the U.S. Navy. Kuwait was technically neutral in the war, but did not conceal its pro-Iraq sympathies; the threat to its shipping came from Iran. Eleven Kuwaiti tankers were reflagged. In addition, Kuwait chartered three Soviet tankers, which were subject to Soviet protection. Thus, both superpowers were in the gulf for the same basic purpose.

Before the U.S.-Kuwaiti arrangements could be completed, the USS *Stark,* a naval frigate, was attacked in the gulf by an Iraqi plane, firing a French missile. The *Stark* was heavily damaged, and thirty-seven men were killed. The Iraqis said that the pilot had made a mistake and that the attack was unintentional, and the United States accepted this explanation.

Congress spent a good part of the summer and fall of 1987 discussing the applicability of the War Powers Resolution to the situation in the gulf, without reaching any agreement. The administration refused even to consider the matter, because, in its view, the resolution was unconstitutional. But even if it were not, officials said, the level of hostilities was too low for the resolution to apply.[36] Nevertheless, the Pentagon authorized "imminent danger" pay bonuses of $110 a month for personnel on ships operating in the gulf; U.S. forces attacked and seized an Iranian landing craft that was laying mines, and they destroyed an Iranian oil platform in the gulf that had a radar station on it. Reagan reported these actions to Congress. He said the platform had been used as a base for attacks against U.S. helicopters.[37]

In July, before the paperwork for reflagging had been completed, the House rejected, 126-283, a proposal to forbid it. The House then voted, 222-184, to delay it for three months. A similar proposal in the Senate fell victim to a Republican filibuster. The closest it came to passing was when it received fifty-seven votes on a motion to end the filibuster (sixty votes were needed).

Later, Senators Byrd and Nunn devised an amendment to the defense authorization bill that did not mention the War Powers Resolution at all but in effect would have applied its terms to the Persian Gulf. The Byrd-Nunn amendment would have allowed Kuwaiti tankers to fly the U.S. flag, but only under the time limits of the War Powers Resolution. This amendment was also the target of a filibuster. A cloture motion failed, 54-45. Byrd and Nunn then declared that the majority support amounted to a symbolic victory, and they withdrew the amendment.

But the matter was not dead. In October, two senators, Lowell P. Weicker, Jr., R-Conn., and Mark O. Hatfield, R-Ore., introduced a joint resolution to start the sixty-day clock of the War Powers Resolution. Senators Byrd and John W. Warner, R-Va., the ranking Republican on the Armed Services Committee, offered a substitute to require the president to report within thirty days on the policy of reflagging and escorting the Kuwaiti ships. Thirty days after the report, the Senate would act on the policy under special rules precluding a filibuster. The substitute supported a U.S. "presence" in the gulf but expressed congressional "reservations" over the policy of reflagging and escorting. This time the Senate voted cloture, 67-28, and then passed the Byrd-Warner substitute, 54-44. But the bill then died in the House. It was too strong for those who supported the administration and too weak for those who wanted to apply the War Powers Resolution.

The Senate took one more action. Following the attack by U.S. forces on Iranian installations, Sen. Brock Adams, D-Wash., introduced another joint resolution, declaring the United States to be in a situation of hostilities in the gulf and triggering the provision of the War Powers Resolution for expedited consideration of such resolutions. In a bit of parliamentary legerdemain, to which Adams assented, the Senate on December 4 upheld a point of order that the Adams resolution did not come under the War Powers Resolution. The Senate did this by voice vote, so that no senator had to go on record. The Senate then agreed by unanimous consent that, for the balance of the 100th Congress (that is, through January 2, 1989), whenever a question arose as to whether a resolution was covered by the expedited procedures, a vote on the matter would be taken after a maximum of four hours of debate.

Meanwhile, a group of 110 House Democrats, led by Rep. Mike Lowry, D-Wash., had filed suit in federal court seeking to force the president to comply with the War Powers Resolution. In December, Judge George H. Revercomb dismissed the suit, calling it a "byproduct of political disputes within Congress" and saying that to rule on it would be to "impose a consensus on Congress" that Congress had not achieved by itself.[38]

After a lull, congressional nervousness rose again in the spring of 1988. On April 14, the USS *Samuel B. Roberts,* a guided-missile frigate, hit an Iranian mine in the gulf. The ship suffered severe damage, and ten of its crewmen were injured, though none was killed. Four days later, U.S. forces destroyed two Iranian oil platforms and sank or severely damaged six small Iranian naval vessels. A marine helicopter with a two-man crew was lost during the attack. President Reagan reported the actions to Congress the next day, even though he argued that they did not fall under the War Powers Resolution.

On April 29, the president ordered the navy to assist, in certain circumstances, neutral shipping as well as U.S.-flag vessels. The action was taken in response to an increasing number of attacks on neutral shipping by both belligerents, sometimes in sight of U.S. naval ships, which under their prior rules of engagement could do nothing. Announcing the new policy, Secretary of Defense Frank C. Carlucci said:

> Such aid will be provided to friendly, innocent neutral vessels flying a non-belligerent flag outside declared war-exclusion zones that are not carrying contraband or resisting legitimate visit and search by a Persian Gulf belligerent.
> Following a request from the vessel under attack, assistance will be rendered by a U.S. warship or aircraft if this unit is in the vicinity and its mission permits rendering such assistance.[39]

Thus, just as the marines' mission in Lebanon had expanded, so, too, did the navy's mission in the Persian Gulf.

Assessment of the Resolution

The War Powers Resolution has not worked the way its sponsors intended. In part, this is because no president has ever really accepted the spirit of the resolution. More important, Congress has not followed through with the same determination it showed when it passed the resolution. The only real tests have come with respect to the marines in Lebanon and the navy in the Persian Gulf, and on both occasions Congress equivocated. After the first of those occasions, Sen. Jim Sasser, D-Tenn., commented, "The real casualty in this whole chain of events, beyond the young Marines who have lost their lives in Lebanon, has been the War Powers Resolution."[40]

The fundamental problem is that the War Powers Resolution does not contain any sanctions against a president who does not comply with it. There is always the implicit threat of impeachment, but this is so extreme that it has been seriously proposed only twice in two hundred years. The real congressional power to control the deployment of troops abroad lies in withholding appropriations. Sen. Frank Church, D-Idaho, put it well during a 1977 hearing by the Senate Foreign Relations Committee to review the resolution:

> If the President ... uses the Armed Forces in an action that is both swift and successful, then there is no reason to expect the Congress to do anything other than applaud.
> If the President employs forces in an action which is swift, but unsuccessful, then the Congress is faced with a fait accompli, and although it may rebuke the president, it can do little else.
> If the President undertakes to introduce American forces in a

foreign war that is large and sustained, then it seems to me that the argument that the War Powers Resolution forces the Congress to confront that decision is an argument that overlooks the fact that Congress in any case must confront the decision, because it is the Congress that must appropriate the money to make it possible for the sustained action to be sustained.

So I wonder really whether we have done very much in furthering our purpose through the War Powers Resolution.[41]

However, Congress has been extremely reluctant to use its power of the purse in these matters. The House rejected attempts to do so with respect to Lebanon, even while it was waxing indignant about its war powers. "In difficult foreign policy matters," one commentator has written, "Congress often wants a role but not responsibility. It wanted to be consulted, and to have something to say, about the stationing of Marines in a situation where they were in obvious danger, but it didn't want to take it upon itself to decide when they should be removed."[42] The same could be said about the Persian Gulf.

Problems of the Congressional Role

Consultation

Quite apart from dealing with Congress because of statutory requirements such as those contained in the War Powers Resolution, presidents are sensitive to congressional opinion for political reasons. Support in Congress for the president's moves can broaden the base of public support for U.S. policy, both domestically and abroad. Conversely, congressional opposition can complicate and frustrate a president's policies.

Although presidents are jealous of their prerogatives as commander in chief, they almost always go through the motions of consulting with Congress about major decisions on the use of troops abroad. (A notable exception was the Nixon incursion into Cambodia, and that was one of the reasons it provoked such an outcry on Capitol Hill.) Chief executives usually do this after the decision has been made, so that the policy is a *fait accompli.* They generally limit themselves to giving selected members information in advance of its public release.

This procedure is not at all what Congress has in mind when it demands to be consulted. The House Foreign Affairs Committee, in its report on the War Powers Resolution, reflected a widely held congressional view when it rejected "the notion that consultation should be synonymous with merely being informed." The report said:

> Consultation in this provision means that a decision is pending on a problem and that Members of Congress are being asked by the President for their advice and opinions and, in appropriate circumstances,

their approval of action contemplated. Furthermore, for consultation to be meaningful, the President himself must participate and all information relevant to the situation must be made available.[43]

Even without these conceptual differences, the process of executive-legislative consultation itself involves difficult problems. The initiative almost always rests with the president, and the question immediately arises as to which legislators should be consulted. Especially during crises or other occasions when time is a factor and when considerations of national security information may be involved, it is obviously not practical to consult with Congress as a whole—for example, through the device of a presidential message to a joint session. There must be some selectivity in choosing legislators to be included, and that is an exceedingly delicate issue among members of Congress. Most problems cut across rival committee jurisdictions, and the party leaders in the House and Senate must be included in such consultations as well.

Thus, the executive branch faces a dilemma. The fewer the members of Congress involved in consultations, the less likely it is that there will be leaks of sensitive information and the more likely it is that a consensus will emerge from the discussions. But when consultations are limited to a small group, the decisions made are less likely to be representative of opinion in Congress as a whole—particularly in this era of dispersion of power on Capitol Hill. Furthermore, the smaller the group consulted, the more likely there are to be hurt feelings on the part of those left out. Finally, if Congress is not in session, some or all of the members to be consulted may not be in Washington or even in the country.

As the House Foreign Affairs Committee pointed out, if there is to be meaningful consultation, there has to be a sharing with Congress of all relevant information. Not infrequently, the executive branch is reluctant to do this. In part, executive reticence stems from a fear of leaks; but more importantly, administrations are reluctant to share with Congress information that may be relevant but that does not support a particular policy. The problem of leaks may be more an excuse than a reason for not engaging in consultations. Over any given time period, Congress certainly leaks no more, and quite possibly less, than the executive branch. Most of the time, Congress has shown no disposition to insist on access to all relevant information, although it has been demanding—and getting—somewhat more in recent years.

It is equally true that many members of Congress are unwilling to devote the time necessary not only to absorb all the relevant information but also to consider seriously all the policy options available to the United States. It took the Kennedy administration a week to decide on its policy in the Cuban missile crisis. The members of Congress who were then "consulted" had less than an hour; yet one can scarcely imagine any of them being willing, even if given the opportunity, to devote a week to the problem in the midst of a political campaign.

There is also a question of how much some members of Congress really want to be consulted, despite congressional fulminations on the subject. Particularly in crisis situations, there is a tendency in Congress to give the president the benefit of the doubt. There is also reluctance to take the political responsibility for potentially disastrous decisions. Better, in this view, that the president should get the credit for something that turns out well than that an individual member of Congress should share the blame for something that turns out poorly. It was not for nothing that Truman had a sign on his desk that read, "The buck stops here."

Policy versus Management

The increasing assertiveness of Congress about troop deployments raises the question of where to draw the line between broad policy, on the one hand, and day-to-day management or administrative decisions, on the other. This not only involves constitutional problems that can be argued at length; it also involves the practical, more immediate problem of the allocation of time—a scarce commodity in Congress. The more Congress devotes itself to the minutiae regarding which troops are sent where, the less it can address the larger policy questions with which it is better equipped to deal. The distinctions between these categories, however, are not always clear.

If Congress is to say, as the House Armed Services Committee did in 1978, that x thousand troops of the Second Division are to be kept in Korea, then there is no reason it cannot say that y thousand troops of the Eighty-second Airborne Division are to be kept at Fort Bragg, North Carolina, or transferred to Fort Knox, Kentucky, or that z ships of the Atlantic Fleet are to be based at Guantanamo, Cuba. No one has seriously suggested this level of congressional involvement in military decision making, but Congress has come close to it in ordering certain domestic bases kept open against the wishes of the White House and the Defense Department.

Nor is the question of where to draw the line between policy and management limited to troop deployment. It is equally, perhaps more, important with respect to weapons systems. One of the functions of a defense budget is to allocate resources among the different elements of the national military establishment. Should the navy build a few giant aircraft carriers or more small to medium-sized ones? Should the air force develop a new manned bomber or put more reliance on missiles— and where should it base the missiles? These and many similar questions come to Congress for decision, because only it has the constitutional power to appropriate money for the armed forces. And of course the armed forces are not the only claimants on federal funds. Even in an era of very large defense budgets, there is never enough money to pay for everything; choices must be made.

Sometimes this process presents Congress with large questions of fundamental policy: Should the United States pursue the SDI? Should it put more resources into the production of nerve gas? Other questions are trivial: Should the parade ground at Fort Sill, Oklahoma, be repaved? How many days' ammunition should be stockpiled in Europe? Somewhere in between a line must be drawn, but the area through which to draw it is murky.

Complicating the problem are the parochial interests that are never far from the consciousness of a member of Congress. Many debates over defense budget items are influenced by whether a particular outcome will result in more or less spending in a member's state or district. At work here is the military-industrial complex that President Dwight D. Eisenhower warned about as he left office in 1961.

Whether for reasons of parochial politics or of high policy, Congress regularly influences the nature of the U.S. defense establishment. It has killed air force plans to develop a new transport plane called the C-X and told the air force to improve the existing C-5 instead. It has chosen one training plane over another. It has told the navy what kind of cargo ships to buy. Many other examples could be cited.

Declarations of War

Increasing legislative assertiveness over troop deployments overseas in part represents an attempt to compensate for the erosion of the power of Congress to declare war, as explained in Chapter 2. This erosion occurred primarily because of changes in international relationships, in military technology, and in the nature of modern warfare.

At various times during the Vietnam War, for example, several senators considered introducing a declaration of war to focus the issue of U.S. involvement in the conflict more sharply. The idea did not, however, gain support on Capitol Hill. Legislators who opposed it believed that a declaration of war would have given U.S. participation a legitimacy it otherwise lacked; and the declaration might have escalated the war to an even higher level of intensity, possibly involving a direct Soviet-American or Sino-American confrontation. There was also the practical and perplexing question of whom to declare war against— North Vietnam or the rather shadowy Viet Cong, or both?[44]

The United States fought the Korean War under the aegis of the United Nations. A declaration of war by Congress in that conflict would have presented the risk of grave consequences by triggering North Korean-Chinese-Soviet defense alliances. In both the Korean and the Vietnam experiences, the absence of a declaration of war was one important way to keep a limited war limited. And in an age of megaton nuclear missiles, that is the only kind of war that can be tolerated.

Hawks versus Doves

"Where you stand," Sen. Hubert Humphrey once remarked, "depends on where you sit." Congress reasserts its powers over the armed forces or acquiesces in the erosion of its powers depending on its prevailing view of a particular presidential policy. Even those senators, such as Taft, who thought Truman exceeded his authority in Korea, muted their criticism because they approved of the substance of the policy if not of the procedure by which it was decided. A year later, during the MacArthur hearings, many of the same senators complained that Truman's conduct of the war was too restrained.

Most of the impetus behind the War Powers Resolution came from members of Congress who disapproved of the Nixon administration's policies in Indochina. And the members of Congress who were most vocal in asserting the power of Congress to keep troops in Korea were those who most strongly opposed the Carter policy of withdrawal.

Arguments over the proper role of Congress in connection with the armed forces usually center on the propriety of restraints on the president. As a legacy of Vietnam, and in the terminology of that era, the arguments tend to assume a division between doves in Congress and hawks in the White House and Pentagon. This is not always the case. There are numerous historical examples, going back to the War of 1812, when Congress has been more militant than the president in dealing with other countries. In any event, history provides abundant evidence that there is no monopoly on wisdom—or for that matter on bad judgment—at either end of Pennsylvania Avenue. Nor is there any guarantee that the president and Congress will not both be mistaken at the same time. It is the modest theory of the Constitution only that they are less likely to be.

Notes

1. Dean Acheson, *Present at the Creation: My Years in the State Department* (New York: W. W. Norton, 1969), 407.
2. Tom Connally, as told to Alfred Steinberg, *My Name Is Tom Connally* (New York: Thomas Y. Crowell, 1954), 346.
3. Harry S Truman, *Years of Trial and Hope*, vol. 2 of *Memoirs* (Garden City, N.Y.: Doubleday, 1956), 338.
4. Acheson, *Present at the Creation*, 409.
5. Connally, *My Name Is Tom Connally*, 347-348.
6. *Congressional Record*, 81st Cong., 2d sess., June 28, 1950, 9319-9323.
7. Acheson, *Present at the Creation*, 113.

8. Ibid., 414.
9. House, 95th Cong., 1st sess., 1977, H.R. 6689, as reported in the Senate; see also S. Rept. 95-194, pp. 26-27.
10. *Congressional Record,* 95th Cong., 1st sess., 1977, 19442-19443. The final version of the amendment as it emerged from the House-Senate conference and was passed is found in P.L. 95-105, Sec. 512.
11. *Congressional Record,* 95th Cong., 1st sess. 1977, 19444, 19447.
12. Senate Committee on Foreign Relations, *Hearings on War Powers Legislation,* 92d Cong., 1st sess., 1971, 393.
13. *Congressional Record,* 95th Cong., 1st sess., 1977, 19457.
14. Ibid.
15. P.L. 95-384, Sec. 23(d).
16. *Congressional Record,* 82d Cong., 1st sess., January 5, 1951, 55.
17. Ibid., 59.
18. Senate, 82d Cong., 1st sess., 1951, S. Res. 8.
19. Senate, 82d Cong., 1st sess., 1951, S. Res. 99 and S. Con. Res. 18.
20. *Military Construction Appropriations, Fiscal Year 1984,* 98th Cong., 1st sess., 1983, H. Rept. 98-238, 5.
21. A *pair* is an agreement between two lawmakers on opposite sides of an issue to withhold their votes on roll calls so that the absence of one of them from Congress will not affect the outcome of record voting. If passage of the measure requires a two-thirds majority, a pair would require two members favoring the action to pair with one opposed to it.
22. P.L. 88-408, August 10, 1964.
23. P.L. 93-126, October 18, 1973, Sec. 13.
24. *Immigration and Naturalization Service v. Chadha,* 462 U.S. 919 (1983).
25. P.L. 93-148, November 7, 1973.
26. House, H. Doc. 93-171, 93d Cong., 1st sess., 1973.
27. Senate Committee on Foreign Relations, *Hearings on U.S. Policy in the Western Hemisphere,* 97th Cong., 2d sess., 1982, 190.
28. House Committee on Foreign Affairs, Subcommittee on International Security and Scientific Affairs, *The War Powers Resolution: Relevant Documents, Correspondence, Reports,* 1983, Committee Print, 50.
29. Text in *Congressional Quarterly Weekly Report,* October 8, 1983, 2101-2102. Text of Reagan statement on signature is in *Congressional Quarterly Weekly Report,* October 15, 1983, 2142.
30. Quoted in dispatch by T. R. Reid and Helen Dewar, *Washington Post,* September 22, 1983.
31. *Congressional Quarterly Weekly Report,* September 24, 1983, 1964.
32. Reagan's remarks are quoted in *Wall Street Journal,* February 8, 1984; for Shultz's criticisms of Congress, see *New York Times,* February 6, 1984.
33. Dispatch by Helen Dewar and Edward Walsh, *Washington Post,* April 16, 1986.
34. *Weekly Compilation of Presidential Documents,* April 21, 1987, 499-500.
35. *Congressional Record,* 96th Cong., 2d sess., 1980, 381.
36. Dispatch by Molly Moore, *Washington Post,* September 28, 1987.
37. *Weekly Compilation of Presidential Documents,* October 19, 1987, 1159-1160, and October 26, 1987, 1206.
38. Dispatch by Helen Dewar, *Washington Post,* December 10, 1987.
39. Quoted in a dispatch by George C. Wilson, *Washington Post,* April 30, 1988.
40. *Congressional Quarterly Weekly Report,* October 8, 1983, 2097.
41. Senate Foreign Relations Committee, *Hearings on the War Powers Resolution,* 95th Cong., 1st sess., 1977, 172.

42. Elizabeth Drew, "A Political Journal," *New Yorker,* September 26, 1983, 143-144.
43. House, 93d Cong., 1st sess., H. Rept. 93-287.
44. The question of whether Congress should have declared war in the Vietnam conflict is discussed more fully in Jacob K. Javits, "The Congressional Presence in Foreign Relations," *Foreign Affairs* 48 (January 1970): 221-235.

CHAPTER 6

The Intelligence Community

In its fundamentals, the relationship of Congress to the intelligence community is, or should be, no different from its relationship to other parts of the executive branch. The role of Congress is to provide basic legislative authority and to oversee how that authority is used. Legislative oversight is a duty that Congress has imposed on itself. The law (2 U.S.C. 190d[a]) requires each standing committee of the House and Senate to "review and study, on a continuing basis, the application, administration, and execution of those laws, or parts of laws, the subject matter of which is within the jurisdiction of that committee."

But several factors make Congress's relationship to the intelligence community unique. One is the necessity for secrecy in an otherwise open government. Another is the failure of Congress to provide basic comprehensive legislation on intelligence activities. A third is the failure of Congress, until 1976 in the Senate and 1977 in the House, to exercise any true oversight. All of these factors combined to create both in the intelligence community and in Congress mental attitudes that made it a traumatic experience for both parties when Congress finally began to assert itself. The intelligence community had been conditioned by more than a quarter-century of experience not to tell Congress what it was doing. And Congress had been conditioned not to ask.

For more than twenty-five years following the passage of the National Security Act, which created the Central Intelligence Agency in 1947, Congress largely ignored the intelligence community. It allowed the National Security Agency and the Defense Intelligence Agency to be created by executive order. It voted for untold billions of dollars in hidden appropriations for intelligence activities with very few, if any, of its members knowing either the amounts or the purposes of the funds. Members of Congress who were actively concerned about the activities of the intelligence community were rebuffed by large majorities on the few occasions when they tried to ask questions or to establish procedures for doing so.

During this period, Congress interested itself in the intelligence community only when something went so horribly wrong that it came to public view, as when the U-2 reconnaissance plane was shot down over the Soviet Union in 1960 or when the Bay of Pigs invasion of Cuba failed in 1961. These crises contributed to what was then still a minority view that Congress ought to do something to keep such things from happening. The emphasis in this view was on preventing mistakes.

Further momentum developed in Congress in the early and mid-1970s with the revelations of CIA activities in Chile and of abuses by the CIA and the FBI of constitutional rights of U.S. citizens. The first serious, broad-scale congressional investigation of the intelligence community, by the Church committee in 1975-1976, was directed almost wholly to the question of "illegal, improper or unethical activities." [1] This investigation and a later, more raucous one in the House laid the groundwork for the creation (in 1976 in the Senate and in 1977 in the House) of the permanent intelligence committees. These committees were given legislative jurisdiction as well as broad powers of oversight. The House committee was in the forefront of the legislative confrontation with the Reagan administration over Nicaragua. Administration efforts to circumvent legal restrictions on its freedom of action in Nicaragua led to the Iran-contra affair of 1986-1987 and to renewed efforts in Congress to improve the oversight machinery. Further revelations in 1988 suggested a recurrence of FBI investigations of opponents of U.S. foreign policies.

Definition of Intelligence Functions

The names and responsibilities of the agencies that comprise the intelligence community were given in Chapter 1. Here, we are concerned with the four main functions that these agencies perform. These are:

Collection: the gathering of information. This can be done in such mundane ways as reading a newspaper or in such exotic ways as taking a picture from space or planting a listening device in an official's office, or by bribery or blackmail.

Analysis: making sense out of the information. The flow of information into the intelligence community is immense but nevertheless incomplete and sometimes conflicting. The analyst's task is to distinguish between the trivial and the significant, as well as between the true and the false and then to send to policy makers judgments as to the meaning of the information. This task is frequently akin to doing a jigsaw puzzle with some of the pieces missing or describing an iceberg when only its tip can be seen. Furthermore, even with complete information, political or economic forecasting is an inexact art.

Counterintelligence: protecting one country's secrets from another country's spies—that is, keeping the other fellow from doing to us what we are trying to do to him. Counterintelligence in the United States is in the domain of the FBI.

Covert action: sub-rosa and theoretically untraceable efforts to influence (sometimes to subvert or overthrow) foreign governments, groups, or economies. These efforts may include the surreptitious dissemination of information, either true or false, but any collection of information is incidental. Covert action has technically been called "special activities" since that term was used in an executive order issued by President Jimmy Carter in 1978, but "covert action" will continue to be used here because it is a more descriptive term.

Whatever technique is used, covert action is done secretly because public identification of the U.S. government with the particular activity would be either counterproductive or embarrassing or both. Some examples of covert action that have become public are the secret subsidies of anticommunist labor unions in Western Europe in the late 1940s and early 1950s, the overthrow of the Mossadegh regime and the restoration to power of the Shah in Iran in 1953, the overthrow of the Arbenz government in Guatemala in 1954, the abortive Bay of Pigs invasion of Cuba in 1961, the attempts to destabilize the Allende government in Chile in 1970-1973, and most recently the operations against Nicaragua that began in 1981.

Problems of Oversight and Control

Over the course of its history, the United States has developed ways of ensuring that the components of its government are responsive to the public will. If the National Park Service, for example, mismanages the national parks, this shortly becomes apparent to large numbers of people, complaints are made, and changes ensue. The process is sometimes slow and cumbersome and may be diverted by arguments over who is at fault, but it usually works. Government agencies are regularly called on to give a public accounting of themselves, and people know from personal experience whether programs are going well or poorly.

Not so with the intelligence community. The time-tested procedures that work for agencies such as the National Park Service are inappropriate for the CIA. This is an anomaly in a country like the United States, where policy is public. Progress has been made in dealing with this problem, but as of 1988, although it is better understood, one cannot say that it has been solved. Nor is it a problem only for Congress; it has haunted such diverse presidents as John F. Kennedy and Ronald Reagan.

Intelligence is an indispensable aid to policy makers; one can scarcely imagine trying to make foreign policy in the dark. But the proper role of the intelligence community stops with its presentation of data and analysis. Some directors of central intelligence—for example, Richard Helms and William Colby—have been very emphatic about this; others, such as William Casey, have actively sought and on occasion played a policy-making role as well.

Collection

Serious questions of public policy are involved in deciding what intelligence to collect. At one time, those who made these decisions were so preoccupied with the threat of communist insurgents that the community expended enormous resources in trying to penetrate ragtag bands of dissidents while paying less attention to more mundane but in the long run probably more important matters, such as economic trends.

Further questions arise about the use of hazardous methods of data collection. When the Soviet Union shot down the U-2 spy plane in 1960, a planned summit meeting between President Dwight D. Eisenhower and Soviet Premier Nikita Khrushchev crashed as well. In the view of some observers, this also cost the Republicans the 1960 election.

Analysis

The main problem of oversight and control presented by analysis is bias. The analyst may be biased, subconsciously or otherwise, toward a particular interpretation of a situation, or may, again subconsciously or otherwise, slant an analysis to fit the bias of the policy maker who is to receive it. Policy makers are ill served by such analysis, but most of them nevertheless welcome information that tends to reinforce their existing predilections. President Lyndon B. Johnson was so dissatisfied with what the CIA was saying about the Dominican Republic in 1965 that he sent the FBI to investigate as well. In 1984, the national intelligence officer for Latin America resigned—after thirty-six years in the CIA—because, he said, of pressure put on him by CIA Director Casey to tailor an estimate about Mexico to fit the Reagan administration's Central America policy.[2] On the other hand, during the Vietnam War, the CIA under Helms resisted, for the most part successfully, pressures from the Johnson administration to distort its reports.

Counterintelligence

The oversight and control problems associated with counterintelligence mainly have to do with safeguarding and respecting the constitutional rights of U.S. citizens. There has sometimes been a tendency to confuse dissent with subversion. Both Presidents Johnson and Nixon suspected that some of the opposition to the Vietnam War was being inspired from abroad, specifically from the Soviet Union. If true, this would have been a classic case of Soviet covert action; but despite considerable efforts, the intelligence community was unable to find supporting evidence. In the process of looking for evidence, however, the CIA violated the legislative injunction against domestic activities, and the FBI, under its legendary director, J. Edgar Hoover, conducted unwarranted surveillance of innocent Americans. In 1988, it was revealed that the FBI had committed the same offenses against opponents of the Reagan administration's policy in El Salvador.

Covert Action

Of all the aspects of the intelligence community, covert action is the most troublesome for people concerned with problems of oversight and control. It is the area in which the community becomes an instrument of policy. It raises three main questions: Should it be done at all? What happens if it is exposed? And is it in furtherance of an objective that most Americans support?

Should It Be Done? Although covert action has been in the U.S. foreign policy tool chest for more than forty years, the argument continues over whether it is a tool that the United States ought to use. More than any other area of foreign policy, it raises the question of whether the end justifies the means. It involves actions that frequently are illegal in another country if not in the United States itself, and that are almost always unethical. These are the kinds of actions that have come to be known as dirty tricks: overthrowing a government, spreading lies to discredit a person, bribing a newspaperman for a favorable story or editorial. Many people find these and similar actions distasteful.

What Happens If It Is Exposed? If it is decided that a given covert action is an appropriate activity for a country like the United States, then it has to be determined whether the action can be carried out in secret, or at least without the role of the United States becoming known, and what the consequences of exposure might be. The revelation of the U.S. role in the Bay of Pigs operation was a severe embarrassment to the Kennedy administration.

Generally speaking, the larger the action and the more people who know about it, the greater the chances of exposure will be. Actions involving paramilitary forces are especially risky. Not only do they typically involve many people; the scale of activity alone will lead observers to ask questions about sponsorship and support.

Is It Acceptable to Public Opinion?   The justification for covert action, if there is one, is that it enables the United States to accomplish a foreign policy objective that could not be accomplished otherwise. It is implicit in this rationale that the objective is one on which there is general national agreement. If this consensus is lacking, then covert action becomes not merely a tool of foreign policy, but also a way for presidents to avoid public debate over controversial policies. Presidents find it difficult to resist the temptation to use covert action in this way. It is a good deal easier for them to tell the CIA to do something in secret than it is to justify the action to a perhaps skeptical Congress or to answer questions about it before a hostile press corps. But when presidents use covert action to bypass public debate, they subvert the democratic policy-making process.

There is, of course, a kind of Catch-22 here: Questioning an action in public makes the action impractical. But the policy that the action is designed to further can be debated in public, and it frequently is. There was no lack of public discussion of U.S. policy toward Fidel Castro's Cuba in 1961. But no public proposal was made to invade Cuba with a force of anti-Castro exiles. Similarly, ten years later, President Salvador Allende of Chile had little support among the U.S. public, but many people would have argued that, if left alone, he would fall without being pushed by the CIA. Most recently, the Reagan administration was rocked in 1986-1987 by the Iran-contra scandal, in which covert action was used to sell arms to Iran, contrary to a long-standing policy against it, and to provide aid to the contras opposing the Sandinista government of Nicaragua, despite an explicit legal provision forbidding it.

To deal with questions such as these, it has long been felt that there should be a mechanism independent of the intelligence community to oversee it and to act as a check on it. The National Security Act of 1947 provided such a mechanism in the form of the National Security Council. But the drafters of the National Security Act did not contemplate a large role for covert action. After President Harry S Truman left the White House, he expressed regret that the CIA had even been created: "I think it was a mistake. And if I'd known what was going to happen, I never would have done it." [3]

An inherent problem in relying on the NSC to control the CIA is that the NSC is the creature of the president; if the president wants to use the CIA covertly to avoid public debate, or to subvert established public policy, the NSC is powerless to stop him, unless its members resign in protest (which has never happened). Beginning with Eisenhower, presidents have sought independent outside advice and judgment about the intelligence community's activities. The entities supplying this advice and judgment have been variously named. During the Reagan administration, there were two: the Foreign Intelligence Advisory Board and the Intelligence Oversight Board, neither of which had any independent authority.

In the system of checks and balances which is the basis of the U.S. government, Congress is a principal check on the president. Congress, therefore, is the logical institution to serve as a check on the intelligence community as well. But Congress did not seriously concern itself with the problem for thirty years after creation of the CIA. Then, in the mid-1970s, it created intelligence committees with real powers of oversight.

That system lasted scarcely ten years before it, too, was proved ineffective by the Iran-contra affair, which left both the intelligence community and the oversight mechanism in such disarray as had rarely been seen. A system that had been carefully and laboriously constructed had failed, and thoughtful people at both ends of Pennsylvania Avenue were asking themselves what had gone wrong and how it could be put right. The rest of this chapter traces that experience.

The Era of Congressional Neglect

The National Security Act

The CIA was created by the National Security Act of 1947 (50 U.S.C. 403[d]). Of the agencies whose sole concerns are intelligence and covert action, it is the only one created by legislation (and, even at that, the principal purpose of the National Security Act was to establish the Department of Defense). The act made the CIA responsible to the president but put it under the general supervision of the National Security Council. It gave the director of the CIA the responsibility of coordinating the activities of the intelligence community as a whole, as well as managing the CIA.

Four other provisions are especially important for present purposes. First, the act says that the CIA "shall have no police, subpena, law-enforcement powers, or internal security functions." This restriction has generally been interpreted (perhaps too broadly) as meaning that the CIA is to conduct no domestic operations other than the administrative and analytical work that is performed in its headquarters. One of the factors that eventually prompted Congress to begin investigating the activities of intelligence agencies was the revelation that the CIA had collaborated with local police departments in investigating dissenters against U.S. involvement in the Vietnam War.

Second, the act provides that the director of central intelligence "shall be responsible for protecting intelligence sources and methods from unauthorized disclosure." Successive directors fell back on this as authority for refusing to respond to questions from Congress. It has also been used as the excuse for some of the CIA's domestic activities.

Third, the CIA is "to perform, for the benefit of the existing intelligence agencies, such additional services of common concern as the National Security Council determines can be more efficiently accomplished centrally." The National Security Council, as noted in Chapter 1, is the highest-level executive agency for advising the president on national security problems. Fourth, the CIA is to "perform such other functions and duties related to intelligence affecting the national security as the National Security Council may from time to time direct."

Since 1947, these catchall provisions have been invoked as authority for numerous intelligence operations, some of which have subsequently aroused public and legislative opposition. They form the basis of the legislative authority for the CIA's intelligence gathering and covert action.

Because the act establishing the Department of Defense was also used as the legislative vehicle for creating the CIA, an anomaly was created. Jurisdiction over the CIA in Congress, as to both legislation and oversight, was lodged in the armed services committees. The way the CIA does its job has at least as many political ramifications in the field of foreign policy as military ramifications in the field of defense, yet the foreign policy committees in Congress were effectively excluded from contact with the CIA for many years.

Following the passage of the National Security Act of 1947, subcommittees on the CIA, or on intelligence (they were variously named), were created in the armed services committees of both houses. The meetings of these subcommittees were not announced, and they were infrequent. A subcommittee sometimes went a whole year without meeting. Similar subcommittees were created in the two appropriations committees to provide funds for the intelligence agencies.

CIA officials have maintained that all of the agency's significant actions were reported to these oversight committees. The members of the committees, however, were clearly not prepared to ask questions and usually accepted whatever they were told about intelligence operations. Leverett Saltonstall, R-Mass., one of the senators concerned with intelligence activities for many years, once said flatly that there were some things about these activities that he did not want to know. Most legislators agreed with Saltonstall or, at the very least, were content to accept existing arrangements. So was the CIA, which operated only under the restraints imposed by the National Security Council; in the 1950s, even the nature of these restraints was a tightly held secret.

Some members of Congress, however, were uncomfortable about this situation. Their unease stemmed from a feeling that the CIA was inadequately supervised, that Congress was shirking its responsibilities, and that sooner or later this state of affairs would cause trouble for the United States abroad.

One of those most deeply concerned about this possibility was Sen. Mike Mansfield, D-Mont., who later became majority leader and later still ambassador to Japan, in which position he had the responsibility of overseeing intelligence operations in that country. For a number of years after he came to the Senate in 1953, Mansfield introduced resolutions to create a CIA oversight committee. The only time he was ever able to get a Senate vote on his resolution was in 1956, when it was rejected 27-59. Ten years later, the Senate effectively killed a somewhat different resolution with the same purpose by voting 61-28 to refer it to the Armed Services Committee. On the face of it, things had not changed very much in a decade.

An important factor at work throughout this period was trenchantly described in 1971 by Francis Wilcox, former chief of staff of the Senate Foreign Relations Committee and a former assistant secretary of state:

> What is basically involved is something it pains the Senate to talk about—personality differences and bureaucratic jealousies. To be blunt about it, and perhaps to overstate it, neither the CIA nor the people who now watch over it fully trust the people who want to watch over it; and the people who want to watch over it do not fully trust either the agency or its present watchers.[4]

Although the votes in 1956 and 1966 were almost identical, the underlying concerns in the Senate had changed. By 1966, evidence had accumulated that intelligence operations or covert actions could have adverse foreign policy repercussions. Two particularly sensitive situations deserve special mention.

The U-2 Incident

The program of U-2 flights over the Soviet Union was developed in the 1950s to give the United States an aerial reconnaissance capability by flying above the range of Soviet antiaircraft weapons and using what were then sophisticated cameras. The intelligence it produced was remarkable and valuable. In May 1960, on the eve of a scheduled summit conference, the U-2 developed a mechanical problem during one of its flights and had to descend to a lower altitude. The plane was shot down inside the Soviet Union, and its pilot was captured. After an initial period of confusion and contradiction, President Eisenhower admitted that the plane's purpose was espionage, and Soviet Premier Khrushchev angrily canceled the summit meeting.

The Senate Foreign Relations Committee held extensive hearings about the incident in closed session and published a censored version. In 1982, the committee published the most significant deletions that had been made in 1960, as well as the full transcript of its seven closed-door debates.[5] Administration witnesses had refused to answer the key question: What was the plane looking for the day it was shot down? The answer was crucial to a determination of whether the intelligence that it hoped to acquire was sufficiently important to justify the political risk of failure on the eve of a summit. It was also crucial to a determination of what would have been lost if the flight had been postponed until after the summit. Nevertheless, the administration was more forthcoming than it had previously been with respect to intelligence matters.

The Foreign Relations Committee's review raised disturbing questions about the extent to which foreign policy consequences were taken—or not taken—into account in the process of approving intelligence operations. A program consisting of several U-2 flights over a period of months had been personally approved by the president, but he had not concerned himself with individual flights within the overall program. The flight that was shot down was scheduled on technical considerations of the weather without regard to the political considerations of the approaching summit conference. Furthermore, the success of previous flights had bred complacency.

The Bay of Pigs

By 1960, the Eisenhower administration became convinced that if the Castro regime survived much longer in Cuba, it would so consolidate itself that it could never be dislodged, and Soviet power would thus be established in the Caribbean. At that time, such a prospect seemed totally unacceptable. Accordingly, plans were made for a covert action in which the CIA would train and support a group of Cuban exiles to overthrow Castro.

The plans and training were well advanced when the Kennedy administration took office in January 1961. After some hesitation, President Kennedy gave the go-ahead, and an invasion was launched at the Bay of Pigs in April 1961. It promptly ended in a disastrous defeat, with the U.S. involvement clearly revealed.

Again the consequences were primarily political—acute embarrassment for the United States—and again it was the Foreign Relations Committee, not Armed Services, that investigated. The closed hearings, in which the executive branch cooperated, went on for weeks. They proved mainly that President Kennedy had received, and acted on the basis of, some very bad advice. The hearings did serve, however, to increase senatorial skepticism of the intelligence community and of the methods by which it was supervised. (The Bay of Pigs incident also increased Kennedy's skepticism along the same lines; he shortly moved to improve White House control over intelligence activities.)

It also developed that the only good advice Kennedy received about the Bay of Pigs undertaking had come from Congress, but not through any established channel for congressional-executive communication. Because of a combination of circumstances—the most important being the personal relationship between Kennedy and Sen. J. William Fulbright, D-Ark., then chairman of the Foreign Relations Committee—the president invited Fulbright to join him in a meeting with his advisers to discuss the projected invasion of Cuba before the decision was made to proceed. Fulbright was the only person present to speak against the plan.

One other incident is also worth mentioning, as an indication of congressional inconsistency in approaching oversight. The Foreign Relations Committee, as noted, spent weeks rehashing the failure of the Bay of Pigs mission. After the success of U.S. policy in the Cuban missile crisis the following year, Secretary of State Dean Rusk all but begged the committee to investigate the performance of the intelligence community and of the administration in crisis management. The committee declined. The point is that Congress as a general rule tends to be more interested in investigating failures than successes.

The Beginning of Real Oversight

After these false starts, what prodded Congress out of its lethargy about overseeing the intelligence community was a series of events in the early and mid-1970s. One impetus was provided by revelations stemming from the Watergate affair. Other reasons were more directly related to developments in foreign policy.

Chile

In 1972, columnist Jack Anderson published internal documents of the International Telephone and Telegraph Company indicating that ITT had tried to persuade the CIA to intervene in Chilean politics in 1970 to prevent a socialist, Salvador Allende, from becoming president. The Senate Foreign Relations Committee responded by creating a Subcommittee on Multinational Corporations to investigate this report and also to conduct an in-depth study of multinational corporations in general.

A year later, in March 1973, the subcommittee held lengthy hearings, which revealed that ITT had indeed sounded the alarm all over Washington at the time of the Chilean elections in September 1970. The company had even offered to furnish as much as $1 million for the expenses of clandestine intervention but had found no takers. Past and present CIA officials testified that the agency had a policy of not accepting contributions from private businesses. John McCone, a director of ITT and a former director of the CIA, was one of the officials who testified to this effect. (In 1980, Congress passed legislation specifically authorizing the director of central intelligence to accept gifts, bequests, and property on behalf of the CIA.)

Notwithstanding ITT's efforts, Allende had been elected and had taken office. He soon encountered a sea of troubles, most of them of his own making but some of them complicated by a cutoff of U.S. credits, both private and public. The Nixon administration never made any secret of its dislike of Allende but maintained that the policies it was following to impede his regime were all open and aboveboard.

In September 1973, six months after the ITT hearings, Allende was overthrown in a bloody coup d'état. The unseen hand of the CIA was again suspected and again denied. CIA Director Colby testified on the matter before the Subcommittee on Western Hemisphere Affairs of the Senate Foreign Relations Committee in the fall of 1973 and before the CIA subcommittee of the House Armed Services Committee in the spring of 1974. Colby reported in greater detail than had ever been done before (but still incompletely) about CIA activities in Chile. According to his account, the agency's principal activity was the covert funneling of subsidies to certain political parties, newspapers, and groups opposing Allende. The objective was to enable the opposition to survive until the next regularly scheduled Chilean presidential election in 1976, at which time it was hoped that a non-socialist candidate could be elected (since Allende was constitutionally unable to succeed himself). In September 1974, the substance of Colby's hitherto secret testimony in the House was leaked to the press.

The Hughes-Ryan Amendment

Partly inspired by the Chile affair, Congress used the 1974 foreign aid bill as a vehicle to require that covert actions (as distinguished from purely intelligence operations) conducted "by or on behalf of" the CIA be reported to "the appropriate committees of the Congress." The amendment by which this was accomplished was the handiwork of Sen. Harold E. Hughes, D-Iowa (a member of the Armed Services Committee), and Rep. Leo J. Ryan, D-Calif., and was known by their names.

The Hughes-Ryan amendment designated the Senate Foreign Relations and the House Foreign Affairs committees as two of the committees to receive the reports; the other "appropriate committees" were not specified. By general agreement, they were defined to be the Appropriations and Armed Services committees in each house and later—after they were established in 1976 and 1977—the two intelligence committees as well. In 1980, Congress provided that only the intelligence committees would receive the reports, and in especially sensitive cases only the chairmen and the ranking minority members, along with the Speaker and minority leader of the House and the majority and minority leaders of the Senate.

In addition, the Hughes-Ryan amendment tightened administrative control of covert action by requiring, as a precondition, that the president find "that each such operation is important to the national security of the United States." The report to the committees was to be made "in a timely fashion" and was to include "a description and scope" of the activity.[6] The CIA had long maintained that it already reported covert actions to its oversight subcommittees in the Appropriations and Armed Services committees; but given the infrequency of the meetings of those subcommittees, the timeliness of the reports could be questioned.

The executive branch never liked the Hughes-Ryan amendment, even after its application was restricted to the two intelligence committees. Before that, much was made of the fact that the membership of the eight committees receiving the reports totaled 220. Telling this many people, it was said, was no way to keep a secret. In practice, not nearly that many people were told, or even wanted to be. In the Senate Foreign Relations Committee, for example, the reports were received orally from the CIA director by the chairman and the ranking minority member. The committee's chief of staff was present and was authorized to brief any other committee member who asked. Not many did. If a member disapproved of a particular covert action, his recourse was to present his objections, not to the CIA but to higher political authority—namely, the State Department or the president.

Angola

A covert operation that aroused a number of objections involved the African country of Angola. At the end of 1974, Angola, then a Portuguese colony, was on the verge of achieving independence after fourteen years of guerrilla warfare. Differing tribal loyalties and ideological disputes sharply divided the political factions; agreements among them concerning the government that was to replace Portuguese authority proved to be short-lived.

U.S. covert activity in Angola began in a very small way, mainly through the payment of a cash subsidy to one of the non-Marxist leaders and his group. Another faction was receiving support from the Soviet Union and later from Cuba, and yet another from South Africa. As the fighting intensified, U.S. involvement increased, ultimately entailing a budget of millions of dollars and the shipment of supplies as well. Senatorial concern grew correspondingly and was expressed in meetings with officials of the State Department and the CIA. To the embarrassment of the senators and the irritation of the CIA, substantial portions of what transpired at some of these meetings were leaked to the press. As a result, Director Colby fired off a letter to the committee that implicitly threatened to stop cooperating with it. "Publicity of this sort," Colby wrote, "obviously casts serious doubts on my ability to provide sensitive information to the Foreign Relations Committee, its subcommittees, and its staff."

While this was going on, the Defense Department appropriations bill for fiscal year 1976, with its hidden funds for the CIA, was making its way through Congress. Sen. John Tunney, D-Calif., who had not been privy to any of the secret briefings from the CIA but who read the newspapers, offered an amendment prohibiting use of any funds in the bill "for any activities involving Angola directly or indirectly." It was agreed to by a vote of 54-22 on December 19, and the House concurred, 323-99, on January 27, over the strenuous objections of the Ford administration.

The Tunney amendment applied only to the funds in that particular appropriation bill. In 1976, Congress approved an amendment offered by Sen. Dick Clark, D-Iowa, to a foreign aid bill prohibiting as a matter of general law any kind of assistance for any kind of military or paramilitary operation in Angola. Angola had by then received its independence, and after bitter fighting a communist government was installed that was supported by the Soviet Union and Cuba. Opposition groups launched a guerrilla war against the government.

In 1980, the Clark amendment was modified to allow aid to the Angolan rebels if Congress approved; that was essentially a meaningless concession to the amendment's opponents. By 1985, however, support for the anticommunist groups—fueled, perhaps by sympathy for the Nicaraguan and Afghan rebels—had grown so much that the Clark amendment was repealed altogether. The key vote in the House was 236-185 on an amendment offered by Rep. Samuel S. Stratton, D-N.Y., to the foreign aid authorization bill, and perhaps the turning point in the debate was an emotional appeal on behalf of the Angolan rebels by Rep. Claude Pepper, D-Fla., the oldest member of the House and chairman of the Rules Committee. Almost forty years before, Pepper, then a senator, had been one of the strongest opponents of President Truman's Greek-Turkish aid program to help those countries oppose communist insurgencies. Among the things that had happened in the meantime was the exponential growth of Cuban-Americans in Pepper's Miami congressional district. These strongly anticommunist constituents were disturbed by the presence in Angola of twenty thousand Cuban troops supporting the government.

Following repeal of the Clark amendment, debate shifted to the question of the kind of aid, if any, that was to be provided to the Angolan rebels. Proposals for overt aid were defeated as the 1985 session of Congress ended. President Reagan said publicly that he preferred that aid be covert, and the State Department tended to oppose all aid on the grounds that it would interfere with negotiations then in progress toward a political settlement. By this time, the Angolan faction originally supported by the United States had faded away, and U.S. support was transferred to the group backed by South Africa, which was known as UNITA.

After the House had voted to repeal the Clark amendment, Rep. Lee Hamilton, D-Ind., chairman of the Intelligence Committee, had assured the opponents of repeal that any request for covert aid would be subject to the normal procedures—that is, it would be submitted to the Intelligence Committee, which, while it could not block the aid, could certainly raise objections to it. However, Hamilton reckoned without the CIA contingency fund. This is a secret fund, variously estimated to contain between $50 million and $500 million. Some of this money was used to start an Angolan program in February 1986, when President Reagan ordered the CIA to provide up to $15 million in arms, ammunition, and supplies to UNITA, whose leader, Jonas Savimbi, had been in the United States actively lobbying for aid.

The House Intelligence Committee put a provision in the intelligence authorization bill for fiscal 1987 that barred aid to the Angolan guerrillas unless the matter had been publicly debated and approved by Congress. This meant, of course, that any aid would have to be overt instead of covert. In its report, the Intelligence Committee succinctly stated the problem with covert action when it said the president "cannot expect sustained support for foreign policy initiatives, including covert action operations, that are generally unpopular or where a covert action mechanism can be viewed as having been chosen to avoid public debate or a congressional vote on the matter." [7] Nevertheless, the Angolan prohibition was deleted in the House by a vote of 229-186. The Intelligence Committee tried again in a separate bill, but this one did not even reach the House floor, mainly because of the opposition of Rep. Pepper and Rep. Dante Fascell, who was also from Miami and was chairman of the House Foreign Affairs Committee.

Congressional Investigations

The creation of the intelligence committees followed separate investigations of the intelligence community in the House and the Senate. In each instance, the focus was on past misdeeds, and thus the committees evolved from a background in which there was a heavy emphasis on preventing mistakes, principally in covert action.

The Church Committee

Early in 1975, by a vote of 82-4, the Senate established the Select Committee to Study Governmental Operations with Respect to Intelligence Activities (a name that the resolution creating it said was given "for convenience of expression"!).[8] It was headed by Sen. Frank Church, D-Idaho, who had presided over the investigation of CIA-ITT activities in Chile. Between January 1975 and April 1976, the Church committee published seventeen volumes of reports and hearings dealing with everything from domestic intelligence activities of questionable legality to assassination plots directed against foreign leaders.

The Church committee soon discovered how extraordinarily difficult it is, even with full access to files and records, to learn the full truth about covert actions in the past. This applies to both executive management and legislative oversight of the intelligence community. Intelligence is a highly compartmentalized business. In order to enhance security and to preserve plausible deniability, intelligence officials are given to speaking, and especially to writing, in circumlocutions. And generally they write very little, so as not to leave a paper trail.

It was not until after the Church committee had completed its work that the facts about CIA involvement in Chile came out—and even then no one could be sure it was the full story. The State Department, the American embassy in Santiago, and eventually Congress knew about CIA subsidies for Allende's opponents; but until the Church committee's investigation, they did not know that President Nixon had directly instructed CIA Director Helms to "destabilize" the situation in Chile so much that Allende could not continue in office. For denying the existence of these activities before the Foreign Relations Committee, Helms was subsequently fined $2,000 when he pleaded nolo contendere to charges of failing to testify "fully . . . and accurately." What emerged from the Church investigation was that, although in a technical sense the CIA might not have been involved in the coup that overthrew Allende, its whole course of action in Chile for three years had been designed to create a situation in which such a coup would occur.

The Church committee's work had two principal results: the creation of a standing committee on intelligence, oriented more to continuing oversight than to investigations of past misdeeds; and a recommendation for legislative charters for all intelligence agencies, spelling out permissible and impermissible behavior. Drafting these charters has proven to be more difficult than it once appeared. By 1988, they had still not been written.

The Pike Committee

The work of the Church committee in the Senate had been quiet but ultimately sensational. In contrast, the House was kept in turmoil for a year and a half over how to go about substantially the same job. The House created a Select Committee on Intelligence in February 1975, with Rep. Lucien Nedzi, D-Mich., as chairman, but its members quarreled among themselves so much that in July the House took the unusual step of abolishing the committee and creating another one with the same name and the same terms of reference but without some of the more contentious members. The new committee was headed by Rep. Otis Pike, D-N.Y. It spent the fall of 1975 wrangling with the administration over access to classified documents.

On January 23, 1976, the Pike committee voted 9-4 to release its final report, despite administration objections that it contained material that should remain classified. Three days later, before it was actually released, a summary of the report appeared in the *New York Times*. On January 29, the House took the extraordinary action of voting 246-124 to prohibit the committee from releasing a report containing classified material until it had been "certified by the President as not containing information which would adversely affect the intelligence activities of the Central Intelligence Agency" or other agencies.[9] Then, on February 11, the *Village Voice* in New York published a twenty-four-page supplement containing lengthy excerpts from the report. Two days later, CBS correspondent Daniel Schorr confirmed that it was he who gave a copy of the report to the *Voice*.

Schorr's refusal to say where he got the copy set off yet another acrimonious investigation. The House Committee on Standards of Official Conduct tried, and predictably failed, to determine Schorr's source. In the meantime, the Pike committee made these recommendations:

- that the House create a permanent intelligence committee;
- that the president put an overall figure for the intelligence community in his budget;
- that transfers and reprogramming of intelligence funds be subject to the approval of the intelligence and other committees;
- that the General Accounting Office be empowered to investigate and audit intelligence agencies on the same basis as other agencies;
- that a Foreign Operations Subcommittee be created by statute in the National Security Council to deal with covert action and hazardous collection of intelligence;
- that the intelligence community be reorganized to separate the director of central intelligence from the CIA and the National Security Agency from the Defense Department, as well as to abolish the Defense Intelligence Agency;
- that there be no recruitment by the intelligence community of American citizens associated with religious, educational, or communications organizations.

The Permanent Oversight Committees

In accordance with the recommendations of the Church and Pike committees, the Senate created a Select Committee on Intelligence in

1976, and the House established a Permanent Select Committee on Intelligence in 1977. Both resolutions provided for overlapping memberships with the Appropriations, Armed Services, Foreign Relations (Foreign Affairs in the House), and Judiciary committees, the last being included because of its jurisdiction over the FBI. In the Senate, two members from each of these committees (one Democrat and one Republican) are to be assigned to intelligence; in the House, only one. The vice chairman of the Senate committee is elected by its minority members; no provision for a vice chairman was made in the House. In both House and Senate, the majority and minority leaders of the full chambers are ex officio members without votes.

Continuous service of a member is limited on both committees—to eight years in the Senate, to six years in the House. This limitation is designed as a safeguard against co-option, the subtle process by which the overseen persuade their overseers to become their handmaidens. Co-option is particularly noticeable among the regulatory agencies of the government, and it has existed, at one time or another and to one degree or another, in the relations between most other congressional committees and the executive agencies for whose legislation they are responsible. Prior to 1975, it certainly existed with respect to the Appropriations and Armed Services committees, on the one hand, and the CIA on the other.

Sen. Daniel K. Inouye, D-Hawaii, the first chairman of the Senate Select Committee on Intelligence, resigned as chairman (while continuing on the committee) at the end of 1977. In a report to the Senate, he stated:

> I believe rotation of Chairmanship is the best way to assure that the combination of close detailed work with the agencies and a vigilant attitude toward their activities can be maintained. I am resigning because I believe it is important for the Senate and for the intelligence agencies who are under the charge of the Select Committee to have overseers who come to the issues as I have come to them—with an open, fresh and relatively objective point of view, so necessary for the important task of oversight.[10]

Inouye was succeeded by Sen. Birch Bayh, D-Ind., who served as chairman for three years. Bayh was defeated in the 1980 election, and Sen. Barry Goldwater became chairman in 1981, when the Republicans took control of the Senate in the 97th Congress. Sen. Dave Durenberger, R-Minn., became chairman in 1985, and Sen. David L. Boren, D-Okla., in 1987. In the House, Rep. Edward P. Boland, D-Mass., was chairman of the Intelligence Committee from its creation until 1984. (The six-year limitation on service of the committee did not go into effect until 1979.) Boland was succeeded by Representative Hamilton, who in turn was succeeded in 1987 by Rep. Louis Stokes, D-Ohio.

At the beginning of Goldwater's term as chairman, there were several signs that the Senate committee had indeed been co-opted. Goldwater himself said in an interview that he did not believe the committee should exist, and in the Senate that he would have preferred that there be no congressional oversight of intelligence agencies. "The Russians have a very fine system. . . . No part of their government has any idea of what is going on [in the KGB, the Soviet secret service]. That is the way . . . I wish it were here in our country, but it is not." [11] Goldwater brought in, as staff director, John Blake, who had previously worked for the CIA for thirty-two years, holding positions as high as acting deputy director. Blake was succeeded by Robert R. Simmons, who had worked for the CIA for ten years before moving to Capitol Hill to become legislative assistant to Sen. John H. Chafee, R-R.I. Conversely, the committee's senior budget officer left in 1982 to become comptroller of the CIA. (This sort of staff movement back and forth does not *necessarily* mean co-option or even an undesirably close relationship. There are many examples of committee staff members drawn from executive agencies who are extremely valuable because they know what questions to ask and where to look in the bureaucratic maze. In the case of both intelligence committees, however, even a former CIA director, Stansfield Turner, concluded that "the Congress is now co-opted.")[12]

Intelligence Appropriations

Both the House and the Senate Intelligence committees get their real power from their jurisdiction over authorizations for appropriations for the intelligence agencies and from congressional rules that specifically prohibit appropriating funds that have not first been authorized. This means that the committees not only have access to information about the secret intelligence budget, but they also can approve or disapprove the budget in whole or in part.

Subcommittees of the Appropriations committees have always been in this position, of course, but the intelligence committees have taken the job more seriously. They consider the budget on a line-item basis—they vote separately on each major category of expenditure, including each covert-action project. The authorization bill resulting from this process is unique in that it says "funds are hereby authorized to be appropriated" but does not contain any figures. These are shown only in the committees' classified reports, which are made available to the Appropriations and Armed Services committees and to the executive branch. The published portions of the bill contain only the authorizations for the counterterrorism activities of the FBI, for the intelligence community staff, and for the CIA retirement and disability fund. The appropriations made pursuant to the authorizing legislation are still concealed in the Defense Department appropriation bill. It may fairly be said that since the establishment of the two intelligence committees, the intelligence budget has been subject to a more searching congressional review than ever before. The committees' ultimate power, of course, lies in withholding money or in prescribing the purposes for which it is to be spent.

On the face of it, Congress has delegated extraordinary powers to its intelligence committees. Yet it is no more power than the Appropriations and Armed Services committees once had and failed to exercise. (The Appropriations committees still have it; they actually provide the money that the intelligence committees authorize.)

Furthermore, any member can read the intelligence committees' classified reports, although few legislators actually do. If the member does not like them, he or she can precipitate a debate in closed session; if enough legislators are persuaded to agree, the committees can be overridden. This has never happened. Except for the fact that the debate would take place in closed session, the procedure is not significantly different from that followed with respect to any other issues considered by a House or Senate committee.

The Flow of Information

One of the more important consequences of the new relationship that was established between Congress and the intelligence community in the mid-1970s was a greatly improved flow of information to Congress. This put Congress on a much more nearly equal footing in dealing with other government agencies concerned with the making of foreign policy. It has also been a source of friction and tension between the CIA and the policy agencies, principally the State and Defense departments.

Twice while William Colby was CIA director (1973-1976), Secretary of State Henry Kissinger intervened to reduce the flow of information from the CIA to the Senate Foreign Relations Committee. The committee protested both times and the flow resumed, but once only after Senator Mansfield, who was majority leader at the time, threatened to take the matter to the president.

One of the earliest substantive intelligence bills that Congress considered would have imposed a requirement on the CIA to send Congress periodic intelligence digests and analyses. The bill was sponsored in the 1960s by Sen. John Sherman Cooper, R-Ky., who had been ambassador to India and thus in a position to observe intelligence from the executive-branch perspective. His bill was the subject of hearings before the Foreign Relations Committee, but it was ahead of its time. By the late 1980s, the flow of informtion about intelligence (not including covert action, however) seemed sufficiently institutionalized to survive most swings of the political pendulum.

Nicaragua

The roots of the Nicaraguan problem run deep into the history of that country and of its relations with the United States, but for our purposes, we may begin with the revolution that culminated in the overthrow of the dictatorial regime of Anastasio Somoza in the summer of 1979. Somoza was the last of a family dynasty that had greatly enriched itself while ruling Nicaragua with an iron hand for more than forty years. All the Somozas were friendly to the United States; the youngest was even a graduate of the U.S. Military Academy at West Point, and his wife was a U.S. citizen. Significantly, the principal faction in the ultimately successful revolutionary movement took its name after César Augusto Sandino, who was the leader of a rebel group against the U.S. marine occupation of Nicaragua in the 1920s and early 1930s.

As the revolution gathered momentum in 1978 and 1979, the United States distanced itself from Somoza and sought, with only partial success, to encourage the broadening of the revolutionary leadership so as to dilute radical Sandinista influence. In the summer of 1979, the Carter administration was also worried about getting the implementing legislation for the Panama Canal treaties through the House and was reluctant to offend Somoza's friends in that body, of whom the most prominent and influential was Rep. John M. Murphy, D-N.Y., chairman of the Merchant Marine and Fisheries Committee, which had primary jurisdiction. With the triumph of the revolution, the Carter administration adopted a policy of cooperative, friendly relations and of trying to help, in a modest way, in the recovery of the war-damaged Nicaraguan economy. Congress, on the other hand, delayed for nine months before passing a $75 million aid bill and then hedged it with restrictions. Many members were apprehensive of growing Cuban influence in Nicaragua (the fall of Somoza was followed by an influx of Cuban teachers, doctors, and technicians), and the leftist rhetoric of the Sandinistas caused some nervousness on Capitol Hill. U.S.-Nicaraguan relations began a long slide downhill.

The slide picked up momentum in January 1981 with the advent of the Reagan administration, which was less inclined than its predecessor to be cooperative; with growing evidence of Nicaraguan support for a leftist rebel movement in El Salvador; and with the continued drift of the Sandinistas to the left. As early as March 1981, CIA Director Casey reported to the Intelligence committees on a covert action aimed at protecting Nicaragua's neighbors, Honduras and Costa Rica, against the spread of revolution; more specifically, the action was intended to stop the flow of arms from Nicaragua through Honduras to the guerrilla movement in El Salvador.[13] By December, Casey's plan had evolved into a $19-million program to train and support a force of five hundred anti-

Sandinista Nicaraguans—the so-called contras—based in Honduras, with the objective of disrupting the flow of Cuban support through Nicaragua to the Salvadoran guerrillas.

By early 1982, some of this began to leak to the press. One of the unlearned lessons of the Bay of Pigs was the difficulty of maintaining the secrecy of operations involving large numbers of people. Also, as shown by both the Bay of Pigs and Angola, these operations tend to grow beyond what was intended. The Nicaraguan action started with five hundred men; by 1987, there were sixteen thousand.

The House Intelligence Committee became concerned enough to put a secret amendment in the fiscal 1983 intelligence authorization bill. It prohibited support for military activities "to any group or individual, not part of a country's armed forces, for the purpose of overthrowing the government of Nicaragua or provoking a military exchange between Nicaragua and Honduras." When the House considered the 1983 Defense Department appropriation bill, Rep. Tom Harkin, D-Iowa, offered an amendment that would also have banned assistance to such groups "for the purpose of . . . carrying out military activities in or against Nicaragua." [14] Chairman Boland of the Intelligence Committee then offered as a substitute the text of the amendment that was already secretly in the intelligence authorization bill. The Boland amendment passed by a vote of 411-0 and became law.

The next year, another Boland amendment was attached to the fiscal 1984 defense appropriations bill. It provided that no more than $24 million could be used "for the purpose or which would have the effect of supporting, directly or indirectly, military or paramilitary operations in Nicaragua by any nation, group, organization, movement or individual." [15] That money was spent by May 1984, and Congress approved no more military aid for the contras until October 1986. Thus, there was a period of seventeen months when no government money was available for such aid.

Meanwhile, the Reagan administration's early anti-Sandinista bent had become an obsession. At first, the administration said U.S. policy was limited to interdicting supplies to El Salvador, even though the Nicaraguan rebels themselves made no bones about their own intention to overthrow the government. Later, Reagan said aid to the contras would stop when the Sandinistas "keep their promise and restore the democratic rule and have elections," and that "the United States does not seek to destabilize or overthrow the government of Nicaragua; nor to impose or compel any particular form of government there." [16] But these statements were made in the context of a flow of strident rhetoric about the danger that Nicaragua represented as a Western Hemisphere outpost of Soviet communism. At a news conference in February 1985, when Reagan was asked if U.S. policy was to remove the Sandinista government, he replied, "Well, remove it in the sense of its present structure, in which it is a communist, totalitarian state." He added that the United States would ease the pressure "if they'd say: 'Uncle,' or 'All right and come on back into the revolutionary government and let's straighten this out.' " [17]

In April 1984, it was reported that the CIA had supervised the mining of Nicaraguan harbors by contra commandos, and a storm of criticism erupted in Congress. Complaining that the Senate Intelligence Committee had not been told about this, Senator Goldwater wrote a vituperative letter to Casey and gave copies to the press. Representative Boland admitted that the House Intelligence Committee had been told, and a member of the Senate committee said privately that that committee had also been told "but you had to be listening carefully to hear it."

Nicaragua brought suit against the United States in the International Court of Justice (World Court). The Reagan administration announced that it did not recognize the court's jurisdiction, though the United States had accepted (and had urged other countries to accept) the court's jurisdiction for almost forty years. The court found in favor of Nicaragua, which was represented, among other lawyers, by Professor Abram Chayes of the Harvard Law School, who had been legal adviser to the State Department in the Kennedy administration.

The combination of the harbor mining, the World Court decision, and the frenetic efforts to win U.S. public support for the contras increased suspicion and distrust of the administration in Congress. The distrust was such that during the summer of 1985, when all but humanitarian aid to the contras was banned, members of the intelligence committees asked pointed questions about whether the ban was being complied with. They received categorical—but false—assurances that it was.

The Iran-Contra Affair

Over the course of several months beginning in October 1986, a series of theretofore secret activities related to the Nicaraguan rebels emerged into public view. These activities—which, together with their aftermath, came to be known as the Iran-contra affair—were essentially of three kinds. First, as public funds for the contras were exhausted, the administration turned to private donors and even to foreign governments for contributions. Second, in conjunction with the government of Israel, arms (mainly antiaircraft and antitank missiles) were secretly sold to Iran by U.S. officials or persons acting on their behalf, at a time when such sales were prohibited by the United States. The immediate objective of this action was to secure the release of U.S. hostages being held by pro-Iranian groups in Lebanon. A longer-range objective was to establish a relationship with putative moderates in the Iranian government. Third, some of the proceeds of the arms sales were diverted to the contras through secret Swiss bank accounts.

The initial revelations set off a number of investigations. The first, by Attorney General Edwin Meese III, was conducted hurriedly over a weekend; it uncovered the first evidence of the contra diversion. President Reagan then appointed a Special Review Board, headed by former senator John Tower, R-Texas; the other members were former senator and former secretary of state Edmund Muskie, and Brent Scowcroft, who had been President Ford's national security affairs adviser. The Senate Intelligence Committee also conducted an investigation. Finally, the House and Senate both created special committees: in the House, the Select Committee to Investigate Covert Arms Transactions with Iran, and in the Senate, the Select Committee on Secret Military Assistance to Iran and the Nicaraguan Opposition. The committees were headed, respectively, by Representative Hamilton and Senator Inouye. They held joint hearings in 1987 and issued a joint report.

Meanwhile, an independent counsel was appointed under the Ethics in Government Act to investigate whether any crimes had been committed.

The activities of the Iran-contra affair were managed and directed by the staff of the National Security Council (see Chapter 1), principally Vice Adm. John M. Poindexter, who was national security adviser during most of this time, and Marine Lt. Col. Oliver L. North, an NSC staff member. North worked largely through private individuals recruited for that purpose. Various officials of the State Department and the CIA played a subordinate role. Participation by the Defense Department was minimal.

The report of the congressional committees that investigated the affair said it "was characterized by pervasive dishonesty and inordinate secrecy." [18] All the established processes of the government were ignored or bypassed. The regular procedure for considering covert action in the NSC was not followed. The affair went forward despite the strongly stated opposition of the secretaries of state and defense. The Tower Commission found that "on one or more occasions Secretary Shultz may have been actively misled by VADM Poindexter." [19]

At the insistence of the CIA, the president was given a document to sign that gave a color of legality to the Iranian arms sales. This was a presidential "finding" that the secret sales were "important to the national security." The law requires such a finding before a covert action can be undertaken; in this case, the finding was signed retroactively—after the action had been taken. The law also requires that it be reported to Congress "in timely fashion"; in this case, the finding specifically ordered the CIA director not to report it to Congress.

Poindexter maintained that Congress had no right to legislate restrictions that applied to the president or his staff, strongly implying that the president was above the law. He readily admitted that he withheld information from Congress and directed others to do the same: "Our objective here all along was to withhold information." [20] His reason was simply that if Congress had known, it might have objected and interfered with the policy. North went further and held Congress responsible for making the whole operation necessary in the first place: "The Congress is to blame because of the fickle, vacillating, unpredictable, on-again-off-again policy toward the ... contras." [21] In other words, if Congress had given the president what he wanted to begin with, the president's staff would not have had to controvert the will of Congress. That attitude would relegate Congress to a role of appropriating money on request, without asking questions.

Even when the NSC staff encountered objections from the secretaries of state and defense, it went ahead anyway. Although some of the CIA bureaucracy raised objections, North said Casey was excited by the idea of a permanent "off-the-shelf" covert-action capability that would be so secret it could be controlled only by those who had access to the secret numbers of Swiss bank accounts. (Casey himself could not be questioned. He underwent brain surgery in December 1986 and died in May 1987.) The staff took special pains to deceive Congress. Poindexter kept the contra diversion even from the president himself.

The Tower Commission's principal recommendations emphasized maintaining the integrity of the policy-making process and the centrality of the role of the national security adviser in ensuring that the president had the benefit of dissenting views.

The congressional committees produced a report that was subscribed to by all the Democrats and two of the four Senate Republicans, William S. Cohen of Maine and Paul S. Trible, Jr., of Virginia. The other Republicans issued a dissenting minority report. There were also thirteen sets of additional views issued by individual members or groups of members.

The principal conclusion of the majority report was:

Covert actions should be consistent with publicly defined U.S. foreign policy goals. Because covert operations are secret by definition, they are of course not openly debated or publicly approved. So long as the policies which they further are known, and so long as they are conducted in accordance with law, covert operations are acceptable. Here, however, the Contra covert operation was carried out in violation of the country's public policy as expressed in the Boland Amendment; and the Iran covert operation was carried out in violation of the country's stated policy against selling arms to Iran or making concessions to terrorists. These were not covert actions, they were covert policies; and covert policies are incompatible with democracy. [22]

The recommendations in the majority report, like those in the Tower Commission report, generally focused on process. The majority said, among other things, that the texts of presidential covert-action findings (instead of only summaries, as at present) should be transmitted to Congress; that findings should be more specific and should be circulated to the statutory members of the NSC; that the NSC adviser should not be an active military officer; and that a time limit should be placed on the service of active officers in other NSC capacities. The minority recommended tighter protection of security information and a line-item veto for foreign policy limitation amendments on appropriation bills.

One of the majority's recommendations was approved by the Senate, 71-19, in March 1988. It required that Congress be notified of covert actions in advance under "ordinary circumstances" and in any event no more than forty-eight hours after they had begun.

Members of the committees generally took the view that they had asked appropriate questions before the Iran-contra affair came to light (for example, was the Boland amendment being complied with?) but had received dishonest answers. This represented a breakdown of the system, for which Congress was not responsible. The remedy was to fix the system. This was the approach taken by the Framers of the Constitution in providing for checks and balances.

Other people with intelligence oversight experience on Capitol Hill were not willing to let Congress off so easily. In their view, the intelligence committees might have been asking appropriate questions, but they were not asking enough people. The affair was closely held in the NSC staff, but there were people in the CIA, and even in the State Department, who knew at least something about it but who were not asked. One knowledgeable source has stated that the affair was known to sixteen people at the State Department and fifty-five at the CIA.

In March 1988, Lawrence E. Walsh, the independent counsel who had been appointed to investigate the possibility of criminal actions in the affair, obtained an indictment against Poindexter, North, and two of their collaborators from outside the government, retired air force general Richard V. Secord and Secord's business associate, Albert Hakim. The indictment charged conspiracy to defraud the government, theft of government property (the diversion of profits from the Iranian arms sales), and wire fraud. In addition, Poindexter was charged with obstruction of Congress and with making false statements; North, with obstruction of Congress, obstruction of a presidential inquiry, obstruction of justice, making false statements, and accepting illegal gratuities; and Secord and Hakim, with conspiring to pay illegal gratuities to North at the time he was a government official.

A few days earlier, Robert McFarlane, Poindexter's predecessor as national security adviser, had pleaded guilty to charges of withholding information from Congress. (In April 1987, Carl Channell, one of the private fund-raisers involved in the affair, had pleaded guilty to defrauding the government by falsely representing that contributions for the purchase of arms for the contras were tax exempt.)

Meanwhile, events continued to unfold in Central America. In August 1987, President Reagan and House Speaker Jim Wright, D-Texas, joined in proposing a peace plan featuring a cease-fire, the institution of political freedoms in Nicaragua, and cessation of foreign aid to the contras by the United States and to the Sandinistas by the Soviet Union. Shortly afterward, however, President Oscar Arias of Costa Rica proposed a regional peace plan (for which he was subsequently awarded the Nobel Peace Prize) that was agreed to by the five Central American countries at a conference in Guatemala. This plan provided for, among other things, a cease-fire, civil and political rights, amnesty for political prisoners, reconciliation, and democratization, all to be carried out according to a specific time table.

Wright immediately endorsed the plan; the Reagan administration did not. The Organization of American States met in Washington in November. President Daniel Ortega of Nicaragua attended, as did several contra leaders and Miguel Cardinal Obando y Bravo, who had been trying to mediate between the contras and the Sandinistas. Wright saw them all, in a flurry of diplomatic activity that was unprecedented for a Speaker of the House and that caused unhappiness in the Reagan administration.

As the end of the 1987 session of Congress neared, the question of aid to the contras arose anew because the $100-million appropriation that Congress had made in 1986 was expiring. The House wanted to end all aid; the Senate was willing to continue a modest amount. A compromise was reached providing $14 million for January and February 1988, subject to several restrictions—among them, that there were to be no U.S. forces with the contras in Nicaragua or within twenty miles of the border and that the CIA contingency fund was not to be used without the approval of the Appropriations and Intelligence committees. There was also provision for another vote on aid in the House on February 3, 1988, and in the Senate on February 4. The report with these provisions squeaked through the House 209-208, and passed the Senate 59-30.

The votes in February came on a new administration request, this one for $36.25 million. The House turned it down, 211-219. In a vote which had only symbolic importance, the Senate approved it, 51-48.

The House leadership next presented a plan for $30.8 million in what it called "humanitarian" aid—food, clothing, shelter, and medical help. This was unsatisfactory to the administration because it included no military aid. Most Republicans voted against it, and it was defeated in the House, 208-216.

Later in March, representatives of the contras and the Sandinistas agreed to a cease-fire as well as a framework for continuing negotiations and for democratization in Nicaragua. This broke the impasse in Congress. On March 30, 1988, the House voted 345-70 for a $47.9 million six-month aid package, and the Senate followed suit the next day, 87-7.

Conclusion

No more dramatic example of the new congressional assertiveness with respect to foreign policy is to be found than that of the changed relationship between Congress and the intelligence community. Yet more than forty years after creation of the CIA, the precise nature of that relationship had not been defined. The efforts to agree on a definition in the 1980s were hampered by the extent to which Nicaragua dominated the discussion. The issue was highly partisan. Because the House was controlled by Democrats throughout the Reagan administration, the issue provided an unusual case in which the House was more assertive in foreign policy than the Senate.

Congress did not seriously bestir itself with regard to intelligence oversight until the mid-1970s, when revelations of gross abuses led to the establishment of the House and Senate Intelligence committees. The CIA during this period was led by directors who were generally cooperative with Congress. (One of them, George Bush, later became Reagan's vice president.) The 1970s marked the end of a cycle of abuse and reform in the intelligence community and in the oversight process.

The advent of the Reagan administration in 1981 marked the beginning of another cycle. William Casey, who was director of central intelligence from 1981 to 1987, firmly believed in an active CIA. In July 1987, Senator Trible revealed that Reagan had approved thirty-three covert actions. These numbers are ordinarily not announced, but that was certainly more than Reagan's immediate predecessors had approved. Even so, according to CIA Deputy Director Robert M. Gates, in September 1987 only "about three percent of CIA's people are involved in covert action." [23]

While process is important, it will not work unless the people in it want it to work. In the Iran-contra case, far from wanting it to work, those involved viewed it as an impediment. Both the president and Congress should have been paying closer attention to what was happening. The Iran-contra affair represented a triumph of ends over means. It remains to be seen whether this was an aberration brought on by a single-minded (and singularly ideological) administration or whether it will serve as a precedent for other actions. In the meantime, it has galvanized Congress into renewed oversight activity, and in this sense, it may be said to mark the end of a second cycle of abuse and reform.

Congress has responded to the recurrence of these cycles with investigations and with attempted remedies for the immediate problems. Yet, more than ten years after the Church committee report, there are still no statutory guidelines for the intelligence community, and important underlying questions such as these have not received the attention they deserve:

> Since covert action has caused so much trouble, should the United States abandon it altogether, or at least forswear its paramilitary form?
>
> Does the United States have a sensible system of setting priorities for the kinds of intelligence to be collected?
>
> Is there a sensible system for insulating analysts from pressures to shape analysis to fit policy?

Finally, there is the most fundamental question of all: How does a democratic society deal with secret activity engaged in by its government? Congress has not answered this question, but it has at least become more aware of the question's complexities.

Notes

1. S. Res. 21, 94th Cong., 1st sess., 1975, establishing the Select Committee to Study Governmental Operations with Respect to Intelligence Activities, which was chaired by Senator Church.
2. John Horton, "Why I Quit the CIA," *Washington Post,* January 2, 1985.
3. Merle Miller, *Plain Speaking: An Oral Biography of Harry S Truman* (New York: G. P. Putnam's Sons, 1973), 391.
4. Francis O. Wilcox, *Congress, the Executive, and Foreign Policy* (New York: Harper and Row, 1971), 86.
5. *Executive Sessions of the Senate Foreign Relations Committee* (Historical Series), 86th Cong., 2d sess. 1960, 12: 251-404 (released November 1982).
6. Sec. 662 of the Foreign Assistance Act of 1961 as amended, 22 U.S.C. 2422.
7. House Permanent Select Committee on Intelligence, *Intelligence Authorization Act, Fiscal 1987,* H. Rept. 99-690, pt. 1, 99th Cong., 2d sess., 1986, 7.
8. Senate, 94th Cong., 1st sess., 1975, S. Res. 21.
9. House, 94th Cong., 2d sess., 1976, H. Res. 982.
10. Senate Select Committee on Intelligence, *Report to the Senate on the Work of the Senate Select Committee on Intelligence,* n.d., 15.
11. *Congressional Record,* daily ed., 96th Cong., 2d sess., June 3, 1980, S6147.
12. Dispatch by George Lardner, Jr., *Washington Post,* December 9, 1981.
13. A good account of the development of the covert action program against Nicaragua is given in a dispatch by Don Oberdorfer and Patrick E. Tyler, *Washington Post,* May 8, 1983. See also House Permanent Select Committee on Intelligence, *Amendment to the Intelligence Authorization Act for Fiscal Year 1983,* H. Rept. 98-122, pt. 1, 98th Cong., 1st sess., 1983.

14. *Congressional Record,* 97th Cong., 2d sess., December 8, 1982, 29457.
15. P.L. 98-212 (approved December 8, 1983), Sec. 775.
16. As quoted in *New York Times,* March 29, 1984, and April 5, 1984.
17. Text of news conference in *New York Times,* February 22, 1985.
18. House Select Committee to Investigate Covert Arms Transactions with Iran and Senate Select Committee on Secret Military Assistance to Iran and the Nicaraguan Opposition, *Iran-Contra Affair,* H. Rept. 100-433, S. Rept. 100-216, 100th Cong., 1st sess., 1987, 13.
19. *The Tower Commission Report: The Full Text of the President's Special Review Board* (New York: Bantam Books and Times Books, 1987), 81.
20. House Select Committee, *Iran-Contra Affair,* 123, 142, 387.
21. *New York Times,* July 10, 1987.
22. House Select Committee, *Iran-Contra Affair,* 17.
23. Robert M. Gates, "CIA and the Making of American Foreign Policy," CIA press release (speech delivered at Princeton University, September 1987), 3.

CHAPTER 7

Trade Policy

The growing importance of economics in foreign policy has been a principal reason for the increase in congressional assertiveness. It is in connection with economic issues that foreign policy and domestic policy become inextricably mixed. Nowhere is this more evident than with respect to trade. This chapter examines congressional action on foreign trade as a case study of an area of foreign policy that has direct and immediate domestic effects.

The Constitution gives Congress two foundations for involving itself in foreign trade policy. First, Congress is given the power "to lay and collect Taxes, Duties, Imposts and Excises ..." (Art. I, Sec. 8). All bills for raising revenue must originate in the House of Representatives (Art. I, Sec. 7), and a great deal of foreign trade policy is concerned with duties, or tariffs, on imports, so this provision involves the House in foreign policy in a most important way. (The Senate can amend a revenue bill, but only after it has first passed the House.) Second, the Constitution gives Congress the power to "regulate Commerce with foreign Nations ..." (Art. I, Sec. 8). Thus, Congress has power over foreign trade even apart from its taxing power.

The last half-century has seen sweeping changes in Congress's approach to using these powers. In 1934, Congress gave up much of its power over trade by delegating it to the president. In 1974, Congress began to take this power back, in part because it was becoming clear that trade policy could not be considered in isolation from economic policy generally.

A serious problem that heightened congressional interest in foreign trade during the second term of the Reagan administration was the enormous excess of imports into the United States over exports out of the United States. It was generally recognized that this problem could not be resolved without also dealing with the government's budget deficit, the dollar's position in international markets, and even the U.S. economy's efficiency. Thus, the foreign and domestic questions were so interrelated that none could be considered in isolation from the others.

It is with respect to such questions that members of Congress most keenly feel conflicting pressures from their constituents and from larger interest groups. One group wants to be protected from imports of a particular product; another group wants to be able to buy the same product at the lowest possible price. Trade issues tend to bring out the parochialism in Congress.

Finally, the trade bill that was the subject of a great deal of congressional debate in 1987 and 1988, and that will be the focus of this chapter, illustrates how complex and cumbersome congressional organization and procedures are when Congress takes an integrated approach to interrelated but separate issues. Parts of the 1987-1988 bill came under the jurisdiction of thirteen committees in the House and eight in the Senate. The conference committee appointed to resolve the differences between the House and the Senate had 199 members.

Background

The tariff is one of the oldest issues in U.S. politics. In the beginning, when the government had far fewer sources of revenue than it has today (there was no income tax, for example), the question was whether tariffs should be levied for revenue only or whether they should be used to protect industry against foreign competition. In general, agricultural interests, whose power base was the great southern plantations, wanted low tariffs. Farmers exported what they produced and relied on imports for many of the things they used; they did not want the prices of these imports increased by tariffs. On the other hand, manufacturing interests, centered in the North, wanted protection from the competition of European goods, and tariffs provided that protection precisely by raising the prices of imports. Over time, the Democratic party became identified with low tariffs or free trade, and the Republican party became identified with high tariffs or protectionism.

The first revenue act passed by the first Congress in 1789 relied mainly on tariffs, and they remained the principal source of the federal government's revenue for more than a century. But that first act also declared in favor of protection as a principle. President George Washington had said that U.S. industries should be promoted and that the country should be "independent of others for essential, particularly for military, supplies." [1]

The strongest statement of the case for a protective tariff came from Alexander Hamilton, the first secretary of the treasury, in his famous *Report on Manufactures* in 1791. Among other things, he argued that tariffs would protect "infant industries" from competitors who were already established abroad. He also made the point that an expansion of industry would permit the employment of more women and children, thereby making them "more useful." [2] The House took no action on the Hamilton report, but the argument over the issues it raised has persisted. In the twentieth century, this argument has been taken up by many of the industrializing countries of the Third World, while voices have been raised in Congress to keep out the products allegedly made by child labor in Third World sweatshops.

As the U.S. economy became more complex during the nineteenth and twentieth centuries, so did congressional consideration of tariff bills. So fierce were the conflicting pressures that, following the deliberations on one such bill, Sen. Arthur Vandenberg, R-Mich., a member of the Finance Committee, expressed to a staff member the hope that "the Lord will take me before I have to deal with another tariff bill."

Protectionism reached its height with passage of the Smoot-Hawley Act of 1930, an omnibus trade measure named after its principal sponsors, the chairmen of the Senate Finance and House Ways and Means committees, respectively. Smoot-Hawley almost doubled tariffs, raising them from an average of 26 percent to an average of 50 percent. This provoked retaliation against U.S. goods by other countries, and world trade plummeted, intensifying the Great Depression.

Congress Yields Power

The Roosevelt administration, coming to office in 1933, adopted a new approach to trade, which was embodied in the Reciprocal Trade Act of 1934. This act authorized the president to negotiate reciprocal tariff reductions of up to 50 percent with other countries. Further, under what was known as the *most-favored-nation principle,* concessions granted to one country would automatically be extended to all others (though certain kinds of exceptions were allowed).

Thus, Congress would no longer write tariffs into law item by item. Instead, within limits set by Congress, tariffs would be negotiated with the nation's trading partners by the president or his representatives. This represented a considerable shift of power from the legislative to the executive branch, and that was one of the issues during congressional consideration of the 1934 act. Finally, and especially since the institution of the income tax in 1913, the tariff had become a minor source of revenue. It was now purely a question of trade policy.

By 1945, much of the tariff-cutting authority of the 1934 act had been used. But since the cuts were measured from the high levels

196 Invitation to Struggle

enacted in Smoot-Hawley, the 50 percent reduction did no more than return tariffs to their pre-1930 level. Hence, early in 1945, President Franklin D. Roosevelt asked for, and Congress gave him, authority to negotiate cuts of 50 percent in the existing rates. Later, the president was authorized to cut 15 percent from the 1955 level and in 1958 to cut 20 percent from that level. By 1961, 39 percent of U.S. imports were entering free of duty, and tariffs on the remainder averaged only 12 percent. The three decades from 1930 to 1960 had seen a major change in U.S. trade policy, almost all of it produced by presidents using authority delegated by Congress.

The General Agreement on Tariffs and Trade. World War II seriously disrupted international trade. Efforts to restore it in the immediate postwar period brought another major change in trade policy, not only for the United States but for its principal trading partners as well. In 1947, twenty-three major trading countries, including the United States, drew up a General Agreement on Tariffs and Trade (GATT). This provided the ground rules by which international trade has been conducted and trade agreements negotiated ever since. It came into force on January 1, 1948. By the end of 1987, ninety-five countries had adhered to it.

President Harry S Truman did not submit GATT to Congress. Instead, he committed the United States to it under the authority of the Trade Agreements Act of 1945. Many members of Congress complained that this was stretching the authority of that act, but Congress did not seriously challenge U.S. membership in GATT. Congress did, however, refuse to approve U.S. membership in the International Trade Organization (1948) and the Organization for Trade Cooperation (1955), both of which were intended as administrative bodies for GATT. Neither came into being, mainly because of U.S. nonparticipation. These were two of the few times between 1934 and 1974 that Congress asserted its trade powers in a major way.

The Reciprocal Trade Act of 1934 had moved trade policy from unilateral U.S. determination to bilateral negotiation. GATT made the negotiating forum multilateral. GATT's basic principle is nondiscrimination. Most-favored-nation treatment is fundamental to it; a trade concession extended to one nation must be extended to all nations. Thus, the phrase "most favored nation" becomes something of a misnomer. A nation receiving this treatment is really not favored above most other nations; it is the nation *not* receiving it that is discriminated *against*.

The thrust of GATT is trade liberalization, and there have been a number of multilateral negotiations under its auspices. By its fortieth anniversary on January 1, 1988, GATT had brought average tariffs down from 40 percent to 5 percent. Partly for this reason, there had been an increase in nontariff barriers and "voluntary" restraint agreements, and these new devices assumed greater importance in debates over trade policy.

Trade Expansion Act of 1962. During the 1930s, 1940s, and 1950s, the Reciprocal Trade Act of 1934 was extended eleven times. By itself, this fact indicated a degree of reluctance in Congress to delegate its authority to the president; the successive delegations were always for short periods. The eleventh extension expired in 1962. President John F. Kennedy decided to let it expire and to seek to replace it with a new bill, embodying a new trade policy.

The impetus for this change was the formation in 1958 of the European Common Market, whose original members were West Germany, France, Italy, Belgium, the Netherlands, and Luxembourg. (It was expected that Great Britain would eventually join as well, as indeed it did.) The Common Market, which has since evolved into the larger European Economic Community (EEC), created a single economic entity comparable to the United States, one that presented major opportunities and challenges to U.S. trade. The chief opportunity was access to the enormous and growing market in Europe, which opened prospects for substantial increases in U.S. trade. The challenge was to ensure that this market remained open to the United States. There was a fear in Washington that the Common Market might become closed to outsiders, for it was big enough that such a step would not be wildly impractical. It was felt that the United States had to be forthcoming itself if it was to maintain its access to Europe.

Kennedy asked Congress for five-year authority to cut tariffs by 50 percent and to remove them completely on products traded predominantly between the United States and the Common Market. The president included in the bill he sent to Congress a provision for adjustment assistance to workers and companies hurt by imports. According to his counsel, Theodore C. Sorensen, Kennedy put this provision in the bill both for bargaining purposes and in order to make it easier for organized labor to support the bill. Even at that, Kennedy did not expect it to pass.[3] But it did pass, and it has since become a fixed part of U.S. trade policy.

The Trade Expansion Act of 1962 also created a position of special representative for trade negotiations. This official was to be responsible directly to the president and was to be in charge of all trade negotiations. This represented a major shift of power within the executive branch. In the Reciprocal Trade Act of 1934 and its successors, Congress had delegated much of its power over tariffs to the president, but the president had exercised this power mainly through the State Department. In the 1962 act, Congress transferred the power to this new official and at the same time reduced the president's flexibility in organizing the executive branch. The moving force behind this change was Rep. Wilbur D. Mills, D-Ark., then chairman of the House Ways and Means Committee. By 1962, along with many others in Congress, Mills had lost confidence that the State Department would put U.S. trade interests ahead of diplomatic objectives. Creating the position of special representative for trade negotiations directly under the president not only removed negotiations from State but avoided putting them in the Commerce Department, where they would probably have been even more exposed to bureaucratic pressures and jealousies.

Congress Reclaims Its Power

The negotiating authority provided by the 1962 act expired in 1967, and Congress did not act on President Lyndon B. Johnson's request for an extension to 1970. For the first time since 1934, the president had no authority to negotiate trade agreements. This was the first hint that the congressional mood was changing. It was possibly related to a general deterioration in executive-legislative relations during the late 1960s.

When President Richard M. Nixon came to office in 1969, he asked that this presidential authority be restored, though by that time there were few tariffs left to cut. However, Congress was then in a different mood, disposed toward restricting imports by means of nontariff barriers (NTBs). Thus, the House response to Nixon's request was a trade bill that placed quotas on imports of shoes and textiles and provided for quotas on other products whenever imports reached specified shares of the U.S. market. The bill also wrote into law the oil-import quotas that President Dwight D. Eisenhower had established by proclamation in 1959. The bill was killed by a filibuster in the Senate, but it revealed the strongest protectionist sentiment in Congress since the days of Smoot-Hawley. Congress was moving to assert itself again in trade policy, and in a way that President Nixon and his successors did not like.

In 1973, the other members of GATT were ready to engage in another round of trade negotiations, the so-called Tokyo Round. But the government of the world's biggest trading nation, the United States, found itself without authority to participate. GATT marked time while Congress considered another trade bill. It took two years.

The main reason for the delay was tangential to trade: It had to do with Jewish emigration from the Soviet Union. The bill proposed by the Nixon administration included a provision authorizing the extension of most-favored-nation treatment to the Soviet Union and other Communist countries (or "nonmarket economies," as the bill called them). A group of members of Congress, led by Sen. Henry M. Jackson, D-Wash., and, in the House, by Rep. Charles A. Vanik, D-Ohio, sought to make this contingent on the emigration policies of the countries concerned. They were strongly opposed by the administration. In the end, the Jackson-Vanik amendment was agreed to by large majorities, and the Trade Act of 1974 was enacted with the amendment included. As a result, the Soviet Union renounced a trade agreement with the United States (repudiating with it a settlement of World War II lend-lease debts) and in addition cut back on Jewish emigration.

In other respects, the Trade Act of 1974 was noteworthy for the emphasis it put on NTBs—a reflection of the fact that most tariffs had been negotiated away—and for the steps it took to reclaim some of the authority that Congress had previously delegated. The president was authorized for five years to negotiate further tariff reductions: the elimination of tariffs of 5 percent or less and reductions of up to 60 percent in higher duties. The president was also authorized to increase tariffs by between 20 and 50 percent.

But Congress reserved to itself the power to review most of the other actions the president was permitted to take under the act. Agreements dealing with NTBs, amendments to GATT substantial enough to require changes in U.S. law, and bilateral trade agreements with Communist countries all had to come back to Congress for specific approval. Special so-called *fast-track* rules were provided for congressional consideration of these matters so as to preclude filibusters or other delaying tactics. The president was required to consult with the House Ways and Means and the Senate Finance committees before making agreements about NTBs. At the beginning of each regular session of Congress, five members of each of these committees (not more than three of whom could be from the same political party) were to be designated as official advisers to the U.S. delegations to international trade meetings. These advisers were to be kept currently informed.

Another noteworthy provision of the 1974 act was that it authorized the president to meet the long-standing desire of less developed countries for nonreciprocal tariff preferences. This had been one of the GATT membership's declared objectives for the Tokyo Round. The outcome was a Generalized System of Preferences, whereby industrial nations give favorable treatment to the products of less developed countries without expecting reciprocal treatment. This nonreciprocal feature was a significant departure for GATT from its firm adherence to most-favored-nation treatment. It was a kind of twentieth-century reverse application of the protection for infant industries that Hamilton had urged, and it ignited such explosive growth in Hong Kong, Singapore, Taiwan, and South Korea that they became known as the "four tigers" of international trade. By 1987, the U.S. trade deficit with the four tigers exceeded its deficit with all of Western Europe, $32.6 billion to $25.1 billion. U.S. electronics companies were making components in

Asia and importing them duty free for assembly. Japanese companies were moving production facilities from Japan to the four and exporting from there to the United States. In January 1988, the Reagan administration withdrew the generalized preferences from the four, on the ground that the preferences had served, or more than served, their purpose. The system remained in effect elsewhere.

The Reagan Years

The decade of the 1980s brought profound changes to the international economic position of the United States, along with changes in the way world trade, world business, and world finance were organized and carried on. The most dramatic of these changes were the following:

At the beginning of the decade, the United States was the world's biggest creditor nation. As the end of the decade approached, it was the biggest debtor.

In 1980, the United States had a surplus of $1.9 billion in its international balance of payments. By 1986, it had a deficit of $141.4 billion.[4]

In 1980, the deficit in the federal budget was $74 billion. In 1987, it was $148 billion. (The federal budget last showed a surplus—$3.2 billion—in 1969.)

A change that had long been building in world trading patterns became starkly clear: Some less developed countries were no longer less developed. Prominent in this group were Brazil, Mexico, South Korea, Taiwan, and Singapore.

The multinational corporation, largely a post-World War II phenomenon, came to dominate world business as never before, and it became more truly multinational, with Japanese firms joining American and European companies.

The world's money and securities markets never closed. The end of the business day in New York was the beginning of the business day in Tokyo, and modern telecommunications tied all the markets together instantaneously.

Each of these changes affected each of the others, and all of them taken together affected the problems with which trade policy had to deal and the environment in which it was made. Some of these interrelationships are imperfectly understood by experts as well as by the man on the street, but the effects on the day-to-day lives of Americans and the consequent impact on Congress are no less real. Let us examine each in turn.

The Foreign Debt

A country's foreign debt is measured by what economists call its *net international investment position*—that is, its total investments of all kinds abroad minus the total investments of foreigners in the country in question. "Investment" in this context means what is sometimes called an IOU but what economists call a *claim on resources*. It includes bank deposits, notes, bonds, stocks, land, and shares of ownership in factories and other businesses. When Americans have these investments abroad, they are considered assets in the United States; when foreigners have them in the United States, they are considered liabilities. At the end of 1981, the United States had a positive net of $141 billion in international investment. At the end of 1986, it had a negative position of $263.6 billion—a change of $405 billion in five years. All forecasts were that this trend would continue. The most optimistic prediction came from the Commerce Department: that the debt would peak at nearly $700 billion by 1993 and then begin to decline. Nongovernmental scholars estimated a peak of $800 billion to $1 trillion.[5]

There is nothing good or bad per se about a country having a foreign debt. The United States had one through most of its history. Much of the industrial and other growth that occurred after the Civil War was financed by foreign money. The United States did not become a creditor until World War I, when it lent large sums to its European allies and the British liquidated many of their foreign investments. What was striking about the change in the U.S. position in the 1980s was its scale and the suddenness with which it occurred.

The foreign debt of the United States is related to its deficits in foreign trade and in the federal budget. The deficit in foreign trade means that the United States has been importing more than it has been exporting. It has therefore been sending more dollars abroad than it has been earning in foreign currency. In order for this to happen, and to continue happening, foreigners had to be willing to hold dollars—that is, to invest them in the United States. Foreigners were willing to do this, at least for most of the decade. The cumulative effect was to increase foreign investment in the United States and thus to increase the U.S. foreign debt.

The deficit in the federal budget likewise had to be made up with borrowed money. (Theoretically, it could also have been closed simply by giving the Treasury more money created by the Federal Reserve System; but given the size of the deficit, that would have been highly inflationary. It was a course strongly opposed both by the Reagan administration and by the Federal Reserve Board [an independent agency], and was never seriously considered.) A great deal of the money that the Treasury borrowed to finance the budget deficit came from foreigners. Again, the cumulative effect was to increase the American foreign debt.

The United States has serviced its foreign debt—that is, paid interest on it—by borrowing more, but in the long run the debt can be serviced only by developing a continuing surplus in the balance of payments. Hence, there has been pressure to increase exports and to decrease imports. However, a U.S. trade surplus would not be universally welcome in the rest of the world. A U.S. surplus is some other country's deficit. Many nations depend on exports, including exports to the United States, to provide jobs, economic growth, even political stability. If the United States is selling more than it is buying, at least some other countries will be buying more than they are selling. The rich countries (Japan, Germany) can afford this; the poor, or even the not-so-poor, countries (Brazil, Mexico, India, Korea) cannot.

There is another complication. The Third World has an international debt of its own, amounting to approximately $1 trillion, much of it owed to U.S. banks. If this debt is ever to be repaid, the Third World has to have a surplus with the United States.

The Trade Deficit

A country with a large surplus in its receipts from foreign investment needs to have a deficit in its balance of trade. Otherwise, its debtors will not earn enough to be able to pay the interest on their loans. Great Britain was such a country in the fifty years before World War I. The United States was such a country in the forty years after World War II. As late as 1986, the United States was still earning more from its investments abroad than foreigners were earning from their investments in the United States, but not much more. The difference was only $21 billion, and it was disappearing.

Conversely, a country with a deficit in its receipts from foreign investment needs to have a surplus in its balance of trade. Otherwise, it will not earn enough to be able to pay the claims of its foreign investors. But in 1987, the United States had a balance-of-payments trade deficit of $159.3 billion. This large and persistent deficit generated a great deal of political pressure to reduce it, pressure in the form both of curtailing imports and of increasing exports.

The effort to reduce imports has been made mainly through nontariff barriers, especially quotas—that is, quantitative limits on imports of particular products. There was remarkably little talk about the traditional method of raising tariffs, though that is the method preferred in orthodox economics. The pressure for quotas came from the industries that were experiencing the greatest competition from imports. Notable among these were textiles, shoes, automobiles, and certain kinds of steel.

To meet the needs of these industries and to blunt their opposition, the Reagan administration and its immediate predecessors negotiated a number of "voluntary restraint" agreements with the principal exporting nations. In the case of textiles, for example, there was a multinational Multi-Fiber Agreement. Exporters were willing to accept these voluntary restraints in order to avoid more rigorous restrictions. In some cases, the exporters adapted to the numerical limits in the agreements by shipping their more expensive and more profitable models to the exclusion of cheaper models. Japanese automobiles are an example. The effect was a double reduction in competitive pressure on the U.S. automobile industry: less overall competition (that is, fewer units imported), and less pressure to produce the smaller, cheaper models that the Japanese had been so successful with.

The U.S. drive to increase exports was two-pronged: to make foreign markets more accessible to U.S. producers and to increase the competitiveness of U.S. industry and agriculture. The focus of efforts to improve market accessibility was Japan. It was with Japan that the U.S. trade deficit was the largest—as much as $50 billion to $60 billion a year. Part of this was accounted for by the large numbers of Japanese automobiles, television sets, and other products that entered the United States, but Japan also has what many Americans believe are bizarre and discriminatory import requirements. For example, although Japan has provided the biggest foreign market for U.S. beef ($500 million in 1986), U.S. beef producers think it should be even larger. Tsutomo Hata, chairman of the governing party in Japan, the Liberal Democrats, told a group of members of Congress (at a steak luncheon) that Buddhist restrictions on eating meat are one reason Japan cannot import more. Further, he said, Japanese have a "much, much larger" digestive system than Americans, and this makes it harder for them to eat beef. Another Japanese official defended barriers to the import of skis with the argument that Japanese snow is different from snow in the rest of the world.[6]

Japan has tried to block implementation of a GATT finding that its restrictions on farm imports violated GATT rules. The U.S. telecommunications industry, supported by the government, has claimed that Japanese specifications for telecommunications equipment are written so as effectively to preclude imports. U.S. automobile manufacturers have made the same complaint about safety and other requirements for cars. Foreign construction firms have been frozen out of contracts in Japan under a kind of Catch-22 requirement: The firms could not bid on the contracts if they have had no experience in construction in Japan—but of course they could not get that experience if they were not permitted to bid on the contracts.

The reaction to all this in Congress was to threaten to impose restrictions on imports from Japan as leverage to reduce Japanese restrictions on imports from the United States. Specifically with respect to construction, Congress passed legislation in 1987 banning Japanese companies from federally funded projects. In March 1988, the Japanese agreed to open fourteen major public-works projects to bidding by U.S. companies.

The drive to increase competitiveness was also two-pronged: increasing the efficiency of U.S. industry (including the productivity of the U.S. worker), and lowering the value of the dollar. Industrial efficiency and labor productivity are dependent on many characteristics of the economy—among others, the extent of mechanization, the level of investment and taxation, and the level of wages and fringe benefits. Some of these are determined by collective bargaining between labor and management; some are determined by Congress when it makes broad domestic policies, usually with little consideration of the impact on foreign trade.

During the 1980s, as foreign competition intensified, U.S. labor accepted some wage and benefit restraints and even cutbacks for the sake of enhanced productivity. By the middle of the decade, productivity, after a long period of stagnation or even decline, did begin to rise. (*Productivity* refers to the volume of production per worker per hour.) However, as competitiveness, efficiency, and productivity came to be seen as directly related to the ability to export and therefore to the size of the trade deficit, two contradictions among U.S. policy objectives appeared.

One of these involved fringe (that is, nonwage) benefits, or, more broadly, social policies that raised costs, to the detriment of export policies. The cost of labor is not simply what workers take home in their pay envelopes each week. It is also the cost of the other benefits they receive as a part of their employment. Some of these are required by law; some are written into collective-bargaining agreements; some are company policy. They include the employer's contribution to the worker's Social Security and in many cases to a company retirement plan; paid holidays and vacations; paid sick leave and health insurance; and in some cases, day-care centers for the children of employees and subsidized lunchrooms and transportation. Sometimes the cost to the employer of these fringe benefits is as much as the worker's wages. In any event, they all add to the employer's cost of production.

The second contradiction involved the relationship between competitiveness and defense. Some of the country's most competitive industries (the computer manufacturers, for example) had difficulty getting export licenses because of fears that the technology would find its way into unfriendly hands. Even when export licenses were issued, the process sometimes took so long that sales were lost to competitors from less finicky countries. A great deal of the research and development carried on in the United States is financed by the Defense Department, which tends to insist on tight controls on exporting the results, whether in military or civilian products. A study by the National Academy of Sciences concluded that unnecessary controls on high-technology exports cost $9 billion in sales and 188,000 jobs in 1985.[7]

When the dollar has a high value (that is, when it is an "expensive" currency), goods made in the United States are relatively costly to foreign buyers and goods made abroad are relatively cheap to U.S. consumers. That situation makes it harder for U.S. companies to sell their products abroad and at the same time encourages people in the United States to buy foreign-made goods, thereby increasing the trade deficit. During the first half of the 1980s, the dollar did have an exceptionally high value: one dollar was worth as much as three German marks and almost 250 Japanese yen.

The reasons for these exchange rates were complex. One was that, during this period, interest rates in the United States were higher than in the rest of the industrialized world. This provided an incentive for foreigners to invest in the United States and created a demand for dollars, which in turn drove the price of dollars up. On the one hand, the United States benefited from this inflow of foreign money, for it made it possible to finance the budget deficit and service the growing foreign debt. On the other hand, it contributed significantly to the trade deficit.

Beginning in 1985, in part because of an agreement on exchange rates among the principal industrial powers, the dollar started to lose value against other currencies. By May 1988, it was worth only 1.68 marks and 125 yen. However, raising the price of imports also raised the general price level in the United States and thereby was conducive to inflation. In addition, it reduced the pressure on U.S. industry to become more competitive.

The Budget Deficit

President Ronald Reagan was elected in 1980 on a platform calling for lower taxes and higher defense spending. He moved immediately to put this program into effect. In 1981, Congress passed a bill cutting taxes substantially, and it adopted a budget increasing defense spending. (It reduced spending on some other programs, but on balance total government spending increased.) The theory behind this tax cut was that it would stimulate the economy so much that total tax revenues would actually increase. Sen. Howard Baker, R-Tenn., the majority leader at the time, called it a "riverboat gamble." It did not pay off, and the United States entered an era of twelve-digit budget deficits (that is, $100,000,000,000 and up). In the eight years from 1980 to 1987, the cumulative deficit was $1.25 trillion.

For the remainder of the Reagan administration, Congress and the president were at loggerheads over the budget and taxes. The president adamantly refused to consider raising taxes while just as adamantly insisting on maintaining a high, and even a rising, level of defense spending. Congress, for its part, refused to make significant cuts in nondefense spending. There were minor compromises from time to time, but none big enough to affect the deficit substantially.

As already noted, the budget deficit was being financed by borrowing from foreigners. This, of course, increased the international debt of the United States. Moreover, the foreign borrowing was facilitated, at least in the first half of the decade, by high interest rates, which served to keep the international value of the dollar high. This, in turn, contributed to the excess of imports over exports.

World Trade

In 1776, the English economist Adam Smith published his famous book, *The Wealth of Nations,* in which he developed the theory of *comparative advantage.* This theory holds that everybody benefits if nations produce the goods that they can make most efficiently and buy from other nations those goods that are most efficiently produced elsewhere. A nation's advantage in production might lie in the availability of raw materials, land, or labor, or in any of a number of other things. After more than two centuries, comparative advantage remains an important part of economic theory and especially an important part of the rationale for free trade.

Comparative advantage has been the root cause for the relocation of much of the world's production. Cheaper labor has sent the shoe industry from New England to Asia and to Brazil. More efficient machinery has given the European steel industry a competitive edge, and cheaper labor has established steel industries in Korea, Brazil, and India.

The production of textiles is another example. In the nineteenth century, textile mills sprang up in New England, where water power was plentiful and cheap. The mills brought cotton from the southern states, where it was grown with the comparative advantage of a favorable climate and cheap labor—until the 1860s, slave labor. The cotton was processed in New England by recently arrived immigrants, who also worked cheaply.

In the twentieth century, the machinery of the New England mills became obsolete and relatively expensive to operate. The workers became unionized and demanded higher wages. As a result, many of the mills moved south, closer to the source of supply and into a nonunion environment. Comparative advantage had shifted.

New England members of Congress reacted by trying to force up the cost of southern labor in order to deprive the South of that element of its comparative advantage. They tried to raise the federal minimum wage and supported changes in federal labor laws that would make it easier for unions to organize, bargain, and strike. The debates in Congress on these subjects, although not always expressed this way, were as much about shifting comparative advantage as about liberal or conservative philosophies of labor-management relations.

After World War II, comparative advantage shifted again, beginning particularly in the decade of the 1960s. This time it moved to the newly industrialized countries around the Asian rim of the Pacific Ocean—South Korea, Taiwan, Hong Kong, Singapore, and the Philippines. These countries had the cheapest labor and the most up-to-date machinery. Again there was a reaction from members of Congress, especially those from South Carolina, which had become the center of the U.S. textile industry. They set up a clamor for protectionist trade legislation, mainly in the form of quotas. Though they did not succeed in their efforts, they did apply enough pressure to force the negotiation of a series of voluntary restraint agreements.

Congress passed a textile import quota bill in 1985, President Reagan vetoed it, and the veto was sustained in the House in 1986. The industry argued that 300,000 U.S. jobs were lost to textile and clothing imports. The bill would have cut these imports from South Korea, Taiwan, and Hong Kong by 30 percent. The Senate added relief for the shoe and copper industries.

At no time did proponents of the bill muster the two-thirds majority needed to override a veto. The bill passed the House initially by 262-159 on October 10, 1985. It passed the Senate with the shoe and copper amendments by 60-39 on November 13. The House concurred in the Senate amendments by 255-161 on December 3. President Reagan vetoed the bill on December 17. The House leadership then postponed consideration of the veto until August 6, 1986.

This unusual delay was an effort to improve the chances of overriding the veto. The vote would come only three months before the 1986 election, and on the day the Multi-Fiber Agreement (MFA) was due to expire. Proponents of the bill were hopeful that the MFA would lapse, or at least have an uncertain future, and that this would win new converts for the bill.

But the proponents were outmaneuvered by the administration. On August 1, fifty-four countries agreed to a new MFA, with tighter limits on some textile imports. In the same period immediately preceding August 6, new trade agreements were reached with South Korea, Taiwan, and Hong Kong. The administration also announced subsidized wheat sales to the Soviet Union; this was done, over the objections of Secretary of State George Shultz, in order to bring the administration support from wheat-growing states. Finally, an agreement was reached with Japan to provide better market access for U.S. exports of semi-conductors. The House sustained the veto by voting 276-149 to override.

Representatives of textile-producing states wanted to make textile quotas part of the omnibus trade bill that Congress considered in 1987 and 1988, but the managers of that bill wanted to avoid a veto. A deal was struck: Textile representatives agreed not to offer amendments to the bill, and in return they were assured of a vote on a separate textile bill. Both sides complied with the bargain. A textile bill passed the House in September 1987 by 263-156. (This again underlines the textile lobby's legislative problem: It had a majority to pass bills, but not two-thirds to override vetoes.) The omnibus trade bill was unencumbered by textile provisions, but was vetoed on other grounds.

Multinational Corporations

The multinational corporations that came into prominence after World War II might be thought of as being companies of American or Japanese or German or some other nationality, depending on their origin and where they have their main offices. In fact, however, they operate largely without regard to national boundaries, taking them into account only when national laws make it advantageous for them to do so. They not only operate across national boundaries; they form joint ventures with each other.

These characteristics sometimes seem to make the traditional approaches of trade policy irrelevant. Trade policy has traditionally been based on the premise that a product has a "national origin." But the products of multinational corporations frequently have no particular national origin, or they may have so many that trying to single out one becomes a meaningless exercise. The "Japanese" television sets that Sony sells in the United States are assembled in Tijuana, Mexico, from parts made in San Diego, California. In 1987, Sanyo announced plans to export color television sets from the United States to Japan. Ford builds Mercury automobiles in a plant in Hermosillo, Mexico, where most of the equipment is Japanese and most of the parts are supplied by Mazda, a Japanese automobile manufacturer. By 1987, Japan was the second largest foreign investor in Mexico after the United States.

A wave of indignation against Toshiba swept Congress and the country in 1987 when it was revealed that the Japanese company had sold technology to the Soviet Union that enabled the Soviets to reduce significantly the noise of their submarines and thereby to complicate the efforts of the U.S. Navy to detect them. Congress prohibited government purchases of Toshiba products, and then discovered that the stores on military bases sold $7 million worth of Toshiba products annually, half of them microwave ovens made in Lebanon, Tennessee.

The International Financial Market

When securities and financial markets open in the morning in Tokyo, Hong Kong, and Sydney, it is early evening the day before in New York. Shortly after Tokyo closes, Frankfurt opens. By the time Frankfurt closes, New York is open; and by the time Chicago closes, Tokyo is almost ready to open again. Somewhere a market is always open. Money is transferred among all of these markets literally at the speed of light. Large banks and securities firms maintain branches and offices around the world to serve their customers in this global market.

An international trade in financial services such as banking has existed since the days of the sailing ships, but it is now much larger and is carried on with great rapidity. It developed after the negotiation of GATT, and the absence of rules covering it is one of GATT's glaring omissions. However, the issue of including financial services in the GATT framework was put on the agenda of the Uruguay Round, the latest in the series of GATT negotiations, which was begun in 1986.

Congress Acts on Trade

The 1980s were a decade of mounting concern in Congress over the economy and especially the deficits in the budget and the balance of payments. This period also saw something of a reversal in the roles of the two political parties.

As noted earlier, the manufacturing industries historically had supported tariffs and other forms of trade protection, whereas agriculture had supported free trade or something close to it. After the Civil War, the Republican party came to be identified with industry and protectionism, the Democratic party with agriculture and low tariffs. These identifications were reinforced by the Smoot-Hawley Act, passed by a Republican Congress and signed by a Republican president in 1930, and by the Reciprocal Trade Act, which was one of the proudest achievements of the Democratic administration of Franklin Roosevelt.

As U.S. foreign trade grew, beginning with the Reciprocal Trade Act and even more after World War II, support for tariffs in the industrial sector began to erode. More U.S. businesses were producing for export, a circumstance that led business leaders to favor liberal trade policies and to oppose high tariffs. On the other hand, organized labor, with which the Democratic party became identified especially in the 1930s, had always had protectionist tendencies, viewing tariffs as a way of protecting jobs. Finally, the Reagan administration pressed its ideological views more than most administrations do, and its ideology was firmly rooted in the principle of private enterprise free of governmental intervention.

Consequently, during the 1980s the Democrats in Congress tended to take the lead in pushing for trade legislation, while the Reagan administration and congressional Republicans resisted what they saw as protectionism. These lines were not absolute, and the differences were frequently more of degree than of principle. Many Democrats, such as Rep. Sam Gibbons of Florida, chairman of the Trade Subcommittee of the Ways and Means Committee, remained staunch free traders, while many Republicans, especially those from districts feeling pressure from imports, wavered in their opposition to protectionist measures. The two senators from South Carolina, Republican Strom Thurmond and Democrat Ernest F. Hollings, were united in fighting for textile import quotas.

The Trade Bill of 1986

The House passed an omnibus trade bill in 1986 by a vote of 295 to 115. The margin was more than enough to override the veto threatened by the administration, but the test never came because no action was taken in the Senate. However, the nature of the bill was a good indication of the temper of the House and foreshadowed things to come.

The bill was long (458 pages) and complicated. Its thrust was at least as much to increase exports as to decrease imports. Its proponents generally lauded it as a "tough" approach: foreigners erecting barriers against U.S. goods would have to face U.S. retaliation against their own goods.

Although the heart of the bill came from the Ways and Means Committee, five other committees contributed parts of it. These were Foreign Affairs; Banking, Finance, and Urban Affairs; Energy and Commerce; Education and Labor; and Agriculture. The result was a package that went well beyond the traditional framework of trade legislation. It included a program of aid to education, in order to improve competitiveness; programs to encourage investment in the Third World, in the hope of increasing those countries' capacity to import; and a requirement (strongly opposed by the Defense Department) that the Commerce Department remove 80,000 items from the list of 200,000 products that required export licenses.

The bill also tried to deal with the issue of intellectual property. It provided for repeal of a requirement that a U.S. company prove injury in cases of alleged patent or copyright infringements. Under the bill, it would be enough to prove that the infringement had occurred.

The administration strongly opposed three elements of the bill. One of them was a complicated procedure for reducing unfavorable trade balances with certain countries. This provision, the work of Rep. Richard A. Gephardt, D-Mo., required the president to negotiate agreements for annual 10 percent reductions in the U.S. trade deficit with those countries with which this deficit was largest. Gephardt said these countries were Japan ($51.5 billion), Taiwan ($13.4 billion), and West Germany ($12.6 billion). If the negotiations did not have the desired result, tariffs would be raised. If tariffs did not work, the president would have to impose quotas, unless he determined that this would cause "substantial harm" to the U.S. economy.

The second element that provoked the administration's opposition was a series of provisions mandating presidential action against specified "unfair" trade practices. The bill defined *export targeting* as one such practice. Under export targeting, a government provides special benefits for certain industries in order to encourage exports. Japan does this for semiconductors and machine tools; the United States does it for farm commodities. The president was required to impose barriers against imports from countries that did not eliminate these practices. The bill even applied to secondary subsidies. Canadian subsidies for the timber industry would become an unfair trade practice, because timber is used to make products that are exported; so would Canadian and Mexican subsidies of natural gas, which is used by industries manufacturing for export. Another unfair trade practice, aimed especially at the cheap labor of Asian countries, was the denial of labor rights.

The Reagan administration opposed these provisions on the ground that they would not open foreign markets to U.S. goods but, on the contrary, would provoke foreign retaliation against U.S. goods and trigger an international trade war, which would leave everybody poorer. A third element of the bill was opposed because it would transfer from the president to the special trade representative decisions about retaliatory actions in cases of unfair trading practices. All presidents are jealous of their powers, but Reagan was more jealous than most. As we saw in Chapter 5, he was reluctant to consult with Congress about sending naval forces to the Persian Gulf for fear that the act of consultation would lend some color of legitimacy to the War Powers Resolution. As we saw in Chapter 6, he resented congressional interference with the intelligence community as another infringement of his powers. So also he bristled at any transfer of powers over trade, even though they were powers given to him by Congress, not by the Constitution. He would raise the same objections in connection with the next trade bill to be debated in Congress.

The Trade Bill of 1987-1988

The Democrats won control of the Senate in 1986, the first time in the Reagan administration that they had a majority in both houses of Congress. Their leaders promptly announced that a trade bill would be one of their top priorities for 1987, and they started the new year on a very fast track.

On January 6, Representative Gephardt, with more than 180 House Democrats as cosponsors, introduced a bill similar in many respects to the House trade bill of 1986. On January 7, Sen. Robert Byrd, once more the majority leader, told Senate committees to report on trade by May 1 so that their bills could be put together into an omnibus bill. On the same day, more than 150 members of the House and Senate announced organization of the Congressional Caucus on Competitiveness, headed by two members from each party: Sen. Max Baucus, Mont., and Rep. Buddy MacKay, Fla., for the Democrats, and Sen. John H. Chafee and Rep. Claudine Schneider of Rhode Island for the Republicans.

During January and February 1987, it appeared that this spirit of bipartisanship might spread beyond the Caucus on Competitiveness and that cooperation between Congress and the White House might replace the hostility that had characterized the 1986 trade debate. When the Senate Finance Committee chairman, Lloyd Bentsen, D-Texas, introduced the Senate trade bill, his fifty-six cosponsors included Minority Leader Robert Dole as well as Majority Leader Byrd. And when the House Ways and Means Committee opened its hearings February 5, House Minority Leader Robert H. Michel, R-Ill., told the committee, "There has been a complete about face in the administration's approach to trade." [8] Bentsen and the Ways and Means chairman, Dan Rostenkowski, D-Ill., agreed.

The administration sent a rival bill to Congress, a massive compendium of two thousand pages. The main provision directly related to trade was an extension of the president's negotiating authority, which was scheduled to expire at the end of 1987 and without which the United States could not fully participate in the Uruguay Round of GATT. In other respects, the bill was a wish list reflecting the administration's conservative, deregulatory philosophy. In the name of competitiveness, it would ease antitrust laws, abolish the Interstate Commerce Commission (the regulatory agency for railroads), limit the liability of corporations for their products, deregulate natural gas, spend more on technical and scientific research, reform banking, improve education, and aid dislocated workers. Many of these provisions were no doubt proposed in the same spirit in which President Kennedy had proposed adjustment assistance for workers in 1962: they could not be passed standing alone but might get through as part of a larger bill.

Democrats in Congress were playing the same game. The White House trade bill was not seriously considered on its merits, but Congress did address many of the same subjects. The 1987-1988 trade bill was the work of a number of different committees. Ways and Means in the House and Finance in the Senate attended to the fundamental provisions dealing with trade. Separate but somewhat related bills came from thirteen committees in the House and eight in the Senate—another consequence of the fragmentation and dispersal of power that characterized Congress in the 1970s and 1980s. The bills were consolidated in the offices of the Speaker of the House and the majority leader of the Senate and were considered in each of the two houses as a single bill.

The main part of the bill was written in the Trade Subcommittee of Ways and Means. The subcommittee modified the 1986 Gephardt amendment and added some provisions of its own. The principal provisions of the subcommittee bill were as follows:

The president's negotiating authority was extended, thereby permitting full U.S. participation in the Uruguay Round. (This was the only part of the bill that the administration really wanted.)

The authority to determine unfair trade practices and to grant import relief was transferred from the president to the special trade representative.

Retaliation was required against countries with "unjustifiable" trade practices, such as violations of international agreements. The president was to determine the type of retaliation, but tariffs were preferred to quotas.

The president was given discretion to retaliate against "unreasonable" or "discriminatory" trade practices, including the denial of workers' rights. These rights were defined as association and collective bargaining, a minimum age for child labor, and a minimum wage that depended on a country's level of economic development.

Retaliation against export targeting was authorized.

Negotiations were required with countries having "excess trade surpluses" (defined as exports that were 175 percent of imports) if those countries had a pattern of unfair trade practices. Retaliation was required if the negotiations failed, unless it would do "substantial harm" to the national interest.

New and easier standards for import and antidumping relief were established.

There was a school of thought in the House, especially among Democrats, that the bill's tough tactics would strengthen the administration's negotiating posture. It was reported that some in the administration thought so, too. Nevertheless, in a letter to members of the Ways and Means Committee, Trade Representative Clayton Yeutter wrote, "If the provisions [objectionable to the administration] are not either eliminated or substantially improved, I would find it exceedingly difficult to recommend that the president sign any trade bill including them." [9]

The omnibus bill that was the subject of House debate also included the bills that had been produced by the various other committees taking part. Some of these dealt with trade only as part of a larger
economic policy. They reflected the pet peeves and pet projects of the
committees that had produced them. For example:

> The president was authorized to stop foreign attempts to take
> over U.S. companies and was required to do so if the Commerce
> Department found that a takeover would threaten national secu-
> rity. This provision, which originated in the House Energy and
> Commerce Committee, was directed primarily at the effort, since
> abandoned, by the Fujitsu Company to take over the Fairchild
> Semiconductor Company. Fairchild was already owned by French
> interests, but Congress was annoyed by Japan, not by France.
>
> There would be an increase from $1.5 billion to $2.5 billion in
> the Export Enhancement Program, under which government-
> owned surplus farm commodities are given to exporters. This is the
> kind of export subsidy that Congress complains about when other
> countries do it.
>
> The Third World's capacity to import would be increased by a
> provision to ease its debt burden by seeking the creation of a new
> international financial entity.
>
> Export controls would be relaxed, and there would be more
> money for education and job training, new rules to ensure that more
> U.S. exports would be carried on U.S. ships, an expanded Office of
> International Trade in the Small Business Administration, and new
> protection for U.S. patents, copyrights, and trademarks.

The centerpiece of the House debate was the amendment that
Representative Gephardt offered from the floor. Similar to his amendment which had prevailed in 1986, it went beyond the protectionist
provisions of the Ways and Means Committee bill, and it split the
Democratic leadership. Speaker Jim Wright, D-Texas, supported it;
Majority Leader Thomas S. Foley, D-Wash., and Ways and Means
chairman Rostenkowski opposed it. It set off feverish lobbying activity
by the administration and by business and labor groups.

The AFL-CIO strongly supported the amendment and made it one
of the crucial votes on the scorecard that labor keeps on members of
Congress. Business was split. The automobile and steel industries and
some companies such as Motorola were for the amendment. Chrysler
president Lee Iacocca even urged Chrysler suppliers to work for it.
Opponents included the National Association of Manufacturers, the
Chamber of Commerce of the United States, the Emergency Committee
for American Trade (an organization of corporate chief executive offi-

cers), and such companies as Hewlett-Packard (a high-tech manufacturer that exports), and K Mart (a retailer that sells low-price imports).

In the end, the Gephardt amendment passed the House by a vote of 218-214. The whole bill, as amended, was then sent to the Senate by a vote of 290-137.

The Senate Finance Committee produced a bill generally along the lines of the House bill. As was done in the House, a number of other committees contributed parts to it, and these, too, were similar to what had been done in the House. A notable exception was the action of the Governmental Affairs Committee and the Commerce, Science, and Transportation Committee. They proposed that the assistant secretaries of commerce for international economic policy and for trade administration be transferred to the Office of the Trade Representative and that that office itself be transferred out of the White House and made semiautonomous. An Advanced Civilian Technology Agency would be created to fund high-risk areas of research and development, and the National Bureau of Standards would be transformed into the National Institute of Technology and given the mission of converting technological advances into salable products.

The Senate debated the 1,013-page bill from June 25 to July 25. In this time, it considered more than 160 amendments, none so dramatic as Gephardt's in the House. It accepted more than 120 and defeated 20. The others were withdrawn or otherwise left in legislative limbo.

The administration objected to a number of provisions in the Senate bill. It did not like (and business liked even less) a requirement that companies give workers notice of intended plant closings. It also opposed provisions that limited presidential authority, ordered sanctions against unfair trade practices, mandated relief for industries and workers hurt by imports, and denied most-favored-nation treatment to Romania.

Nonetheless, the bill passed the Senate in July by 71-27. This was more than enough to override a veto, but it was not indicative of Senate sentiment on the merits of the bill. Some senators had cast yea votes simply to keep the legislative process moving.

Given the length and complexity of the bills and the number of committees involved, the process was cumbersome at best. It took until October to appoint conferees to resolve differences between the House and Senate bills, and then there were 199 of them—155 from the House and 44 from the Senate. They organized themselves into seventeen subgroups, some of which had sub-subgroups. In the meantime, the principal conferees, those from Ways and Means and Finance, had become preoccupied with the negotiations between Congress and the administration over reducing the budget.

On November 10, Minority Leader Michel moved to instruct the

House conferees to recede from the Gephardt amendment. His motion was defeated, 175-239, but that was more reflective of House views on procedure than on substance.

Nothing more was done in 1987. By the time the second session of the 100th Congress convened in January 1988, the bill was caught up in the presidential election campaign. The House trade conferees, led by Rostenkowski and Sam Gibbons, D-Fla., wanted to dump the Gephardt amendment. But Gephardt was then an active candidate for the Democratic presidential nomination. He was making trade policy a major issue, and his House colleagues did not want to disavow him in those circumstances. So one of the major issues in the bill was held in abeyance until March, when Gephardt, not having done well in the early primaries, withdrew from the race. At that point, the Gephardt amendment was removed from the bill, and the conference began to move forward.

One at a time, the seventeen subgroups completed their work, and a final omnibus bill was produced. It was less protectionist than either the House or Senate bills had been and also carried fewer extraneous provisions. Among other things, there remained authority to participate in the Uruguay Round of GATT, better protection for patents and copyrights, tougher rules against unfair trade practices, training and other assistance for displaced workers, easier export controls for business, and more export subsidies for farmers.

There also remained the provision requiring companies to give sixty days' notification of plant closings to workers. Labor strongly insisted on this. Business equally strongly resisted it. The administration was also opposed and promised a veto if the provision stayed in the bill. The remaining Democratic presidential candidates—Massachusetts Governor Michael S. Dukakis and the Rev. Jesse Jackson—announced their support.

The House agreed to the conference report, 312-107, on April 21, 1988, with the plant-closing notification and without the Gephardt amendment. Gephardt was one of two Democrats who voted against the conference report. The Senate agreed on April 27 by 63-36, three votes short of the two-thirds necessary to override a veto.

In an effort to gain more votes in the Senate, House Democrats then resorted to a highly unusual procedure. They called up and passed, 253-159, a resolution instructing House clerks to remove from the official copy of the bill two provisions restricting the export of Alaskan oil. This would be done before the bill was sent to the president. These provisions had been opposed by Alaska's senators, both Republicans, and the Democrats hoped that this conciliatory gesture would win the Alaskans' support. But this ploy was blocked in the Senate by the bill's opponents, and the bill went to the president unchanged.

The expected veto came May 24. The president's veto message cited the Alaskan oil provisions, but it was clear that his principal objection was to the plant-closing notification.[10] The House overrode the veto the same day it was received by a vote of 308-113. In early June the matter was still pending in the more closely divided Senate.

Conclusion

As recently as a quarter-century ago, it was axiomatic on Capitol Hill that members who looked after the particular interests of their state or district could vote as they pleased on foreign policy without fear of political repercussions. That piece of political wisdom seems to be valid no longer. The line between local interests and foreign policy has disappeared. Similarly, it is now impossible to separate trade policy from policies affecting the federal budget, the position of the dollar in international finance, Third World debt, the role of multinational corporations, even the condition of education and the cost of social programs. In short, no one element of economic policy can be isolated from the whole. This was recognized during debates on the trade bill in 1987 and 1988. Indeed, strictly speaking, the trade bill was not even a trade bill; it was an economic policy bill. No one thought that the trade provisions by themselves would close the U.S. trade deficit.

Because of the importance to Congress of local interests, Congress tends to take a more protectionist view of trade policy than does the president, who has a broader constituency. Before Congress surrendered most of its tariff-setting powers to the president in 1934, it typically approached trade policy item by item. Congress abandoned this approach after it began to reclaim some of its powers in 1974. Trade legislation of the last two decades has been couched in more general, less product-specific, terms.

It is characteristic of Congress to delegate power, or to acquiesce in the presidential use of power, so long as Congress finds the results satisfactory. It is characteristic of presidents to attempt to retain all the power they have acquired, however it came to them. Congress began to be uncomfortable with the results of U.S. trade policy in the 1970s. By the 1980s, Congress was seriously disturbed. The range of issues in trade policy by then encompassed the whole of the economy. There was no simple mechanism for delegating to the president powers confined to trade. Policy making had become an endless series of trade-offs. If the value of the dollar goes down to discourage imports, there is a danger of inflation. If interest rates go up and attract foreign investment, there is a danger of a depression. Finally, the process of making policy amid these precarious circumstances is complicated by cumbersome congressional procedures.

Notes

1. Quoted in Charles A. Beard and Mary R. Beard, *The Rise of American Civilization* (New York: Macmillan, 1942), 349.
2. Nathan Schachner, *Alexander Hamilton* (New York: D. Appleton-Century, 1946), 276.
3. Theodore C. Sorensen, *Kennedy* (New York: Harper and Row, 1965), 411.
4. U.S. Congress, Joint Economic Committee, *Economic Indicators*, 100th Cong., 2d sess., April 1988, 36.
5. U.S. Congress, Joint Economic Committee, *The Economy at Midyear: A Legacy of Debt* (staff study, August 5, 1987), 18, 21.
6. Dispatch by Stuart Auerbach, *Washington Post,* December 18, 1987, F3.
7. National Academy of Sciences, *Balancing the National Interest: U.S. National Security Export Controls and Global Economic Competition* (Washington, D.C.: National Academy Press, 1987).
8. *Congressional Quarterly Weekly Report,* February 7, 1987, 238.
9. Ibid., March 21, 1987, 519.
10. *Congressional Record,* daily ed., 100th Cong., 2d sess., May 24, 1988, H3531-H3532.

Conclusion

Part I (Chapters 1 and 2) provided a general discussion of the roles of the executive branch—focusing upon the powers of the president and of Congress in the foreign policy process. In Part II (Chapters 3-7), five specific issues from recent American diplomatic experience were selected to illustrate the role of Congress in foreign policy since the Vietnam War. These case studies had two common elements: they addressed significant questions confronting the United States in foreign relations, and they identified one or more important prerogatives of Congress and the president in the foreign policy field.

In the final chapter of this study, which comprises Part III, we have two purposes. The first is to identify congressional behavior patterns in the recent era of legislative activism in foreign relations. What approaches has Congress taken to a series of diverse external problems? In what respects has Congress's approach in recent years marked a change from the long preceding period of legislative acquiescence in presidential diplomatic leadership?

Second, what are the noteworthy long-term implications of an active and independent role by Congress in foreign affairs? To answer that question, we must consider the factors that have sustained congressional assertiveness in confronting foreign policy questions. How durable are these factors? Are they likely to provide momentum for forceful legislative initiatives in foreign relations in the years ahead? Or can they be expected to diminish as memories of the Vietnam conflict recede and as the United States confronts new and difficult problems in the international system? On balance, what has been the impact of an assertive Congress upon American diplomacy?

The era of congressional dynamism in foreign policy was to no inconsiderable degree an inevitable outgrowth of the Vietnam War. That traumatic experience brought about a reappraisal of the whole process of reaching foreign policy decisions. In Southeast Asia, the United States found itself embroiled in a massive military conflict because of a series of separate, unrelated, and often modest steps—an approach to foreign policy sometimes called *incrementalism.*

In effect, the war "just happened" as the result of no conscious or deliberate design by policy makers or citizens. (In fact, officials in Washington frequently denied their intention of expanding America's responsibility for the defense of South Vietnam, even while they were in the process of doing so.) In time, however, the United States found itself saddled with the dominant responsibility for the Vietnam War effort—primarily because officials in Washington and informed citizens failed at each stage to perceive the cumulative effect of a series of isolated steps that collectively produced America's involvement in that conflict.

From the end of the Vietnam War until the late 1970s, American diplomatic behavior was massively influenced by what was sometimes called the post-Vietnam syndrome. Its principal elements were a pervasive feeling of guilt and disillusionment with the results of America's involvement in Southeast Asia, an evident reluctance to become embroiled in "another Vietnam" abroad, and a preoccupation with internal problems (many of which had been neglected during the Vietnam conflict).

By the end of the decade, however, Americans had become genuinely concerned about such developments as the deterioration of the nation's influence abroad; potential or actual Soviet gains in regions like the Persian Gulf, East Africa, and Latin America; and the "indecisiveness" of national leadership, as epitomized by the Carter presidency. While domestic economic factors were perhaps the crucial element in the outcome, these foreign policy issues unquestionably contributed to the election of a Republican president in 1980. Many of these same foreign policy concerns also contributed to Reagan's reelection to the White House in 1984. Moreover, such changes in the public-opinion context of foreign policy decision making fundamentally affected congressional attitudes and behavior toward foreign policy questions.

What are the principal implications of congressional activism in foreign affairs for the future? What specific forms does this activism take? How has congressional assertiveness in foreign relations affected the ability of the United States to respond effectively to diverse challenges abroad? What kind of new balance may be emerging in executive-legislative relations in the years ahead? Such questions are fundamental in any attempt to understand the American foreign policy process. Our answers to them must be tentative; they are perhaps inescapably conditioned by underlying value judgments; and they cannot anticipate the conditions that will confront the United States in its relations with more than 150 independent nations. With due recognition of these uncertainties, Chapter 8 presents an assessment of the overall impact of Congress upon the foreign policy process in the United States.

Congressional Assertiveness
and Foreign Affairs:
A Balance Sheet

Late in President Ronald Reagan's second term, Secretary of State George Shultz publicly decried the "seemingly inexorable encroachment of Congress into the conduct of foreign policy" by the United States. While the executive branch welcomed "a constructive dialogue with the legislative branch" on foreign policy questions, Shultz said, "increasing congressional restrictions" upon the president's diplomatic freedom of action were severely hampering the ability of the United States to achieve its foreign policy objectives. In remarkably blunt language for a secretary of state who had cultivated cooperative executive-legislative relations, Shultz stated, "This is no time for the Congress to be hauling down the American flag around the world." Secretary Shultz's observations supported what a recent British ambassador described as the "extraordinary power of . . . Congress over foreign policy" in the United States.[1]

Executive policy makers have increasingly acknowledged the crucial role that Congress plays in the foreign relations of the United States. Although before entering government service, Henry Kissinger had been dubious about undue legislative influence in foreign affairs, as secretary of state he called for "a new national partnership" between the president and Congress in dealing with international issues.[2] During the early 1980s, the chairman of the Senate Foreign Relations Committee, Sen. Charles H. Percy, R-Ill., observed that unless there was "a joint approach to U.S. foreign policy, which both branches of government backed by substantial elements of both parties must work to forge," the United States would be unlikely to achieve its foreign policy goals.[3] Early in his administration, President Reagan sought to revive the bipartisanship in foreign affairs that had characterized executive-legislative relations under the Truman and Eisenhower administrations, and he periodically repeated his call for a return to bipartisan collaboration in dealing with foreign policy questions. Reagan and his White House aides acknowledged that successful dialogue between executive and legislative leaders was indispensable for unified efforts in the foreign policy field.[4]

Although executive officials and informed students of American foreign policy are becoming increasingly aware of the expanding role of Congress in foreign policy, they are often far from enthusiastic about its implications. Presidents Johnson, Nixon, Ford, Carter, and Reagan vocally opposed legislative efforts to limit their powers abroad and to exercise powers they believed to be constitutional and historical prerogatives of the executive branch.

From the perspective of the White House, President Gerald R. Ford, himself a representative from Michigan for more than twenty years, lamented that congressional activities not infrequently impeded America's ability to achieve its foreign policy objectives. "The pendulum has swung so far," he once said, "that you could almost say we have moved from an imperial Presidency to an imperiled Presidency. Now we have a Congress that is broadening its powers in foreign relations too greatly." [5]

Similar judgments were expressed by informed students of the American governmental system during the Reagan administration. An experienced State Department official, for example, feared that legislative activism in foreign affairs had brought about a reversal in the traditional contributions of the president and Congress to the foreign policy process—to the detriment of American diplomatic undertakings. Sen. Alan K. Simpson, R-Wyo., complained that Congress was so internally "fragmented" that it was perhaps incapable of providing leadership in foreign and domestic affairs. Another experienced observer of the U.S. political scene asked: "How does a nation live with a Congress that counts more brilliant men than ever before but cannot lead, and will follow no leadership?" Since the Watergate crisis of the Nixon administration, Congress had been "in revolt" against the presidency. Yet Congress itself "can offer no solutions" to urgent internal and external problems.[6]

What have been the principal causes of recent congressional activism in the foreign policy field? What can be identified as the most significant consequences of forceful legislative influence upon American foreign relations? And what will be the future balance between executive and legislative influence in the foreign policy process? These three important and interrelated questions provide the framework for discussion in the concluding chapter of our study.

Congressional Assertiveness:
Background and Causes

According to the provisions of the Constitution, as we saw in Part I, Congress possesses a number of prerogatives that allow it to influence foreign relations. Congress must appropriate funds needed for innumerable programs in foreign affairs. It has the power to declare war; and it must raise and support the armed forces. The Senate has two unique constitutional functions not shared with the House of Representatives: the requirement that treaties receive the advice and consent of the Senate, and the provision that most of the president's major appointments be confirmed by the Senate. From the foundation of the American republic, therefore, it was envisioned that Congress would be involved in the solution of diplomatic problems, although in many important respects the exact scope and nature of its involvement was left to be determined by experience.

The powers of the chief executive in foreign relations expanded significantly over the course of time—leading by the mid-1960s to a condition of virtually unchecked presidential authority in diplomacy. The accretion of the president's diplomatic influence became particularly pronounced after the United States emerged as a superpower at the end of World War II. Perhaps the most remarkable fact about this growth in presidential authority in foreign relations was how seldom it was challenged by Congress. In fact, during several eras the enhancement of presidential power could have occurred only with the explicit or tacit concurrence of Congress. The Roosevelt administration's conduct of World War II and the escalation of the Vietnam War under Presidents Kennedy and Johnson are two examples.

Today, the era of congressional passivity or acquiescence in presidential decisions in the foreign policy field has ended. As a former official of the Johnson administration has expressed it: "In the present world situation, far greater congressional and public involvement in formulating our foreign policy seems to me not only right but nearly inevitable."[7] One reason for greater congressional involvement in foreign policy making is the interrelationship between foreign affairs and domestic issues. According to a former member of the House of Representatives, "foreign and domestic policy have merged into a seamless web of interlocking concerns."[8]

Since the New Deal program of the 1930s, American society has also witnessed what might be called a legislative explosion of vast dimensions. Untold thousands of new laws have been enacted by Congress during the past half-century. An increasing proportion of Congress's time is devoted to adding to this list, to making needed changes in existing legislation, and to overseeing the administration of the laws already enacted. Much of this activity is based upon the premise that the solution to pressing national problems lies in the enactment of legislation.[9]

In America's approach to problems beyond its own borders since World War II, basically the same tendency can be discerned. The Truman administration's adoption of the containment strategy for resisting Communist expansionism in 1947 committed the United States to a new diplomatic role, inescapably enhancing the powers of Congress in foreign affairs. For over a generation thereafter, the continuity of American foreign policy—from ongoing economic and military assistance programs, to the defense of NATO, to the creation and maintenance of an adequate defense establishment—has depended upon favorable action by Congress. Moreover, congressional behavior in confronting closely related domestic issues, such as the level of taxation, overall governmental spending, and the development of natural resources, has directly affected U.S. relations with other countries.

Internal Changes in Congress

A number of identifiable changes have occurred within Congress in the past ten years that have contributed to legislative activism in foreign affairs. We will examine three of the most important of these changes.

Diffusion of Power.   Partly as a result of efforts to reform Congress since World War II, the problem of dispersed power within the House and Senate has become increasingly acute in recent years. As noted in Chapter 2, most congressional committees are involved in some aspect of foreign affairs, and their jurisdictions over foreign policy issues frequently overlap. Congressional deliberations today seem more disunified than at any other stage in American history. According to an experienced observer of the Washington scene, "Never since the Senate defied Woodrow Wilson on the importance of creating a League of Nations ... has the Congress ... seemed as parochial, personal or divided as it does now." [10]

The problem of internal disunity within the legislative branch did not diminish perceptibly during the Reagan administration. Thus, in 1982 one study of how American legislators themselves perceive Congress found widespread complaints about the lack of effective leadership in the House and Senate, about the independence enjoyed by the principal committees of Congress, and about the degree to which overlapping committee jurisdictions and responsibilities inhibited a unified legislative approach to major policy issues. Despite several efforts since World War II, the need for far-reaching reforms within Congress remained compelling.[11]

Expansion of Staff. A second change that has affected the ability of Congress to play a more assertive role in foreign policy making is the expansion of legislative staff. In mid-1979, Sen. William Proxmire, D-Wis., confounded his colleagues by conferring the "Golden Fleece Award" for questionable expenditures of taxpayers' money on none other than Congress itself. Proxmire pointed out that the staff of the Senate and House had risen sharply, with over seven thousand in the former and eleven thousand in the latter in 1987. In 1969, the average number of staff employees per senator was thirty-four; ten years later, it was sixty-eight. The cost of maintaining this legislative bureaucracy had climbed from $150 million to $550 million annually.[12]

Today, members of the House and Senate can no longer legitimately complain about staff shortages on Capitol Hill. One study of Congress has asserted that "Congress ... has developed a virtual counter-State Department composed of predominantly young, experienced and aggressive experts who are out to make their own marks on the foreign policy map."[13]

A greatly expanded staff has had a twofold impact upon Congress's role in foreign affairs. A larger staff provides Congress the means to assert its own independent position vis-à-vis the executive branch with regard to major international questions. It also supplies national legislators with a new incentive to become active in a field where, during an earlier period, they often had neither the interest nor the expertise to become deeply involved.

Staff expansion has also added momentum to centrifugal tendencies within Congress itself. Hardly a committee or individual member of Congress lacks (or is unable to acquire) adequate staff assistance for dealing with international issues. As one commentator has observed, now each member of the House and Senate is better equipped than ever "to go his separate way and establish his own domain of power and prestige."[14]

Increased Participation by the House. Until the period of the Vietnam War, the House of Representatives usually played a subordinate role in the foreign policy process. Although members of the House sometimes chafed at their inferior position vis-à-vis the Senate in external policy making, they were normally content to accept understandings worked out between executive officials and influential senators and Senate committees with jurisdiction over foreign policy questions.[15] In recent years, however, the era of passivity by the House in foreign relations has ended. For example, members of the House tried to influence the new Panama Canal treaties, negotiated and ratified by the Carter administration. Members of the House objected to being excluded from the treaty-making process. Before the agreements were formally ratified, committees and subcommittees in the House played an active role in efforts to influence their provisions relating, for example, to the nation's defense commitments in the Panama Canal area.

Increased participation by the House in foreign affairs can be explained on several grounds other than mere jealousy of the Senate's constitutional prerogatives. The growing interrelationship between domestic and external problems dictates a more dynamic role by the House in diplomatic decision making. As never before, Congress is called upon to enact legislation and to appropriate funds for implementing foreign policy proposals and programs. Advocates of greater House influence are convinced that the House can make a vital and distinctive contribution in Congress's deliberations on international questions. Since its members must stand for election every two years, the House provides the kind of "recurrent plebiscite on the foreign policy of the United States" that no other institution of the American government can contribute.[16]

External Influences on Congress

Legislative activism in foreign affairs has been influenced not only by changes within Congress, but also by several new forms of external pressure: by the nature and dynamics of American public opinion, by increased lobbying efforts by interest groups, and by lobbying on the part of executive agencies. Let us examine each of these influences.

Public Opinion. Since the Wilsonian era, public opinion has emerged as an influential force affecting the course of American diplomacy. Mounting public opposition to Soviet expansionism, for example, was a potent factor inducing the Truman administration to adopt the policy of containment against the Soviet Union. Conversely, a generation later, growing public disenchantment with the nation's role in Southeast Asia was crucial in the Nixon administration's decision to terminate the war in Vietnam. In the late 1970s and the 1980s congressional opinion and public opinion were significant factors in inducing the Carter and Reagan administrations to stiffen their positions toward Soviet interventionism and to strengthen the American defense establishment. Then during the late 1980s, public sentiment was again a significant influence leading to intensive Soviet and American efforts to reduce the level of global armaments. In such instances, legislators were instrumental in communicating the nature and force of public sentiment to executive officials.

In keeping with the idea that Congress is the most representative branch of the American government, legislators believe that viewpoints expressed in the House and Senate provide the most authoritative expression of public thinking available to the president and his advisers.

The House International Relations Committee (now the Foreign Affairs Committee) emphasized this point in a 1977 report on Congress and foreign policy:

> Congressmen, by being in continuous contact with the people and representing their disparate interests and concerns, have served not only to ensure democratic control over the foreign policymaking process, but have also been the conveyors of sometimes ambivalent and occasionally vociferous public opinion.
>
> Recent events have demonstrated that without a genuine public consensus of support, the executive branch cannot legitimately and effectively pursue any foreign policy.[17]

Congress's perception of its relationship to public opinion as it bears upon foreign relations has several specific implications. Many legislators believe it is uniquely incumbent upon Congress to foster public awareness and better understanding of foreign policy issues. As the chairman of the Senate Foreign Relations Committee defined its responsibilities in 1979, the committee had an obligation to "stimulate public debate"; it was the "main forum" for promoting public discussion of external policy questions.[18]

Alternatively, some legislators believe it is the responsibility of Congress to confront executive policy makers with public sentiment concerning a particular course of action in foreign affairs. This contribution by Congress to the American foreign policy process was well illustrated in the early 1980s by legislative insistence that President Ronald Reagan and his military advisers rethink the proposed MX missile system. As a result of legislative opposition, the president appointed a bipartisan commission to study the question; the commission's recommendations (which clearly reflected a number of public and congressional apprehensions about the MX missile system) went far toward providing a broader and more defensible rationale for the administration's nuclear strategy.[19]

On most foreign policy questions, however, the American people seldom speak with a unified voice. Particularly since the Vietnam War, popular attitudes toward foreign affairs have been marked by confusion, ambiguities, and contradictions. On the one hand, as the election of Ronald Reagan in 1980 indicated, by the end of the 1970s the American people had once again become apprehensive about communist gains and the deterioration of U.S. power abroad. Reflecting public sentiment, Congress clearly supported the Reagan administration's effort to strengthen the defense establishment and to bolster American power in regions like the Persian Gulf area. On the other hand (as has been illustrated by the continuing controversy over American diplomacy in Central America), Americans were alarmed by the prospect that they would become involved in another Vietnam. In another sphere, Soviet-

American relations, American opinion showed the same ambivalence: the people remained apprehensive about the Kremlin's diplomatic goals and behavior, but they also called for the Reagan administration to undertake serious negotiations with Moscow to reduce the level of global armaments and to resolve other outstanding issues.[20] Even on a single issue such as better Soviet-American understanding, American attitudes oscillated between approbation and fear of its consequences and implications.[21] As one commentator has pointed out:

> We may simply have to learn to conduct foreign policy for a very long time without a single unifying theme on which to base a broad national consensus. Both the nature of the problems abroad and their diverse impact on American public opinion at home now point strongly to such a conclusion.[22]

A national consensus is also lacking on such issues as the operations of the intelligence community and human rights practices abroad. As noted in Chapter 6, Congress responded to the American people's apprehensions about certain questionable activities of the CIA and other members of the intelligence community. Yet as demonstrated by developments like the Iranian revolution and the discovery of a large Soviet military presence in Cuba during the late 1970s, the American people questioned the adequacy of U.S. intelligence operations and called for their improvement. During the Reagan administration also, fundamental questions were raised about covert CIA operations in the Persian Gulf area, in Central America, and in other regions. Some of these activities violated either the letter or the spirit of the law—and in some instances, perhaps both. At the same time, Congress and the American people remained concerned about Communist gains abroad. Accordingly, there was no discernible sentiment in favor of dismantling the CIA or prohibiting covert intelligence activities overseas. Similarly, Congress has actively sought to protect and promote human rights in other countries. At the same time, evidence of human rights violations did not deter Congress from providing economic and military aid to such countries as the Philippines, South Korea, and El Salvador.[23]

The public has approached major international questions since Vietnam eclectically, pragmatically, and with a good measure of common sense. As one commentator explained:

> Faced with some different ideas and a changing world, Americans chose eclectically what they thought made sense and rejected what they thought didn't.... Such, then, has been the pattern of accommodation, eclecticism and shameless synthesis that the American public has demonstrated in recent years.... Exposed to new doctrines [in foreign policy], the public made careful choices.... They put their choice to one essential test: Did it make common sense? If it did—fine. If not—back on the shelf.[24]

Inevitably, Congress's approach to foreign policy issues is heavily colored by these dominant characteristics of American public opinion.

Lobbying by Interest Groups and Foreign Governments. While lobbying is not a new phenomenon in the nation's history, some members and former members of Congress believe that legislators have become increasingly responsive to the campaigns of well-funded and highly organized pressure groups.[25] A number of factors have produced a favorable environment for pressure group activity in recent years: the expanding role of government in all spheres of American life; the lack of a public consensus in the United States on foreign policy issues; the decline of party identification by citizens and the weakening of party discipline on Capitol Hill; the emergence of single-issue politics (in which one issue, such as gun control or abortion, can dominate a political campaign); and the growing diffusion of power within the House and Senate. One recent study called attention to the "385 standing committees and subcommittees [of Congress] being pursued by more than 1,300 registered lobby groups." Instead of the traditional two-party system, there now appeared to exist on Capitol Hill "a 385-party system." [26]

Lobbying by foreign governments, whose efforts are frequently supported by internal pressure groups, has also had momentous consequences for recent American foreign policy. In many cases, foreign governments appeal White House decisions in foreign affairs to the more sympathetic legislative branch. Governments abroad now routinely ignore the once firmly established principle that the president is "the sole organ" of the nation in its relations with other countries.[27]

Many foreign governments today have a direct stake in supporting a more active and independent foreign policy role for Congress.[28] As we saw in Chapter 4, the pro-Israeli lobby has repeatedly mounted intensive campaigns to have Congress block or reverse White House decisions thought inimical to Israel. Early in the 1980s, a report on lobbying by foreign interests referred to "multimillion dollar lobbying campaigns aimed at swaying U.S. policies" abroad. It is estimated that overall spending by lobbyists representing governments and political groups overseas exceeds $100 million annually. Justice Department records show that 701 persons were registered as agents of foreign governments in 1982 (compared to 452 in 1970). Among this group were a number of former senators and representatives.[29]

Lobbying by the Executive Branch. Lobbying activities by executive agencies on behalf of the president's programs and policies can be another crucial factor in determining Congress's role in the foreign policy process. Most executive agencies have one office that is primarily responsible for communicating to Congress the views of the executive branch. For example, within the State Department the legislative liaison function is performed by the Bureau of Congressional Relations. Sometimes executive agencies also form alliances with private citizens' organizations to influence attitudes both within Congress and throughout American society.[30]

A correlation exists between effective lobbying activities by the executive branch and the level of congressional activism in foreign affairs, as illustrated by the record of the Carter administration. On numerous occasions President Carter and his advisers complained about congressionally imposed restraints upon executive management of foreign affairs. Yet President Carter's aides were inexperienced in legislative relations and, in some instances, their tactics in dealing with legislators generated resentment and irritation on Capitol Hill.[31]

The record of the Reagan administration in respect to executive-legislative relations was quite clearly mixed. On the one hand, during Reagan's first term especially, the president and his advisers called for a revival of bipartisanship in the conduct of foreign relations; and the White House adopted such measures as appointing bipartisan commissions to advise the president on such controversial issues as the proposed MX missile system and American foreign policy toward Central America. (Critics charged that the latter commission particularly, chaired by former secretary of state Henry Kissinger, had been constituted to yield a predetermined result.)[32] Despite such steps, it could be questioned whether, on balance, the Reagan White House actually achieved a high level of executive-legislative cooperation in the foreign policy field. Certainly by 1987, the well-publicized Iran-contra affair—resulting ultimately in a highly critical document by Congress denouncing the management of foreign relations by the president and his principal aides[33]—did little to promote collaboration between executive and legislative policy makers in Washington. In fact, as the Reagan administration drew to an end, executive-legislative relations seemed as strained and as unproductive in dealing with foreign policy issues as in any era since the end of the Vietnam War.

The failure of a president and his subordinates to engage in effective legislative liaison activities produces a condition tailor-made for legislative diplomatic activism. Not only does it ensure that Congress will exert its viewpoints and prerogatives forcefully in the foreign policy process; it also contributes to making congressional efforts episodic, uncoordinated, and inconsistent.

Leadership Failure in the White House

By the late 1970s, a deep-seated anxiety existed on Capitol Hill and among many segments of American public opinion that the influence of the United States abroad had declined in recent years. In the years that followed, the fear that the United States would find itself involved in another Vietnam was at the forefront of legislative and popular sentiment toward foreign policy issues.

Advocates of a more forceful congressional role in external affairs have brought two somewhat contradictory indictments against recent chief executives. Presidents Johnson, Nixon, and Reagan were criticized for using (or threatening to use) the vast powers of the presidency in behalf of ill-conceived foreign policy ventures, such as the Vietnam conflict and military intervention in Latin America. By contrast, Presidents Ford and Carter were criticized widely for failing to use the powers at their command to respond forcefully and successfully to external challenges, such as the ongoing Soviet military buildup, the Soviet invasion of Afghanistan, and Communist gains in the Caribbean and Central America. Critics declared that a precipitous decline in American power and influence abroad had resulted. During the late 1970s Senate Minority Leader Howard Baker of Tennessee expressed a typical opinion when he complained that Americans were tired of being "pushed around" by other countries. They wanted President Carter "to be firmer, more consistent, a little less smiling, and Mr. Nice Guy." Baker and other Republicans accused the Carter administration of "presiding over the decay of American influence and the decline of American military power." [34]

Then by the early 1980s (as American society confronted a serious domestic recession and a mounting federal deficit), the opposite viewpoint was widely expressed. Critics charged that President Reagan and his advisers had become preoccupied with a massive defense buildup, that they were neglecting the nation's internal well-being, and that they were engaging in diplomatic adventurism that entailed unwanted foreign commitments and burdens. Informed critics of President Reagan's diplomacy noted that, on the one hand, the Reagan White House had the highest defense budget in history. On the other hand, it had not yet produced a clear and consistent strategy or rationale for using the nation's potent military arsenal in behalf of diplomatic objectives.[35]

Divisions within the executive branch have also invited strong legislative initiatives in foreign affairs. As one American political commentator lamented: "The misconduct of foreign affairs in the United States has lately become something of an international scandal. You can seldom pick up a newspaper these days without reading about some self-appointed Secretary of State who is embarrassing the country." [36] A newsworthy example was provided in 1987, when House Speaker Jim Wright (D-Texas) injected himself into negotiations between the Sandinista government of Nicaragua and anticommunist groups who were seeking to find a formula for political stability in Central America. In the White House view, Wright's action raised major questions about who was really in charge of American foreign policy.[37]

President Carter's secretary of state, his chief national security adviser, and his special envoy to the Middle East all held different views on the steps to be taken in resolving the Arab-Israeli conflict. During the Reagan administration the problem of intra-executive conflicts on major foreign policy issues showed no signs of disappearing. Secretary of State Alexander Haig's resignation less than eighteen months after he took office called attention to ongoing conflict among Reagan's advisers on external problems. The problem did not disappear with Haig's replacement by George Shultz. In the months ahead, not only Secretary of State Shultz, but also Secretary of Defense Caspar Weinberger found themselves relegated to the sidelines of policy making by members of President Reagan's staff on the National Security Council. As the revelations in the Iran-contra affair indicated, some of these staff members, working closely with high officials in the Central Intelligence Agency, undertook independent policy initiatives in the Middle East and Central America; in some instances, even the president was unaware of these activities, although other activities had explicit or implicit presidential approval. Some of these steps, as in making arms available to the revolutionary government of Iran, were in direct conflict with the president's own foreign policy declarations and directives.

Perhaps more than any other comparable development since the Vietnam War, the Iran-contra affair raised fundamental questions about who was in fact "conducting" American foreign relations—if indeed anyone actually was! Such conditions in turn invited forceful attempts by Congress to take control of the nation's diplomatic efforts. Yet, as events during and after the Iran-contra affair indicated, it was at best debatable whether Congress was really able to discharge such a responsibility effectively.[38]

Congressional Assertiveness: Consequences and Implications

What impact has a more assertive and independent diplomatic role by Congress had upon American foreign policy? What have been its consequences—both positive and negative—upon the conduct of foreign relations by the United States? These questions merit more detailed examination in the light of our case studies and of other examples of Congress's recent dynamism in the foreign policy field.

Independent Legislative Initiatives

Until the period of the Vietnam War, it was a clearly established principle that negotiations with foreign governments were an executive prerogative. For example, long-standing precedent supports the view that the president or his designated agent makes or negotiates treaties with other governments. One of the earliest enactments of Congress was the Logan Act, which prohibits unauthorized contacts or negotiations between Americans and foreign officials.[39] Although such contacts today have become commonplace—and no citizen has ever been prosecuted for violating its terms—the Logan Act remains the law of the land.

In the period since World War II, legislators have frequently been involved in the conduct of diplomatic negotiations—but nearly always at the invitation of the president. Today the appointment of legislators as members of American negotiating teams is an accepted technique for creating bipartisan support for the nation's foreign policy. The Carter administration attempted to win widespread congressional support for the proposed SALT II agreements with the Soviet Union by allowing "26 Senators, 14 Republicans and 12 Democrats, including opponents and critics, and 46 members of the House of Representatives, to sit in on the arms negotiations in Geneva" at one time or another.[40] President Reagan utilized legislators as "observers" of national elections in El Salvador in 1982; in 1983, he appointed a former senator, Richard Stone, to serve as his special envoy in an effort to promote political stability in Central America.

The novel feature of Congress's involvement in diplomatic negotiations today is the tendency of legislators to engage in them independently—without White House approval, and sometimes in the face of presidential opposition. In 1979 Sen. Jesse Helms, a member of the Foreign Relations Committee, sent two staff members to London to observe diplomatic discussions (to which the United States was not even a party) designed to end the long-standing civil conflict in Zimbabwe (formerly Rhodesia). Senator Helms's justification was candid: "I don't trust the State Department on this issue." [41]

Another newsworthy example of Congress's direct intervention in foreign relations occurred after Iranian students seized the American embassy in Tehran on November 4, 1979, and held some fifty Americans hostage. After early White House efforts to gain the release of the hostages failed, Rep. George Hansen, R-Idaho, undertook his own self-appointed peace mission to Iran, where he visited the hostages and sought to obtain their release. Hansen's efforts also failed, and his unauthorized negotiations during the crisis were criticized by executive and legislative officials alike, who feared his initiatives would undermine the president's authority and would provide evidence of disunity within the American government during the crisis.[42]

Earlier, reference was made to House Speaker Wright's involvement in efforts to negotiate a political settlement in Central America. Once again, the White House criticized this legislative intrusion into the

236 Invitation to Struggle

sphere of diplomatic negotiations. These examples clearly support the precedent that legislators may now engage in the negotiating process freely. Perhaps legislators do so on the theory that, in the absence of overt White House objections, they have the president's tacit approval. In any case, the practice is bound to raise questions abroad about who is ultimately in charge of American foreign policy and about how durable agreements reached with a variety of American officials are likely to be.

The recognition of other governments is another area—long regarded as an executive province—into which Congress has intruded during the past decade. Early in 1979 several senators attempted to make President Carter's decision to recognize the People's Republic of China (PRC) contingent upon Peking's pledge not to use force in exerting its longstanding claim to sovereignty over Taiwan. In effect, these legislators wanted to threaten the PRC with withdrawal of American recognition if it attempted to seize Taiwan by force. While the president and his advisers were mindful of congressional concern about the future of Taiwan, they were unwilling to condition American recognition upon the PRC's behavior in the matter.

Expansion of Treaty-Making Role

As noted in Chapter 2, the Senate has relied upon its constitutional prerogatives in the treaty-making process to assert its influence in the diplomatic field, and the House has sought to use other prerogatives (for example, its dominant role in the appropriations process) to compensate for the Senate's constitutionally unique position. Several significant aspects of Congress's involvement in the negotiation and ratification of treaties have come to the fore in recent years. In contrast to earlier years, since World War II the Senate has shown that it is determined to construe its role in the treaty process actively and to leave its imprint on major international agreements entered into by the United States. Three recent examples—the new Panama Canal treaties, the SALT II arms limitation accord, and demands on Capitol Hill that the Reagan administration negotiate a nuclear freeze with the Soviet Union—are cases in point.

In the instances of the Panama Canal treaties and SALT II, Senate deliberations were prolonged, thorough, and in the end extremely influential. (Mounting Senate opposition to SALT II was one factor motivating President Carter to withdraw the treaty from further Senate deliberation.) The issue of the nuclear freeze presented an essentially different question: Could legislators compel an obviously reluctant chief executive to undertake negotiations with another government in behalf of a nuclear freeze or some other goal favored by Congress? Legally and on the basis of precedents, the answer was not really in doubt: As explained in Chapter 1, under the Constitution the president makes treaties, or enters into negotiations with other governments; the Senate considers treaties submitted to it by the executive branch. Yet realistically, President Reagan and other modern chief executives knew that such forceful expressions of legislative sentiment unquestionably reflected deep public concern about the threat of nuclear devastation; and they were no less aware that, even if Congress could not force a president to negotiate a Soviet-American arms freeze, legislators could demonstrate their discontent about American diplomacy in other ways (such as by cutting defense expenditures).[43]

During the late 1970s another interesting aspect of the Senate's prerogative in treaty making was raised when twenty-five senators contended in federal court that the existing defense treaty with Taiwan could be terminated only with congressional approval. In a decision by a United States court of appeals—sustained by the Supreme Court—the judiciary ruled that the termination of the treaty in this case was a presidential prerogative.[44]

Still another interesting aspect of the treaty power arose during President Ronald Reagan's second term, involving the meaning of the ABM treaty between the United States and the Soviet Union in 1972 (as explained in Chapter 3). As interpreted by the Reagan White House, the provisions of this agreement should be construed flexibly, to permit the administration to move ahead with the development of the Strategic Defense Initiative (or "Star Wars") space-based defense system, designed to protect the nation from enemy missiles. When the Senate considered the treaty, officials of the Nixon administration gave assurances that it prohibited what the Reagan administration said it permitted. A number of leading senators, therefore, contended that the president could not unilaterally decide upon the meaning of an international obligation entered into by action of both branches of the government. This latter point of view, needless to say, was unacceptable to the chief executive and other high-ranking executive officials involved in the foreign policy process. While it is difficult to see how legislators could force a certain interpretation of a treaty upon an unwilling president, critics on Capitol Hill could spearhead a movement to deny the White House funds needed to move ahead with the Star Wars scheme or other programs in national defense and foreign affairs.[45]

The Pattern of Overseas Commitments

Since World War II, Congress has been determined to play a more influential role in the assumption and maintenance of the overseas commitments of the United States. Has there been a consistent pattern of legislative activity concerning these overseas obligations? For the most part, the answer is no. Congress has curtailed some of them, it has expanded others, and it has maintained still other international commitments largely intact. Most important, Congress has insisted far more adamantly than ever before that the nation's international obligations be made a matter of public record.

First, let us examine overseas commitments that have been cut or curtailed by Congress since the late 1960s. The Vietnam War was terminated by act of Congress (although in the Nixon administration's view, that process had already begun before Congress ordered it). In the ensuing years, adverse congressional sentiment was a potent factor in preventing possible consideration of foreign aid to North Vietnam.

By enacting the War Powers Resolution in 1973, Congress imposed several new limitations upon the authority of the chief executive to use the armed forces; yet, as we saw in Chapter 5, congressional insistence upon strict compliance with the terms of the War Powers Resolution has been less than stringent. Toward Angola, Congress denied the White House authority to use military force and to carry on covert intelligence operations (a restriction Congress later lifted). And in several foreign countries with repressive governments that jeopardized the rights of their citizens, Congress has—or has threatened to—cut off American aid and trade.

The limitations imposed by Congress upon the president's management of foreign affairs operate both ways, however. Beginning with the Johnson administration, every chief executive has complained about congressionally imposed restrictions upon presidential freedom of action in foreign relations. President Nixon and his national security adviser, Henry Kissinger, were persuaded that—except for congressional interference in the conduct of the Vietnam War—executive policy makers could have obtained a much more advantageous settlement of the conflict.[46] President Reagan believed that congressionally imposed restrictions upon executive activities in Central America seriously impeded his efforts to contain Communist expansionism in the western hemisphere.

On other occasions, however, executive policy makers have found actual or potential congressional restraints upon their freedom of action diplomatically useful. Former Secretary of State Kissinger has recounted several instances in which the president and his advisers used the threat of a severe congressional reduction in America's overseas commitments as a diplomatic gambit in negotiating with foreign governments. And the Nixon administration repeatedly informed the NATO allies that unless they increased their contribution to the defense of the western alliance, Congress would almost certainly reduce America's troop contribution to the NATO area.[47] Similarly, the Reagan administration unquestionably relied upon actual or potential congressional reductions in economic and military aid to El Salvador in order to induce internal reforms in that country.

Since the Vietnam War congressional activism in foreign affairs has not infrequently taken the opposite course: *expansion* of the nation's overseas obligations. Congress has at least tacitly approved most military base agreements negotiated by executive officials with foreign countries. It did not block efforts by the White House to augment American military power in the Indian Ocean. Despite criticisms about failure to consult Congress, legislators did not fundamentally object to the Reagan administration's use of force against Libya or to the more extensive and costly buildup of American military power in the Persian Gulf area. Significantly, in the latter case, few legislators insisted that the president adhere to the terms of the War Powers Resolution.

Even before the Carter administration left office—and the impetus continued under the Reagan administration—support was evident on Capitol Hill for the acquisition of new naval bases in the Persian Gulf area, along with the creation of a powerful military strike force (the Rapid Deployment Force, RDF) capable of protecting American defense and security interests in the Middle East and other foreign settings. Moreover, although the funds provided for the purpose vary from year to year, Congress continues to support foreign economic and military aid programs. Despite periodic efforts to reduce America's contribution, Congress also continues to support a substantial American military presence in Western Europe. It is perhaps most significant that, despite disagreements on Capitol Hill about the precise allocations for new weapons, manpower needs, research and development, and other budgetary components, year after year since 1980 legislators have approved record-level spending for national defense.

Owing in no small measure to congressional initiatives, contemporary American foreign policy is governed now, more than in any previous era of history, by the Wilsonian principle of "open convenants, openly arrived at." Henry Kissinger's visit to the Chinese mainland in 1971 on behalf of the Nixon administration was remarkable not only because it inaugurated the new era of rapprochement in Sino-American relations, but also because it was a diplomatic initiative by the executive branch that was kept secret for some time from Congress.[48]

To the degree that a better informed Congress and citizenry provide a more secure foundation for effective diplomacy, legislative insistence upon maximum publicity for international commitments has clearly been a gain. The Vietnam War experience demonstrated convincingly that public support is indispensable for military and diplomatic success abroad.

Problems with Congressional Policy Making

Although Congress has adopted a more assertive role in foreign affairs, it may be doubted that the nature of congressional decision making lends itself to effective foreign policy management. A former State Department official has called legislative power in foreign policy a "blunt instrument," which not infrequently has resulted in "a series of uncoordinated actions that annoyed the Secretary of State more than it advanced coherent policy." On some occasions, legislators have threatened to paralyze American foreign policy unless the White House abandoned or changed a proposed course of action.[49] According to one of President Carter's aides, "Congress ties the President's hands on foreign policy, scrutinizing and criticizing every move he makes, sometimes jeopardizing relations with our allies and unpredictable foes."[50]

Even individuals with legislative experience have expressed concern about Congress's intrusion into the foreign policy field. J. William Fulbright, former Senate Foreign Relations Committee chairman, said:

> I confess to increasingly serious misgivings about the ability of the Congress to play a constructive role in our foreign relations. . . . those of us who prodded what seemed to be a hopelessly immobile herd of cattle [Congress] a decade ago, now stand back in awe in the face of a stampede.[51]

Basically the same complaints, as well as others, were expressed about Congress's foreign policy role in the 1980s. Thus, one legislator acknowledged that cabinet members and other officials of the executive branch could justifiably complain about the "repetitious testimony" they were required to give the House and Senate and about the lack of identifiable and effective leadership on Capitol Hill. Another legislator lamented the Senate's apparent inability "to control events," its internal fragmentation, and its growing susceptibility to pressure group campaigns. As legislators were considering such complex issues as the proposed MX missile system and Soviet-American arms-control negotiations, another senator deplored "the incredible lack of knowledge about the Soviet people and Soviet history" that existed on Capitol Hill. After reviewing the consequences of a number of congressionally imposed restrictions upon the president's diplomatic behavior during the 1970s, another experienced legislator called upon Congress to "reexamine its role in the conduct of foreign policy and repeal or amend, as necessary" most of this legislation, since it clearly posed an obstacle to "a unified, coherent and cohesive foreign policy."[52]

In the words of one young, liberal senator, Congress possesses the ability to "foul up foreign policy," and it has done so from time to time in recent years.[53] The congressional response to the discovery in August 1979 of a large contingent of Soviet troops in Cuba, for example, was confusing and ambiguous. One national news journal concluded that the Kremlin was "notoriously loath to let U.S. Senators beat them with sticks" on the Cuban question. Mishandling of the whole affair in Washington, the article concluded,

not only casts still more doubt on the leadership of the Carter administration but also raises a longer-term and more disturbing question
about whether the Congress—recently so assertive about playing a
bigger role in foreign policy—can help solve crises rather than manufacturing and aggravating them.[54]

During the 1970s and 1980s, it might be doubted how much congressional interest in the subject actually advanced the cause of human
rights in other countries. It was at least debatable, for example, whether
legislative initiatives had in fact advanced the cause of freedom in Iran
or Pakistan, although it may have done so in other settings (like Brazil).

Congress often approaches external policy making as an exercise in
law making, and that may be one reason why its assertive role in foreign
affairs has not always been productive. According to a former State
Department official, by the end of the 1970s Congress had imposed
"more than 150 statutory limitations on the United States' relations
with foreign countries." Commenting on the congressional tendency to
envision diplomatic questions in legal terms or as legal contests, he
added: "Foreign policy has become almost synonymous with law making. The result is to place a straitjacket of legislation around the
manifold complexity of our relations with other nations." [55]

Although he was an advocate of bipartisan executive-legislative
collaboration in foreign affairs, Sen. Arthur Vandenberg, R-Mich., was
also concerned about some of the implications of Congress's forceful
intrusion into the foreign policy field. On one occasion he warned: "I
think the Senate is entitled, at any time it pleases, to ... tell the
Executive what it thinks concerning foreign affairs. But I think it would
be a tragic and unfortunate thing if the habit ever became general or too
contagious." [56]

Implicit in Vandenberg's admonition is a distinction, although it
has become increasingly ill-defined, between an expanded legislative
voice in policy formulation and in the conduct or execution of foreign
affairs. The former is a province in which Congress can and should
participate. The day-to-day management of foreign relations, however,
is another matter. This is not a realm into which Congress should
intrude regularly, nor is it really equipped to do so. Nevertheless, as one
study pointed out, Congress has appeared "determined to play havoc
with policy implementation." [57]

Foreigners have always found unique and bewildering the American
system of separation of powers among three coordinate branches of
government. But in no previous era has the foreign policy process in the
United States perhaps proved so mystifying and frustrating for outsiders. Recent diplomatic experience has shown that agreement with the
administration, even when the president's party controls Congress, often counts for little. After arriving at understandings with executive

officials, in many cases foreign negotiators then have "to enter into separate external relations with the American Congress, and renegotiate ... the agreement reached." [58]

Most governments endeavor to arrive at a unified foreign policy position before they enter into negotiations with other states, but judging from recent examples, a unified position among policy makers in the United States is often arrived at only *after* understandings have been reached with foreign governments. This led one Soviet spokesman to ask, "With whom in America can we have dealings?" For foreign officials, it was "still not clear who exactly in the U.S. can speak in international relations on behalf of the United States." [59]

Congressional Assertiveness: Probabilities and Prospects

What is the future of congressional assertiveness in American foreign relations? Has it become a permanent feature of the foreign policy process in the United States, or is it merely a phase that will be followed in time by a new era of executive dominance in external affairs? A number of diverse and contrary factors will determine the answers to these questions in the years ahead.

Factors Favoring an Expanded Role

A persuasive case can be made for the contention that Congress will continue to exercise a powerful—in some instances, a decisive—voice in foreign affairs for the indefinite future. Executive officials, foreign governments, and the public must come to terms with this possibility.

Global and Domestic Setting. Among the forces that engender and sustain an energetic role by Congress in foreign affairs, none is perhaps more important than the changing nature of the global agenda. In the second half of the twentieth century, unique and often extremely difficult issues have come to the forefront of international concern: economic stability, the pressing needs of the less developed societies, the increasingly acute world food shortage, runaway population growth throughout most of the Third World, and worldwide environmental problems. Today the solution to these major international and regional problems requires active participation by Congress.

In the United States and in most other countries since World War II, the role of government has expanded to meet these challenges. This trend is both exemplified and sustained by the volume of legislation produced by Congress in the postwar era. One way of looking at the diplomatic activism of Congress, therefore, is to observe that the legislative branch is finally taking the same approach in dealing with external affairs that it has taken toward domestic issues since the New Deal: Congress is attempting to solve major public policy questions by enacting legislation and by relying upon other powers incident to law making, such as the oversight function.

The assertiveness of the House and Senate in foreign relations can also be attributed to the American cultural milieu. Since the early 1960s sweeping changes have occurred in American life styles, in traditional modes of thought, and in behavior norms.[60] On all fronts, customs and long-established practices have been challenged. Perhaps more in the political realm than in other sectors, established authority has come under attack. Demands are heard on all sides that political decision making be made more democratic. And American voters today are more independent, refusing to identify themselves with either major political party.

In the post-Vietnam War period, there is a deep-seated feeling of disillusionment and skepticism about the results achieved in domestic and foreign affairs by the nation's leaders. In this milieu, the possibility of a fundamentally different approach to foreign relations—with Congress playing a decisive role in the process—finds many advocates on Capitol Hill and throughout the nation as a whole.

Executive Encouragement. As much out of necessity as conviction, perhaps, executive officials today frequently support a more dynamic and meaningful role by Congress in foreign relations. The president, the secretary of state, and other high-ranking executive officials at times have called upon legislative officials to join them in creating a unified approach to foreign policy issues.[61] Moreover, the attitude of executive officials toward congressional activism in foreign affairs is often highly variable and eclectic. While executive officials routinely complain about congressional restrictions upon the president's authority, in particular instances they have favored forceful legislative intrusion into the diplomatic arena.

Early in 1979 Sen. Frank Church, chairman of the Senate Foreign Relations Committee, bluntly notified officials of Saudi Arabia that the United States expected their diplomatic support in its efforts to resolve the Arab-Israeli conflict. Church informed the Saudi government— apparently with the full encouragement of executive officials—that unless the Saudis supported U.S. efforts, there would be a major congressional review of American foreign policy toward the Middle East. (For several months, State Department officials had been reluctant to convey such a warning directly to Saudi Arabia.)[62]

An even more dramatic example of executive encouragement of congressional activism was provided by former national security adviser and secretary of state Henry Kissinger when he testified before the

Senate Foreign Relations Committee in July 1979 on the SALT II agreements. Kissinger encouraged what one commentator called "congressional forays into the foreign-affairs power of the executive" by urging the Senate to make ratification of the accords contingent upon a significant increase in American defense spending—a move not favored by the White House at the time.[63] During the Reagan administration, visits by legislators to El Salvador and other Latin American nations, as well as expressions of active congressional interest in developments in Central America, strengthened the hand of the White House in its efforts to encourage internal reforms within these countries. Legislators also joined with executive officials in calling for sweeping reforms in the Philippines and South Korea.

Congress's Accomplishments.   The positive results Congress has achieved in foreign policy are another factor that has sustained congressional activism in foreign affairs and may continue to do so in the years ahead. Advocates of a more forceful and independent legislative role in foreign affairs believe the track record of Congress is good. Proponents of this view are convinced that it was Congress that extricated the nation from the Vietnam War and, by enacting the War Powers Resolution, ensured that there will be no more Vietnams to mar the nation's diplomatic record. Similarly, it was the Senate that protected American security interests by insisting upon changes in the Panama Canal treaties as negotiated by the executive branch. Owing in large part to Congress's efforts during the 1970s, American intelligence agencies were placed under tighter control, and the United States became identified with the international promotion of human rights, as symbolized particularly by the diplomacy of the Carter administration.

In more general terms, Congress has helped reverse the trend toward virtually unchecked executive authority in the field of foreign relations since the Vietnam War. Congressional influence has also been a potent factor in changing the direction of American diplomacy. It has reversed America's tendency to become overcommitted abroad, and it has endeavored to ensure that another Vietnam does not mar the nation's diplomatic record. The influence of Congress has also been cast in the direction of broadening the base of American foreign policy by insisting that legislative and public opinion be considered early in the stage of policy making—not merely (as in the case of the Vietnam War) after diplomatic defeats have been sustained and in the allocation of blame for these setbacks. In 1987, many citizens believed that the extended legislative investigation of the Iran-contra affair would produce certain long overdue improvements in the foreign policy process, such as tighter supervision of activities of the White House staff and intelligence agencies.

Factors Favoring Restraint

A number of short- and long-term factors, however, point to re-straint and possibly a reversal in the pattern of legislative activism witnessed since the Vietnam War. Initially, we need to be reminded that a forceful and independent role in foreign affairs by legislative bodies is a distinctive phenomenon among modern governments, confined almost entirely to the American system. In nearly all other countries, the tide has been running strongly in the contrary direction; other national legislatures have steadily lost the power to act independently, especially in the foreign policy field.

In Great Britain, France, West Germany, Japan, and other democ-racies today, the responsibility for managing foreign affairs is vested almost solely with executive officials. In the rare cases when the legisla-tive body does successfully challenge the incumbent government's for-eign policy, a political crisis (followed by new national elections) nor-mally ensues. The experience of many countries suggests that the successful conduct of foreign relations inherently militates against a high degree of legislative activism and independence.

Cycles in Diplomatic History.   Moreover, the forceful assertion of Congress's powers in foreign relations has been a cyclical occurrence in the nation's diplomatic experience. The "War Hawks of 1812," who demanded and got another war with Great Britain, had many members on Capitol Hill. Following the end of the Mexican War in 1848, Congress once more asserted its influence dynamically in foreign affairs. And the period before and after World War I marked another era of congres-sional assertiveness.

The cyclical nature of Congress's diplomatic militancy—and of the ensuing struggle between executive and legislative officials for primacy in foreign affairs—may be explained in various ways. No single existing theory adequately accounts for it. To some extent, congressional as-sertiveness in foreign relations may be related to the oscillating isola-tionist and interventionist moods of the American people toward inter-national affairs.[64]

Alternatively, it may be a function of the political balance between the executive and legislative branches and of the shifting political tides within American society. For reasons that are even now difficult to explain satisfactorily, the zenith of bipartisan cooperation in foreign affairs in the postwar era was reached under the Truman and early Eisenhower administrations—when the presidency and Congress were controlled by different political parties. President Truman had much greater success in arriving at a constructive working relationship with a Republican-controlled Congress on foreign policy than President Carter experienced with a House and Senate controlled by his own political party.[65] By contrast, under the Reagan administration the Democratic-controlled House of Representatives was the center of intense congressional activism in dealing with such issues as the national defense budget, the proposed new MX missile system, and political developments in Central America.

Problems with Executive-Legislative Consultation.   The nature of consultation between policy makers in the executive and legislative branches of government is a significant factor in determining the outcome of efforts to achieve constructive bipartisan collaboration on major foreign policy issues, as advocated by the Reagan administration during the early 1980s. Yet, as emphasized in Chapter 5, there is the problem of when to consult—before or after the president has decided upon a particular diplomatic course of action? There is the additional question of which members of Congress should be included in such discussion. Who really represents Congress and can arrive at understandings in its name?

Even if the problems of when and whom to consult can be solved, a third serious inhibition upon successful executive-legislative consultation remains. What responsibility do members of Congress incur by participating in consultation on foreign policy issues? Does a policy decision resulting from such consultations become their decision, fully as much as the president's?

More specifically, does concurrence in a particular intelligence mission by selected members of the House and Senate make Congress as a whole responsible for its success or failure? Does a president's consultation with a selected group of legislators, in adherence to the terms of the War Powers Resolution, make Congress equally responsible with the executive branch when American military forces are used for diplomatic objectives?

If the answer to such questions is yes, how can this fact be reconciled with Congress's traditional role as a critic of executive policies, especially when they miscarry? Alternatively, if the answer is no, what inducement does an incumbent president have to consult legislators on particular domestic questions, when they refuse to share with executive officials responsibility for the outcome of a proposed policy?

The success or failure of executive-legislative consultation may also be determined by individual personalities. During the late 1940s Secretary of State Dean Acheson and other executive officials worked harmoniously and effectively with influential legislators such as Senators Arthur H. Vandenberg and Tom Connally to formulate diplomatic undertakings (such as the Marshall Plan) acceptable to the White House and Congress. Although these officials often belonged to different political parties, an atmosphere of mutual trust and respect governed their deliberations. Agreements reached between them nearly always were subsequently supported by majorities in the House and Senate.[66]

By contrast, during the Johnson administration, legislative and executive officials were often far from agreement on foreign policy issues. Senator Fulbright outspokenly criticized White House policies toward Vietnam, the Dominican Republic, and other areas. The personal animosity and distrust ultimately existing between Johnson and the Senate Foreign Relations Committee chairman served as a major deterrent to constructive executive-legislative relations in the foreign policy field.

Public Attitudes toward President and Congress. "Capacity in government," one informed student of the American system has said, "depends, in the United States as elsewhere, on leadership." [67] By the beginning of the 1980s, the American people's desire for clear and firm White House leadership in meeting the nation's internal and external problems was unmistakable. President Jimmy Carter's inability, for example, to manage Congress—to create and maintain minimal unity on Capitol Hill in behalf of his programs—was a key element in the widespread perception that he was a weak and indecisive chief executive.[68]

Even congressional voices were heard in the chorus calling upon the chief executive to exhibit forceful and dynamic diplomatic leadership. Sen. Adlai Stevenson III, D-Ill., declared that in recent years Congress had excelled at the game of "kick the President"—perhaps an understandable reaction on Capitol Hill to recent abuses of presidential power. Yet, Stevenson informed his colleagues, Congress's "weaknesses will come back to haunt us. I want a strong executive." [69]

A resurgence of executive authority rather than congressional militancy in foreign affairs may be the wave of the future. According to one study of contemporary executive-legislative relations:

> Left and right want a strong Presidency, the left in domestic affairs, the right for foreign policy. . . . Americans not only prefer Presidential leadership but the scope of foreign and domestic problems and the recurrent emergencies facing a world power simply demand Presidential power—particularly when Congress' foreign policy decisions are so often governed by domestic policies.[70]

Or as another study of public attitudes expressed it, for most Americans the presidency is "everyone's first resort." Realistically or not, the American people expect the chief executive to be forthright and successful in solving national problems; they complain vocally about the lack of White House leadership when this does not happen.[71]

The celebrated American comedian Will Rogers once told his audiences, "There's good news from Washington. Congress is adjourned." Such humor always strikes a responsive chord with Americans, for whom the denigration of Congress's deeds and misdeeds sometimes seems a national pastime.[72] Today, as in the past, the American people are aware that Congress's record has been badly tarnished. Influence peddling on Capitol Hill, misuse of campaign contributions, scandalous personal behavior by legislators, recurring disunity within the House and Senate, and obstructionist moves by Congress in dealing with national policy issues have become public knowledge. Legislators can be energetic and decisive in dealing with executive wrongdoing but dilatory and ineffectual in correcting unethical practices, illegal activities, and organizational problems on Capitol Hill.

Public confidence in Congress's performance has fallen steadily in recent years. In 1974, a poll showed that almost half of the American people approved of the way Congress was doing its job; by mid-1979 this figure had declined to 19 percent. According to another study of public attitudes, twice as many Americans blamed Congress as blamed President Carter for deadlocks between the two branches of the government. Another study, in 1983, found that just over 7 percent of those interviewed believed that Congress was doing a better than adequate job of dealing with urgent internal and external issues; almost half (46.5 percent) thought that Congress's performance was disappointing or poor. According to one experienced observer, Congress still needed to display "more backbone in confronting the president" and to be less concerned with "nitpicking, constituency service, and the thousands of small issues" dominating the activities of legislators. A Gallup Poll in 1982 showed that only 29 percent of the public approved of the way Congress was performing its duties, while 54 percent disapproved. Earlier Gallup Polls showed that public approval of Congress's performance varied from a low of 19 to a high of 38 percent. Aware of such public attitudes, even members of the House and Senate deplored the fact that on some occasions, the behavior of legislators was "demeaning," making Congress the "laughing stock of America." [73]

Popular anxieties about the imperial presidency do not automatically translate into heightened public confidence in Congress's performance or leadership potential. Implicit in public criticism of President Carter's lack of leadership was the twofold demand that the White House take charge of the governmental machinery and that the president exercise more leadership in dealing with Congress to produce unified and effective policies and programs.

Public and Congressional Domestic Concerns. Another factor restraining congressional activism in foreign policy is that the American public exhibits a low level of interest in international questions. This has been true of American society historically (it was a major force, for example, sustaining the isolationist approach to foreign relations), and it is no less the case in the contemporary period. Almost invariably, on a list of the dominant concerns of the American people, pollsters have found citizens give highest priority to internal problems. Only some 15 percent of the people belong to the "attentive public"—that minority of opinion which is reasonably interested in and informed about foreign relations.[74] The behavior of Congress is inescapably affected by this public opinion trait.

This leads to another, closely related factor likely to inhibit a dynamic and sustained role by Congress in the diplomatic field. Constituency-related business ranks as a primary claim upon the time and energies of most legislators. Even with greatly enlarged staffs, most legislators today are hard pressed to meet the diverse demands made upon them by their constituents.[75]

As several of our case studies emphasized, relatively few legislators have the time to acquire expert knowledge of a broad range of complex foreign policy questions. Only a minority of legislators has shown any real desire to receive and to assimilate detailed information about the activities of intelligence agencies—although legislators are legally entitled to it. Similarly, few legislators are inclined to read and digest voluminous reports from executive officials regarding human rights problems in more than 150 independent nations.

The high priority accorded to domestic concerns by the American people and their legislative representatives has two specific consequences. First, perhaps even more today than in the past, Congress's approach to foreign affairs is heavily colored by local and domestic considerations vis-à-vis a commitment to the national interest. Late in 1979 one of the nation's most knowledgeable reporters characterized the foreign policy process in the United States in such terms as "chaos" and "an international scandal." To a considerable degree, he blamed Congress for this state of affairs: "Seldom in memory has it seemed so divided, so concerned with personal, local or state interests and so indifferent to its own Congressional leadership or the disturbing problems of the 1980s." [76]

Second, Congress's involvement in external affairs is likely to be characterized by a short attention span and to be heavily conditioned by the current newsworthiness of a particular foreign policy issue. As our discussion in Chapter 6 illustrated, members of the House and Senate were actively concerned for a time about various misdeeds of the CIA. After a relatively brief period, however, the attention of most legislators had shifted to other issues, leaving only a handful of senators and representatives to monitor intelligence activities on a continuing basis. Summing up a conversation about attempts by Congress to restore its powers, one senator characteristically exclaimed, "I think we've made substantial headlines—I mean headway." [77] Basically the same point could be made about the Iran-contra affair during President Reagan's second term. For a period of a few brief weeks, this episode dominated the headlines and appeared to monopolize the energy and attention of Congress. Then interest in the affair waned rapidly and other issues (such as the challenge to U.S. diplomatic interests in the Persian Gulf and the prospects for arms-control agreements between the superpowers) were at the forefront of public and legislative concern. As is true of American public opinion generally, it is difficult for Congress to exhibit sustained interest in a particular foreign policy problem or issue for an extended length of time.

Invitation to Struggle

From the time of George Washington's administration until the present day, the president and Congress have vied for control over foreign relations. And the lively interaction between Congress and the president—the major theme of our study—will continue to be a dominant feature of the American foreign policy process in the future. During some periods (the era from World War II until the closing stage of the Vietnam War), executive authority in the foreign policy sphere has been preeminent. In other periods (during the 1930s and the 1970s), the congressional voice has been louder and more decisive.

Continuation of this institutional rivalry in foreign affairs seems assured by two fundamental conditions: the provisions of the U.S. Constitution and the obligations inherent in America's role as a superpower in a complex and unstable international system. Although many formal and informal changes have been made in the Constitution since 1789, the basic pattern of divided responsibility and power in foreign affairs remains unaltered. The president still serves as commander-in-chief of the armed forces; he alone has the power to recognize other governments; and only he and his agents can officially negotiate treaties and agreements with other countries in the name of the United States.

After two centuries, Congress also retains influential prerogatives in national security and foreign affairs. The size and nature of the American military establishment are determined by Congress; funds for current military operations and for the development of new weapons must be provided by the legislative branch. In addition, Congress must authorize and appropriate funds for a host of other programs and governmental activities in the foreign policy field—ranging from the State Department budget, to foreign military and economic aid programs, to the activities of intelligence agencies. Also implicit in Congress's lawmaking function is its power to investigate the operations of executive agencies and the administration of programs it has authorized and funded—a power the House and Senate have used with telling effect on numerous occasions since World War II.

The nature of the contemporary international system also provides incentives for the executive and legislative branches to use their respective powers vigorously in the foreign policy field. Since World War II, the United States has been one of the two superpowers in world affairs, and all indications are that it will indefinitely remain so. As a superpower, the United States has certain inescapable and continuing global responsibilities; discharging them nearly always entails policies and programs that involve executive and legislative officials.

Continuing Disunity in the Policy Process

Since the Vietnam conflict, the executive and legislative branches of the American government have faced comparable problems with respect to their role in the foreign policy process. Stated negatively, the efforts of both branches have often been seriously weakened by schisms, organizational rivalries, and centrifugal forces that impair their internal cohesion and their ability to arrive at unified positions on major diplomatic issues. Stated positively, policy makers at opposite ends of Pennsylvania Avenue have important contributions to make to the American foreign policy process. Better understanding of their significant and distinctive roles may guide officials in both branches in their approach to foreign policy issues in the years ahead.

Our discussion in Chapter 1 called attention to the fact that within the executive branch the traditional authority and premier position of the State Department in the diplomatic field have been steadily diluted by the proliferation of executive agencies that play a major or minor role in contemporary American foreign policy. Since the Nixon administration particularly—with the emergence of the president's national security adviser as a rival to the secretary of state—executive efforts in foreign affairs appear to have become increasingly disunified and uncoordinated.[78] Under the Reagan administration, the dramatic resignation of Secretary of State Alexander Haig—and in the years that followed, the Iran-contra affair—raised the question anew: Who really speaks for the administration in foreign affairs?

As our case studies have shown, the role of Congress in contemporary American foreign policy is also beset by comparable difficulties. If the House and Senate have now established—and can be expected to maintain—an influential congressional presence in the foreign policy field, how well equipped are they to continue to play this role? Recent experience indicates that the answer must be: rather poorly and inadequately. To date, in terms of organizational, procedural, and behavioral changes required, few members of Congress have faced up squarely to the necessary implications of their demand for a position of equal partnership with the White House in foreign affairs.

By the early 1980s, Congress appeared to be more decentralized, fragmented, and resistant to unifying influences than in any previous period of American history. To date Congress has supplied little evidence to show that it is prepared to adapt its own organizational structure and internal procedures to the demands of the active foreign policy role.

In judging the respective claims of the presidency and Congress to leadership in the foreign policy process, the American people are likely to apply their customary pragmatic and eclectic tests. Has the active intrusion of Congress into many dimensions of foreign affairs improved, or has it detracted from, the ability of the United States to achieve its diplomatic goals? Has congressional assertiveness on foreign policy questions enhanced the domestic well-being of American society? Has the influence of Congress upon the course of the nation's diplomacy reversed, or has it contributed to, the tendency toward weakened American power and influence abroad? As much as any other single factor, how the American people perceive the answers to these questions will determine Congress's future foreign policy role.[79]

Shared Goals

Executive and legislative officials alike, we may safely assume, ultimately seek the same goal: a unified, rational, and successful foreign policy for the United States. Moreover, all participants in foreign policy decision making would no doubt subscribe to the theoretical proposition that continuing discord, disunity, and competing efforts within the American government—regardless of whether they arise within the executive branch, within Congress, or from conflicts between the executive and legislative branches—nearly always impair the ability of the United States to achieve its diplomatic objectives.

If broad agreement exists in Washington on these propositions, it follows that officials in each branch need to devote greater attention to defining their respective contributions to the foreign policy process more clearly. By virtue of their differing constitutional responsibilities, experiences, and resources, executive and legislative policy makers ought to make different contributions to the common effort, reflecting what each group is uniquely prepared to supply.

Presidential Role.   What contributions are the president and his executive advisers singularly qualified to make? The president symbolizes and represents the national interest of the United States both to the American people and to foreign countries. The chief executive alone can speak in behalf of the nation to governments, leaders, and political movements abroad. As commander in chief of the armed forces, only the president is in a position to respond promptly and decisively to external threats.

The president and the executive officials under his jurisdiction also play an indispensable role in policy formulation. Relying upon the State Department's communications system with American embassies overseas and upon the intelligence community's resources for collecting and analyzing data, the White House remains in an unrivaled position to consider available options and to devise diplomatic strategies and programs for which it will later seek legislative support. Moreover, the president's position as a leader and educator of public opinion remains dominant. As the presidency of the "great communicator," Ronald Reagan, illustrated, the chief executive is in a unique position to inform the American people about major diplomatic issues and to elicit their support in behalf of foreign policies and programs advocated by the White House. In the past (and the presidency of Franklin D. Roosevelt provided a graphic example), this has been a potent instrument of presidential influence in foreign relations. In the post-Vietnam War era—when the American people and Congress remained apprehensive about American military commitments abroad—the president's ability to use this instrument effectively depended heavily upon his ability to demonstrate that the security of the United States was at stake in Central America, the Middle East, and other regions in which the United States had major diplomatic interests. Lacking convincing evidence that such security considerations were present (as the Reagan administration discovered in its Latin American diplomacy), the president is likely to find that the legitimacy of his foreign policy ventures is widely questioned at home and abroad.

The Contribution of Congress. Congress also brings certain distinctive powers and perspectives to bear in foreign policy making. First, there is the legislative power to grant or to withhold funds for foreign policy ventures and programs. Although Congress has possessed this prerogative since 1789, only since the closing stage of the Vietnam War has it relied regularly upon its control over the purse strings to influence the course of American diplomacy. In the new era of budget reductions and austerity, Congress will be challenged as never before to use the power of the purse wisely and effectively in allocating funds to a variety of foreign policy undertakings.

Second, Congress makes an essential contribution in supplying a base of legitimacy to American foreign policy. For a democracy, this vital element—a pervasive public belief that the nation's diplomatic goals are rational, are attainable at reasonable cost, and are consonant with American society's cherished values—is a prerequisite for diplo-

254 Invitation to Struggle

matic success. Especially since the Vietnam War, even executive officials have acknowledged this legislative contribution to the foreign policy process. Thus, as the United States prepared to enter the 1980s, one State Department official said that there was "an important need after Vietnam and Watergate to legitimize American foreign policy." [80] During the early 1980s the Reagan administration depended upon this same contribution of Congress to create a foundation of legitimacy under its efforts to counter Communist influence in Central America. Conversely, the administration's military intervention in Lebanon lost the necessary public support, and this fact required the president to withdraw American forces from that country.

Third, as our discussion of legislative activities with regard to the intelligence community illustrated (Chapter 6), Congress can make a positive contribution to foreign policy decision making—and to the future of American democracy—by scrutinizing the activities of executive agencies and by imposing more stringent guidelines upon their operations. This contribution of the legislative branch is highlighted by the continuing challenge of imposing effective controls upon the CIA and other members of the intelligence community, especially with regard to covert activities directed against Communist or unfriendly governments abroad. On the basis of recent experience, it seems safe to conclude that the American people and their legislative representatives have a decidedly mixed attitude about intelligence operations. The vast majority of citizens believes that the United States is required to engage in intelligence operations to preserve its security in a dangerous world. At the same time, Americans remain apprehensive about such operations—especially about "covert" intelligence activities abroad. In many instances, such covert operations are quickly made "overt" by the news media, thereby often defeating the purpose of such undertakings.

A fourth essential and distinctive contribution of Congress to the foreign policy process was brought into sharp focus by our analysis of Congress's role in the disposition and control of the armed forces (Chapter 5). Relying upon its constitutional prerogatives over the military establishment, Congress can prescribe limits to the president's use of armed force for foreign policy ends. By doing so, Congress creates powerful restraints upon diplomatic adventurism, upon a tendency by the United States to become overextended abroad, and upon the tendency to intervene indiscriminately in the affairs of other countries.

Efforts by the House and Senate to impose more stringent controls over the president's use of the armed forces abroad make another singular contribution to American foreign policy. They serve to remind executive policy makers that, although the United States is a superpower, it is not omnipotent. Even superpowers must base their diplomacy upon a set of priorities. They must define and continually redefine their diplomatic vital interests with care and discrimination. As Walter Lippmann cautioned Americans many years ago, success in foreign policy lies in arriving at and maintaining a balance between what the nation would like to accomplish abroad and what it is able to accomplish on the basis of the power available to it. Failure to preserve an approximate balance between these elements can result in a kind of "diplomatic bankruptcy." [81]

The executive and legislative branches of government would do well to concentrate upon the unique contributions each is equipped to make in the foreign policy process. Too often in the past, each branch has jealously guarded and asserted its own powers in foreign affairs, while endeavoring to exercise or usurp those properly belonging to the other. A clearer sense of a division of labor in the diplomatic field by officials at both ends of Pennsylvania Avenue would go far toward achieving the goal of a more unified, stable, and successful American approach to external problems in the years ahead.

Notes

1. See the full statement by Secretary of State George Shultz, "From the Secretary of State," *Foreign Affairs* 66 (Winter 1987-1988): 426-428; and the views of the former British ambassador to the United States, Peter Jay, as quoted in William D. Rogers, "Who's in Charge of Foreign Policy?" *New York Times Magazine,* September 9, 1979, 49. (The author is a former State Department official, but he is not to be confused with former secretary of state William P. Rogers.) See also James Sundquist, *The Decline and Resurgence of Congress* (Washington, D.C.: Brookings Institution, 1981).
2. Dispatch by Bernard Gwertzman, *New York Times,* January 25, 1975.
3. Charles E. Percy, "The Partisan Gap," *Foreign Policy* 45 (Winter 1981-1982): 3.
4. Dispatch by Francis X. Clines, *New York Times,* May 16, 1983.
5. Quoted in Marvin Stone, "Presidency: Imperial or Imperiled?" *U.S. News & World Report,* January 15, 1979, 88. See also Gerald R. Ford, *A Time to Heal* (New York: Harper and Row and the Reader's Digest Association, 1979), 138-139, 150.
6. Warren Christopher, "Ceasefire between the Branches: A Compact in Foreign Affairs," *Foreign Affairs* 60 (Summer 1982): 998; dispatch by Steven V. Roberts, *New York Times,* March 21, 1983; and Theodore H. White, "Weinberger on the Ramparts," *New York Times Magazine,* February 6, 1983, 77.
7. Nicholas DeB. Katzenbach, "Foreign Policy, Public Opinion and Secrecy," *Foreign Affairs* 52 (October 1973): 18.
8. For the views of John V. Lindsay, former member of Congress and mayor of New York, see "For a New Policy Balance," *Foreign Affairs* 50 (October 1971): 1.
9. For a detailed analysis of the "legislative explosion" witnessed since World War II, see James McClellan, "The State of the American Congress," *Modern Age* 21 (Summer 1977): 227-239.
10. Dispatch by James Reston, *New York Times,* September 21, 1979.

11. "What Congress Really Thinks of Itself," *U.S. News & World Report,* March 15, 1982, 22-24. See also the views of Senator Simpson as described in a dispatch by Steven V. Roberts, *New York Times,* March 21, 1983; and Martin Tolchin, "Howard Baker: Trying to Tame an Unruly Senate," *New York Times Magazine,* March 28, 1982.

12. *New York Times,* January 5, 1987; and Marvin Stone, "Proxmire's Well-Placed Jab," *U.S. News & World Report,* September 10, 1979, 84.

13. The study was conducted by Professors Thomas Franck and Edward Weisband, and it is discussed in *New York Times,* November 29, 1976.

14. McClellan, "State of the American Congress," '237. See also Susan W. Hammond, "Congressional Change and Reform: Staffing the Congress," in Leroy N. Reiselbach, ed., *Legislative Reform: The Policy Impact* (Lexington, Mass.: D. C. Heath, 1978), 183-193.

15. See Dean Acheson, *Sketches from Life of Men I Have Known* (New York: Harper and Row, 1961), 124-125. For historical background, see Holbert N. Carroll, *The House of Representatives and Foreign Affairs* (Boston: Little, Brown, 1966).

16. See the views of Rep. Paul Findley, as described in the *New York Times,* October 6, 1966.

17. House Committee on International Relations, *Congress and Foreign Policy,* 94th Cong., 2d sess., 1976, 19. See also the dialogue between executive and legislative officials on the role of public opinion in foreign affairs in William O. Chattick, *State Department, Press, and Pressure Groups* (New York: John Wiley, 1970), 43-45.

18. Senator Church, quoted in a dispatch by Richard Burt, *New York Times,* January 9, 1979.

19. Dispatches by Steven V. Roberts, *New York Times,* May 15, 1983, and May 26, 1983.

20. Useful studies of American public opinion on foreign affairs in the recent period include Ralph B. Levering, *The Public and American Foreign Policy: 1918-1978* (New York: William Morrow, 1978); H. Schuyler Foster, *Activism Replaces Isolationism: U.S. Public Attitudes, 1940-1975* (Washington, D.C.: Foxhall, 1983); John E. Rielly, "America's State of Mind," *Foreign Policy* 66 (Spring 1987): 39-56; Ole R. Holsti and James N. Rosenau, *American Leadership in World Affairs: Vietnam and the Breakdown of Consensus* (Boston: Allen and Unwin, 1984); Eugene Wittkopf, "Elites and Masses: Another Look at Attitudes toward America's World Role," *International Studies Quarterly,* 31 (June 1987): 131-159.

21. Dispatch by James Reston, *New York Times,* January 4, 1980.

22. James Chace, "Is a Foreign Policy Consensus Possible?" *Foreign Affairs* 57 (Fall 1978): 15-16. The variability of American attitudes toward the Soviet Union can be seen in J. D. Jones, "Reagan and Moscow," *Foreign Policy* 67 (October 1986): 62-78, and Charles M. Maynes, "America's Chance," *Foreign Policy* 68 (Fall 1987): 88-100. Current information is contained in "Great Decisions '87: National Opinion Ballot Report" (New York: Foreign Policy Association, 1987) and in subsequent issues in the series.

23. House Committee on International Relations, *Congress and Foreign Policy,* 188-189. The intense congressional interest in international human rights issues is highlighted in Charles McC. Mathias, "Ethnic Groups and Foreign Affairs," *Foreign Affairs* 59 (Summer 1981): 975-999.

24. Ben J. Wattenberg, *The Real America: A Surprising Examination of the State of the Union* (Garden City, N.Y.: Doubleday, 1974), 211-212.

25. The extent of lobbying activities by foreign governments in the contempo-

rary period is conveyed by an examination of the voluminous data in
Washington Representatives, 1986 (Washington, D.C.: Columbia Books,
1986). This work contains a list of organizations engaged in such activities
that occupies ten closely packed pages (633-643). The numbers range from
thirty-three for Taiwan, thirty-seven for France, twenty-three for Israel,
and thirty-four for Mexico to ten for the People's Republic of China, four
for Cuba, eight for Panama, and eight for the Soviet Union. See also later
volumes in the same series.

26. "What Carter's Aides Really Think of Congress," *U.S. News & World
Report,* August 14, 1978, 15.

27. For specific examples of lobbying by foreign governments, see F. C. Ogene,
*Interest Groups and the Shaping of Foreign Policy: Four Case Studies of
United States African Policy* (New York: St. Martin's, 1983); Abdul A.
Said, ed., *Ethnicity and U.S. Foreign Policy* (New York: Praeger, 1981);
Steven Emerson, *The American House of Saud: The Secret Petrodollar
Connection* (New York: Franklin Watts, 1985); *The Washington Lobby,* 5th
ed. (Washington, D.C.: Congressional Quarterly, 1987); Jack Holland, *The
American Connection: U.S. Guns, Money, and Influence in Northern Ire-
land* (New York: Penguin Books, 1988); Mathias, "Ethnic Groups and
Foreign Affairs"; George W. Shepherd, *Racial Influences on American
Foreign Policy* (New York: Basic Books, 1970); "Middle East Lobbying,"
Congressional Quarterly Weekly Report, April 22, 1981, 1523-1530; and
Deborah M. Levy, "Advice for Sale," *Foreign Policy* 67 (Summer 1987): 64-
87.

28. See *U.S. News & World Report,* November 22, 1976, 30.

29. More detailed examination of pro-Zionist and pro-Arab lobbying in the
United States is available in Nimrod Novik, *The United States and Israel:
Domestic Determinants of a Changing U.S. Commitment* (Boulder, Colo.:
Westview, 1986); Abraham Ben-Zvi, *Alliance Politics and the Limits of
Influence: The Case of the U.S. and Israel, 1975-1984* (Boulder, Colo.:
Westview, 1984); "Middle East Lobbying"; Paul Findley, *They Dare to
Speak Out: People and Institutions Confront Israel's Lobby* (Westport,
Conn.: Lawrence Hill, 1985); Edward W. Said, *Covering Islam* (New York:
Pantheon Books, 1981); Elia Zureik and Fouad Moughrabi, *Public Opinion
and the Palestine Question* (New York: St. Martin's, 1987); Cheryl A.
Rubenberg, *Israel and the American National Interest* (Champaign: Uni-
versity of Illinois Press, 1986); Stephen L. Spiegel, *The Other Arab-Israeli
Conflict: Making America's Middle East Policy from Truman to Reagan*
(Chicago: University of Chicago Press, 1985); and Peter Grose, *Israel in the
Mind of America* (New York: Alfred A. Knopf, 1983).

30. For a detailed study of efforts by the executive branch to influence the
deliberations of Congress, see Abraham Holtzman, *Legislative Liaison:
Executive Leadership in Congress* (Chicago: Rand McNally, 1970).

31. Alton Frye and William D. Rogers, "Linkage Begins at Home," *Foreign
Policy* 35 (Summer 1979): 55-56.

32. The findings of the Kissinger Commission are contained in *The Report of
the President's Commission on Central America* (New York: Macmillan,
1984). See also George Shultz, "Implementing the National Bipartisan
Commission Report," Department of State, Special Report, No. 148 (August
1986).

33. See U.S. Senate, Select Committee on Secret Military Assistance to Iran
and the Nicaraguan Opposition, *Report of the Committees Investigating
the Iran-Contra Affair,* 100th Cong., 1st sess., 1987.

34. Dispatch by Hedrick Smith, *New York Times,* February 17, 1979.
35. Informative studies of U.S. defense policies and strategies are James Fallows, *National Defense* (New York: Random House, 1982); Patrick O'Heffernan, ed., *The Search for a Rational Military Policy* (Cambridge, Mass.: Ballinger, 1984); George F. Hudson and Joseph Kruzel, eds., *American Defense Annual, 1985-1986* (Lexington, Mass.: D. C. Heath, 1985), and subsequent volumes in this series; and William A. Buckingham, Jr., ed., *Defense Planning for the 1990s* (Washington, D.C.: National Defense University Press, 1984).
36. Dispatch by James Reston, *New York Times,* September 21, 1979.
37. House Speaker Jim Wright's (D-Texas) personal involvement in these negotiations aimed at producing a political settlement in Central America is examined more fully in the *Congressional Quarterly Weekly Report,* November 14, 1987, 2789-2791, and November 21, 1987, 2867-2868.
38. See the *New York Times'* edition of *The Tower Commission Report* (New York: Bantam Books and Times Books, 1987); and the later *Report of the Committees Investigating the Iran-Contra Affair.* A useful source book on the Iran-contra affair is Jonathan Marshall, Peter D. Scott, and Jane Hunter, *The Iran-Contra Connection: Secret Teams and Covert Actions in the Reagan Era* (Boston: South End, 1987).
39. 1 U.S. Statutes-at-Large 613 (1799).
40. Dispatch by Hedrick Smith, *New York Times,* August 14, 1979.
41. Dispatch by James Reston, *New York Times,* September 21, 1979.
42. Dispatch by John Kifner, *New York Times,* November 26, 1979, and dispatch by Bernard Gwertzman, November 27, 1979.
43. *U.S. News & World Report,* February 19, 1979, 52-54. See also Alan Platt and Lawrence D. Weiler, *Congress and Arms Control* (Boulder, Colo.: Westview, 1978).
44. *Washington Post,* December 14, 1979, and *Congressional Quarterly Weekly Report,* December 15, 1979, 2850.
45. For recent discussions of the ABM agreement, its meaning and implications, see Raymond L. Garthoff, *Policy versus Law: The Reinterpretation of the ABM Treaty* (Washington, D.C.: Brookings Institution, 1987); William J. Durch, *The ABM Treaty and Western Security* (Cambridge, Mass.: Ballinger, 1987); and dispatch by Fred C. Iklé, *New York Times,* June 8, 1987, and dispatches by Gerald C. Smith and David Riley, and by Jonathan Fuerbringer, *New York Times,* October 2, 1987.
46. For the views of the Nixon-Kissinger White House on the results of congressional action toward the Vietnam War, see Richard Nixon, *The Memoirs of Richard Nixon* (New York: Grosset and Dunlap, 1978), 744, 888-889; and Henry Kissinger, *White House Years* (Boston: Little, Brown, 1979), 1413, 1461.
47. Kissinger, *White House Years,* 400-401.
48. Ibid.
49. George W. Ball, *Diplomacy for a Crowded World: An American Foreign Policy* (Boston: Atlantic/Little, Brown, 1976), 204.
50. "What Carter's Aides Really Think of Congress," 15.
51. J. William Fulbright, "The Legislator As Educator," *Foreign Affairs* 57 (Spring 1979): 719-733.
52. Percy, "The Partisan Gap," 12; dispatch by Steven V. Roberts, *New York Times,* March 21, 1983, quoting Senator Simpson; John Tower, "Congress versus the President: The Formulation and Implementation of American Foreign Policy," *Foreign Affairs* 60 (Winter 1981-1982): 229-247; and dis-

patch by Steven V. Roberts, *New York Times,* June 4, 1983, quoting Sen. Dan Quayle, R-Ind.

53. Dispatch by Adam Clymer, *New York Times,* July 3, 1977.

54. See "SALT Debate is Complicated by Soviet Troops in Cuba," *Congressional Quarterly Weekly Report,* September 8, 1979, 1913; the excerpt from the report on SALT II by the Senate Foreign Relations Committee, in *New York Times,* November 20, 1979; and *Time,* October 1, 1979, 100.

55. Rogers, "Who's in Charge of Foreign Policy?" 44, 47, 50. Basically the same criticism is made of Congress's approach to foreign affairs by former secretary of state Henry Kissinger, who contrasts the fields of law and diplomacy. See Kissinger, *White House Years,* 940-941.

56. Senator Vandenberg's views are quoted in Ben H. Brown, Jr., "Congress and the Department of State," *Annals of the American Academy of Political and Social Science,* no. 289 (September 1953): 107.

57. Lee H. Hamilton and Michael H. Van Dusen, "Making the Separation of Powers Work," *Foreign Affairs* 57 (Fall 1978): 39.

58. Genrikh Trofimenko, "Too Many Negotiators," *New York Times,* July 13, 1979.

59. Ibid.

60. For an excellent interpretation of the philosophical and cultural values of modern American society, see Christopher Lasch, *The Culture of Narcissism: American Life in an Age of Diminishing Expectations* (New York: W. W. Norton, 1978). See also Steven J. Kelman, "Youth and Foreign Policy," *Foreign Affairs* 48 (April 1970): 414-427, and the detailed discussion of the cultural values of the 1970s in *Newsweek,* November 19, 1979.

61. For the views of Assistant Secretary of State for Congressional Relations Douglas J. Bennet, Jr., see "Congress: Its Role in Foreign Policy-Making," *Department of State Bulletin* 78 (June 1978): 35-36, and "Congress in Foreign Policy: Who Needs It?" *Foreign Affairs* 57 (Fall 1978): 40-51.

62. Dispatches by Bernard Gwertzman, *New York Times,* January 18 and February 2, 1979.

63. Dispatch by Anthony Lewis, *New York Times,* August 23, 1979.

64. The concept of oscillating isolationist and interventionist foreign policy moods by the American people is identified and explained in F. L. Klingberg, "The Historical Alternation of Moods in American Foreign Policy," *World Politics* 4 (January 1952): 239-273.

65. For a detailed discussion of bipartisan collaboration during the Truman administration, see Cecil V. Crabb, Jr., *Bipartisan Foreign Policy: Myth or Reality?* (New York: Harper and Row, 1957), and Arthur H. Vandenberg, Jr., ed., *The Private Papers of Senator Vandenberg* (Boston: Houghton Mifflin, 1952).

66. Acheson, *Sketches from Life of Men I Have Known,* 123-146.

67. James L. Sundquist, "Congress and the President: Enemies or Partners?" in Lawrence C. Dodd and Bruce I. Oppenheimer, eds., *Congress Reconsidered* (New York: Praeger, 1977), 222.

68. *U.S. News & World Report,* August 27, 1979, 20.

69. Elizabeth Drew, "Why Congress Won't Fight," *New York Times Magazine,* September 23, 1973, 83.

70. The findings of the study, conducted by Thomas E. Cronin and Lawrence C. Dodd, are summarized in a dispatch by Tom Wicker, *New York Times,* November 18, 1977.

71. Dispatch by Terence Smith, *New York Times,* October 28, 1979.

72. For detailed analyses of public attitudes toward Congress, see "What Con-

gress Really Thinks of Itself"; Malcolm E. Jewell and Samuel C. Patterson, *The Legislative Process in the United States,* 3d ed. (New York: Random House, 1977), 315-317; and Roger H. Davidson, David M. Kovenock, and Michael K. O'Leary, *Congress in Crisis: Politics and Congressional Reform* (Belmont, Calif.: Wadsworth, 1971), 38-66.

73. See the survey data presented in *Time,* October 1, 1979, 25; *U.S. News & World Report,* July 16, 1979, 21, March 15, 1982, 22-24, and May 23, 1983, 48; dispatch by Steven V. Roberts, *New York Times,* December 26, 1982; and *Baton Rouge Morning Advocate,* August 1, 1982.

74. Levering, *The Public and American Foreign Policy,* 29.

75. John Bibby and Roger Davidson, *On Capitol Hill: Studies in the Legislative Process* (New York: Holt, Rinehart and Winston, 1967), 111-112. See also McClellan, "The State of the American Congress," 229, 237.

76. Dispatch by James Reston, *New York Times,* September 21, 1979.

77. This unnamed senator is quoted in Drew, "Why Congress Won't Fight," 16.

78. For numerous examples of the decline of the State Department in the foreign policy process during the Nixon administration, see Kissinger, *White House Years.*

79. The influence of pragmatic criteria in shaping American attitudes is discussed more fully in Wattenberg, *The Real America,* 203-213, and George W. Ball, *The Discipline of Power: Essentials of a Modern World Structure* (Boston: Atlantic/Little, Brown, 1968), 343-358.

80. Assistant Secretary of State for Congressional Relations Brian Atwood, as quoted in a dispatch by Martin Tolchin, *New York Times,* December 24, 1979.

81. Walter Lippmann, *U.S. Foreign Policy: Shield of the Republic* (Boston: Little, Brown, 1943); and Walter Lippmann, *The Cold War: A Study in U.S. Foreign Policy* (New York: Harper and Row, 1947). More detailed analyses of the contributions that executive and legislative officials may make to the foreign policy process are in Christopher, "Ceasefire between the Branches," and Tower, "Congress versus the President."

SUGGESTED READINGS

Books

Austin, Anthony. *The President's War: The Story of the Tonkin Gulf Resolution and How the Nation Was Trapped in Vietnam.* Philadelphia: Lippincott, 1971.

Barnhart, Michael, ed. *Congress and United States Foreign Policy: Controlling the Use of Force in the Nuclear Age.* Albany: State University of New York Press, 1987.

Barrett, Laurence I. *Gambling with History: Reagan in the White House.* New York: Doubleday, 1983.

Becker, Abraham, ed. *Economic Relations with the USSR.* Lexington, Mass.: D. C. Heath, 1983.

Becker, William H. *Economics and World Power: An Assessment of American Diplomacy since 1789.* New York: Columbia University Press, 1984.

Bowles, Nigel. *The White House and Capitol Hill: The Politics of Presidential Persuasion.* New York: Oxford University Press, 1987.

Breckinridge, Scott D. *The CIA and the U.S. Intelligence System.* Boulder, Colo.: Westview, 1986.

Brenner, Phillip. *The Limits and Possibilities of Congress.* New York: St. Martin's, 1983.

Brown, Harold. *Thinking about National Security.* Boulder, Colo.: Westview, 1983.

Brown, Seyom. *The Faces of Power: Constancy and Change in United States Foreign Policy from Truman to Reagan.* New York: Columbia University Press, 1983.

Brzezinski, Zbigniew. *Power and Principle.* New York: Farrar, Straus, and Giroux, 1983.

Campagna, Anthony S. *U.S. National Economic Policy, 1917-1985.* New York: Praeger, 1987.

Campbell, Colin. *Governments under Stress: Political Executives and Key Bureaucrats in Washington, London, and Ottawa.* Toronto: University of Toronto Press, 1983.

_____. *Managing the Presidency: Carter, Reagan, and the Search for Executive Harmony.* Pittsburgh: University of Pittsburgh Press, 1986.

Carter, Jimmy. *Keeping Faith: Memoirs of a President.* New York: Bantam Books, 1982.

Cohen, Stephen D. *The Making of United States International Economic Policy: Principles, Problems, and Proposals for Reform.* 2d ed. New York: Praeger, 1984.

Coker, Christopher. *U.S. Military Power in the 1980s*. Salem, Mass.: Salem House, 1983.

Crabb, Cecil V., Jr. *The Doctrines of American Foreign Policy: Their Meaning, Role, and Future*. Baton Rouge: Louisiana State University Press, 1982.

Crabb, Cecil V., Jr., and Kevin V. Mulcahy, *Presidents and Foreign Policy: FDR to Reagan*. Baton Rouge: Louisiana State University Press, 1986.

Deibel, Terry L. *Presidents, Public Opinion, and Power: The Nixon, Carter, and Reagan Years*. New York: Foreign Policy Association, 1987.

Dellek, Robert. *The American Style of Foreign Policy*. New York: Alfred A. Knopf, 1983.

DeMuth, Christopher, et al. *The Reagan Doctrine and Beyond*. Lanham, Md.: American Enterprise Institute, 1988.

Denton, Robert E., Jr., and Dan F. Hahn. *Presidential Communication: Description and Analysis*. New York: Praeger, 1986.

Destler, I. M. *American Trade Politics: System under Stress*. Washington, D.C.: Institute for International Economics, 1986.

Dugger, Ronnie. *On Reagan: The Man and His Presidency*. New York: McGraw-Hill, 1983.

Durch, William J. *The ABM Treaty and Western Security*. Cambridge, Mass.: Ballinger, 1987.

Fisher, Louis. *The Politics of Shared Power*. 2d ed. Washington, D.C.: CQ Press, 1987.

Forsythe, David P. *Human Rights and World Politics*. Lincoln: University of Nebraska Press, 1983.

Franck, Thomas, and Edward Weisband. *Foreign Policy by Congress*. New York: Oxford University Press, 1979.

Garthoff, Raymond L. *Policy versus Law: The Reinterpretation of the ABM Treaty*. Washington, D.C.: Brookings Institution, 1987.

George, Alexander L. *Managing U.S.-Soviet Rivalry: Problems of Crisis Prevention*. Boulder, Colo.: Westview, 1983.

Gilboa, Eytain. *American Public Opinion toward Israel and the Arab-Israeli Conflict*. Lexington, Mass.: D. C. Heath, 1986.

Godson, Roy, ed. *Intelligence Requirements for the 1980s*. Lexington, Mass.: D. C. Heath, 1986.

Goldstein, Walter, ed. *Reagan's Leadership and the Atlantic Alliance: Views from Europe and America*. Washington, D.C.: Pergamon-Brassey Press, 1986.

Goldwin, Robert A., and Art Kaufman. *Separation of Powers: Does It Still Work?* Lanham, Md.: American Enterprise Institute, 1986.

Greenstein, Fred A. *The Hidden-Hand Presidency: Eisenhower As Leader*. New York: Basic Books, 1982.

Haftendorn, Helga, and Jakob Schissler. *The Reagan Administration: Toward a Reconstruction of American Strength*. Hawthorne, N.Y.: Aldine de Gruyter, 1988.

Hahn, Walter F., ed. *Central America and the Reagan Doctrine*. Lanham, Md.: University Press of America, 1987.

Haley, P. Edward. *Congress and the Fall of South Vietnam and Cambodia*. East Brunswick, N.J.: Fairleigh Dickinson University Press, 1982.

Hart, John. *The Presidential Branch*. New York: Pergamon, 1984.

Hogan, J. Michael. *The Panama Canal in American Politics: Domestic Advocacy and the Evolution of Policy*. Carbondale: Southern Illinois University Press, 1986.

Holt, Pat M. *The War Powers Resolution: The Role of Congress in U.S. Armed Intervention*. Washington, D.C.: American Enterprise Institute, 1978.

House Select Committee to Investigate Covert Arms Transactions with Iran and Senate Select Committee on Secret Military Assistance to Iran and the Nicaraguan Opposition. *Report of the Congressional Committees Investigating the Iran-Contra Affair.* 100th Cong., 1st sess., 1987, H. Rept. 100-433, S. Rept. 100-216.

Hunter, Robert E., Wayne L. Berman, and John F. Kennedy, eds. *Making Government Work: From White House to Congress.* Boulder, Colo.: Westview, 1986.

Hyland, William, ed. *The Reagan Foreign Policy.* New York: New American Library, 1988.

Inderfurth, Karl R. *Decisions of the Highest Order: Perspectives on the National Security Council.* Pacific Grove, Calif.: Brooks/Cole, 1988.

Jordan, Hamilton. *Crisis: The Last Year of the Carter Presidency.* New York: G. P. Putnam's Sons, 1982.

Kauppi, Mark V., and R. Craig Nation, eds. *The Soviet Union and the Middle East in the 1980s.* Lexington, Mass.: D. C. Heath, 1983.

Kellerman, Barbara. *The Political Presidency: The Practice of Leadership from Kennedy through Reagan.* New York: Oxford University Press, 1986.

Kernell, Samuel. *Going Public: New Strategies of Presidential Leadership.* Washington, D.C.: CQ Press, 1986.

Kissinger, Henry. *White House Years.* Boston: Little, Brown, 1979.

———. *Years of Upheaval.* Boston: Little, Brown, 1982.

Krickus, Richard J. *The Superpowers in Crisis: Implications of Domestic Discord.* Elmsford, N.Y.: Pergamon-Brassey, 1988.

Landau, Saul. *The Dangerous Doctrine: National Security and U.S. Foreign Policy.* Boulder, Colo.: Westview, 1988.

Laqueur, Walter Z. *A World of Secrets: The Uses and Limits of Intelligence.* New York: Basic Books, 1985.

Lehman, John F. *The Executive, Congress, and Foreign Policy: Studies of the Nixon Administration.* New York: Praeger, 1976.

Leiken, Robert S., ed. *Central America: Anatomy of a Conflict.* New York: Pergamon, 1984.

Leuchtenburg, William E. *In the Shadow of FDR.* Ithaca, N.Y.: Cornell University Press, 1983.

Levering, Ralph B. *The Public and American Foreign Policy, 1918-1978.* New York: William Morrow, 1978.

Lipsen, Charles B., and Stephan Lesher. *Vested Interest: A Lobbyist's Account of Washington Power and How It Really Works.* New York: Doubleday, 1977.

Lowi, Theodore J. *The Personal President: Power Invested, Promise Unfulfilled.* Ithaca, N.Y.: Cornell University Press, 1985.

Mako, William P. *U.S. Ground Forces and the Defense of Central Europe.* Washington, D.C.: Brookings Institution, 1983.

Mann, Thomas E., and Norman J. Ornstein, eds. *The New Congress.* Washington, D.C.: American Enterprise Institute, 1981.

Melanson, Richard A., and Kenneth W. Thompson, eds. *Foreign Policy and Domestic Consensus.* Lanham, Md.: University Press of America, 1985.

Muravchik, Joshua. *The Uncertain Crusade: Jimmy Carter and the Dilemmas of Human Rights Policy.* Lanham, Md.: Hamilton, 1986.

Muskie, Edmund, et al., eds. *The President, Congress, and Foreign Policy.* Lanham, Md.: University Press of America, 1986.

Nathan, James A., and James K. Oliver. *Foreign Policy Making and the American Political System.* 2d ed. Greenview, Ill.: Scott, Foresman/Little, Brown, 1987.

Nelson, Michael. *The Presidency and the Political System*. Washington, D.C.: CQ Press, 1984.

Newsom, David D. *Diplomacy and the Amerian Democracy*. Bloomington: Indiana University Press, 1988.

O'Brien, Lee. *American Jewish Organizations and Israel*. Washington, D.C.: Institute for Palestine Studies, 1986.

O'Heffernan, Patrick, ed. *Defense Sense: The Search for a Rational Military Policy*. Cambridge, Mass.: Ballinger, 1984.

Oisken, Michael, ed. *Trouble in Our Backyard: Central America and the United States in the Eighties*. New York: Pantheon Books, 1984.

Oleszek, Walter J. *Congressional Procedures and the Policy Process*. 3d ed. Washington, D.C.: CQ Press, 1988.

Orman, John. *Comparing Presidential Behavior: Carter, Reagan, and the Macho Presidency*. Westport, Conn.: Greenwood, 1987.

Oye, Kenneth, Robert J. Lieber, and Donald Rothchild, eds. *Eagle Defiant: United States Foreign Policy in the 1980s*. Boston: Little, Brown, 1983.

Packard, David. *Management of America's National Defense*. Lanham, Md.: American Enterprise Institute, 1987.

Pastor, Robert A. *Congress and the Politics of U.S. Foreign Economic Policy, 1929-1976*. Berkeley: University of California Press, 1980.

Pierre, Andrew J., ed. *Arms Transfers and American Foreign Policy*. New York: New York University Press, 1979.

Piper, Don C., and Ronald J. Terchek. *Interaction: Foreign Policy and Public Policy*. Lanham, Md.: American Enterprise Institute, 1984.

Platt, Alan, and Lawrence D. Weiler. *Congress and Arms Control*. Boulder, Colo.: Westview, 1978.

Powers, Francis Gary, with Curt Gentry. *Operation Overflight: The U-2 Spy Pilot Tells His Story for the First Time*. New York: Holt, Rinehart and Winston, 1970.

Powers of Congress. 2d ed. Washington, D.C.: Congressional Quarterly, 1982.

Richelson, Jeffrey T. *The U.S. Intelligence Community*. Cambridge, Mass.: Ballinger, 1985.

Rielly, John E., ed. *American Public Opinion and U.S. Foreign Policy, 1987*. Chicago: Chicago Council on Foreign Relations, 1987.

Rockman, Bert. *The Leadership Question: The Presidency and the American System*. New York: Praeger, 1984.

Romberg, Alan D., ed. *The United States and Japan: Changing Societies in a Changing Relationship*. New York: Council on Foreign Relations, 1987.

Rubin, Barry. *Secrets of State*. New York: Oxford University Press, 1985.

Rubinstein, Alvin Z., ed. *The Great Game: Rivalry in the Persian Gulf and South Asia*. New York: Praeger, 1983.

Said, Abdul A., ed. *Ethnicity and U.S. Foreign Policy*. Rev. ed. New York: Praeger, 1986.

Schneider, Jerrold E. *Ideological Coalitions in Congress*. Westport, Conn.: Greenwood, 1979.

Scott, Robert T., ed. *The Race for Security: Arms and Arms Control in the Reagan Years*. Lexington, Mass.: D. C. Heath, 1986.

Senate Committee on Foreign Relations and Committee on the Judiciary. *The ABM Treaty and the Constitution, Joint Hearings*. 100th Cong., 1st sess., 1987.

Smith, Steven S., and Christopher J. Deering. *Committees in Congress*. Washington, D.C.: CQ Press, 1984.

Stern, Paula. *Water's Edge: Domestic Politics and the Making of American*

Foreign Policy. Westport, Conn.: Greenwood, 1979.

Strong, Robert J. *Bureaucracy and Statesmanship: Henry Kissinger and the Making of American Foreign Policy*. Lanham, Md.: University Press of America, 1986.

Stubbing, Richard A., and Richard A. Mendel. *The Defense Game*. New York: Harper and Row, 1986.

Sundquist, James A. *The Decline and Resurgence of Congress*. Washington, D.C.: Brookings Institution, 1981.

Taylor, William J., and Steven A. Maaranen, eds. *The Future of Conflict in the 1980s*. Lexington, Mass.: D. C. Heath, 1983.

Tivnan, Edward. *The Lobby: Jewish Political Power and American Foreign Policy*. New York: Simon and Schuster, 1987.

The Tower Commission Report. New York: Bantam Books and Times Books, 1987.

Trade: U.S. Policy since 1945. Washington, D.C.: Congressional Quarterly, 1984.

Treverton, Gregory F. *Covert Action: The Limits of Intervention in the Postwar World*. New York: Basic Books, 1987.

Turner, Stansfield. *Secrecy and Democracy: The CIA in Transition*. Boston: Houghton Mifflin, 1985.

U.S. Defense Policy. 3d ed. Washington, D.C.: Congressional Quarterly, 1983.

Vance, Cyrus. *Hard Choices*. New York: Simon and Schuster, 1983.

Walker, Thomas W. *Reagan versus the Sandinistas: The Undeclared War on Nicaragua*. Boulder, Colo.: Westview, 1987.

Waller, Douglas C. *Congress and the Nuclear Freeze: An Inside Look at the Politics of a Mass Movement*. Amherst: University of Massachusetts Press, 1987.

The Washington Lobby. 4th ed. Washington, D.C.: Congressional Quarterly, 1982.

West, Darrell M. *Congress and Economic Policymaking*. Pittsburgh: University of Pittsburgh Press, 1987.

Whalen, Charles W., Jr. *The House and Foreign Policy: The Irony of Congressional Reform*. Chapel Hill: The University of North Carolina Press, 1982.

Wilcox, Francis O., and Richard A. Frank. *The Constitution and the Conduct of Foreign Policy*. New York: Praeger, 1976.

Williams, Phil. *The Senate and U.S. Troops in Europe*. New York: St. Martin's, 1985.

Wormuth, Francis D., and Edwin B. Firmage, *To Chain the Dogs of War: The War Powers of Congress in History and Law*. Dallas: Southern Methodist University Press, 1986.

Wyden, Peter. *Bay of Pigs: The Untold Story*. New York: Simon and Schuster, 1979.

Articles

Adelman, Kenneth L. "Arms Control and Human Rights." *World Affairs* 149 (Winter 1986-1987).

Aspin, L. "The Defense Budget and Foreign Policy: The Role of Congress." *Daedalus* 104 (Summer 1975).

Barilleaux, Ryan. "Executive Non-Agreements and the Presidential-Congressional Struggle in Foreign Affairs." *World Affairs* 148 (Spring 1986).

Bergsten, C. Fred. "Economic Imbalances and World Politics." *Foreign Affairs* 65 (Spring 1987).

Blechman, Barry M., and James E. Nolan. "Reorganizing for More Effective Arms Negotiations." *Foreign Affairs* 61 (Summer 1983).

Blumenthal, W. Michael. "The World Economy and Technological Change." *Foreign Affairs: America and the World, 1987/88.*

Brzezinski, Zbigniew. "NSC's Midlife Crisis." *Foreign Policy* 69 (Winter 1987-1988).

Caldwell, Lawrence T. "United States-Soviet Relations and Arms Control." *Current History* 86 (October 1987).

Christopher, Warren. "Ceasefire between the Branches: A Compact in Foreign Affairs." *Foreign Affairs* 60 (Summer 1982).

Destler, I. M. "Congress as Boss?" *Foreign Policy* 42 (Spring 1981).

_____. "Protecting Congress or Protecting Trade?" *Foreign Policy* 62 (Spring 1986).

Diebel, Terry L. "Why Reagan Is Strong." *Foreign Policy* 62 (Spring 1986).

Diebold, William. "The United States in the World Economy: A Fifty-Year Perspective." *Foreign Affairs* 62 (Fall 1983).

Fascell, Dante B. "Congress and Arms Control." *Foreign Affairs* 65 (Spring 1987).

Finger, Seymour M. "Jeane Kirkpatrick at the United Nations." *Foreign Affairs* 62 (Winter 1983-1984).

Gates, Robert M. "The CIA and American Foreign Policy." *Foreign Affairs* 66 (Winter 1987-1988).

Goodman, Allan E. "Reforming U.S. Intelligence." *Foreign Policy* 67 (Summer 1987).

Henkin, Louis. "Foreign Affairs and the Constitution." *Foreign Affairs* 66 (Winter 1987-1988).

Hough, Jerry F. "The Future of Soviet-American Relations." *Current History* 85 (October 1986).

Javits, Jacob. "Congress and Foreign Relations: The Taiwan Relations Act." *Foreign Affairs* 60 (Fall 1981).

Jervis, Robert. "Intelligence and Foreign Policy: A Review Essay." *International Security* 11 (Winter 1986-1987).

Johnson, Loch, and James M. McCormick. "The Making of International Agreements: A Reappraisal of Congressional Involvement." *Journal of Politics* 40 (May 1978).

Kenworthy, Eldon. "United States Policy toward Central America." *Current History* 86 (December 1987).

Krasner, Stephen D. "Trade Conflicts and the Common Defense." *Political Science Quarterly* 101, no. 5 (1986).

Luard, Evan. "Western Europe and the Reagan Doctrine." *International Affairs* 63 (Autumn 1987).

Lustick, Ian S. "Israeli Politics and American Foreign Policy." *Foreign Affairs* 61 (Winter 1982-1983).

"The Media and the Presidency" (symposium). *Presidential Studies Quarterly* 16 (Winter 1986).

Owens, MacKubin T. "The Hollow Promise of JCS Reform." *International Security* 10 (Winter 1985-1986).

Percy, Charles H. "The Partisan Gap." *Foreign Policy* 45 (Winter 1981-1982).

Quandt, William B. "The Electoral Cycle and the Conduct of Foreign Policy." *Political Science Quarterly* 101, no. 5 (1986).

Rhodes, John J. "The Far Side of the Hill." *Foreign Affairs* 61 (Winter 1982-1983).

Schlesinger, Arthur, Jr. "Foreign Policy and the American Character." *Foreign Affairs* 62 (Fall 1983).

Sharpe, Kenneth E. "The Real Cause of Irangate." *Foreign Policy* 68 (Fall 1987).

Sherr, Alan B. "Sound Legal Reasoning or Policy Expedient? The 'New Interpretation' of the ABM Treaty." *International Security* (Winter 1986-1987).

Silk, Leonard. "The United States and the World Economy." *Foreign Affairs* 65 (Spring 1986).

Solarz, Stephen J. "When to Intervene." *Foreign Policy* 63 (Summer 1986).

Sorensen, Theodore C. "The President and the Secretary of State." *Foreign Affairs* 66 (Winter 1987-1988).

Spero, Joan E. "Information: The Policy Void." *Foreign Policy* 48 (Fall 1982).

"The State and American Foreign Economic Policy" (symposium). *International Organization* 42 (Winter 1988).

Thurow, Lester C., and Laura D. Tyson, "The Economic Black Hole." *Foreign Policy* 67 (Summer 1987).

Treverton, Gregory F. "Covert Action and Open Society." *Foreign Affairs* 65 (Summer 1987).

Turner, Stansfield, and George Thibault. "Intelligence: The Right Rules." *Foreign Policy* 48 (Fall 1982).

van Voorst, I. Bruce. "The Churches and Nuclear Deterrence." *Foreign Affairs* 61 (Spring 1983).

Williams, Phil. "The Limits of American Power: From Nixon to Reagan," *International Affairs* 63 (Autumn 1987).

INDEX